THE VICTORIAN MODE IN AMERICAN FICTION

1865-1885

The Victorian Mode
in American Fiction
1865-1885

by

ROBERT FALK

MICHIGAN STATE UNIVERSITY PRESS

1965

We know a man imperfectly until we know his society, and we but half know a society until we know its manners. This is especially true of a man of letters, for manners lie very close to literature.

HENRY JAMES

Preface

This study of a twenty-year period of American literary experience and social history was written in the hope of saying something new about an old subject—the late-lamented Victorian Americans of the post-Appomatox decades. Its aim is to isolate and define the phenomenon which has been called "Victorian Realism" and to focus upon the significance of that phrase as cultural and literary history. A ready-made historical orthodoxy lay at hand to assist me in interpreting the relationship between the tone and character of the 1870's and 1880's and the literary ideals of the period. However, the collective portrait of the age as drawn by earlier historians and critics was essentially a negative one, and much as I admired the skill of certain of its spokesmen, I became convinced that there was room for a more affirmative evaluation of the evidence. In short, I was anxious to establish my own reading of the so-called "Gilded Age" as a necessary background for tracing the growth of an aesthetic of realism in the fiction and criticism of the major writers of that time.

As I progressed with the work, it became more and more apparent to me that the period between 1865 and about 1885 contained a certain homogeneity of mind which marked it off from the decades immediately preceding it and those which followed. More than that, the twenty years seemed to follow a "cycle" of development, in literary, social, and cultural affairs, from a kind of youthful experiment and hesitation toward a greater measure of fulfillment and maturity of mind. In broad terms, Victorian realism was a different thing from Victorian romanticism, on the one hand, and *fin de siècle* realism, or naturalism, on the other. What I sought to describe was the particular "vision of reality" which prevailed during those years and the steps by which it was given expression in fiction and critical theory. This tone or temper could be dimly seen in the popular tastes, arts, fashions, social and political history of the nation. But its clearest definition and meaning are found in the work of its major literary figures—Henry James, Howells, De Forest, and Mark Twain.

The method chosen to make visible this rather evanescent quality may best be described as "narrative portraiture." That is, I wanted to tell the "story" once more of that phase of the American experience and thus to avoid using arbitrary topical or critical divisions which often make history lifeless and which reflect too insistently twentieth-century standards of judgment. The challenge lay in bringing some harmony to a study which involved both historical "facts" and literary tendencies. The effect intended was a combination of chronological narrative and literary interpretation. The period as a whole was set in a frame, like a landscape with figures, and the ultimate aim was to view the whole as a self-contained unit of social, intellectual, and literary history.

In the center of the picture is the novel as it reflected and gave meaning to the generation of Victorian Americans of that time. Although still at that period of history uncertain of its role as a picture of conditions or a reforming and guiding force, the novel in the best hands became the finest expression of the age. It helped to translate the formal arrangements of society and the standard expressions of democratic idealism into the subtle forms of individual experience and dramatic meaning. The shock of recognition which followed upon Appomatox involved, among other things, a diminished confidence in the power of the grand old phrases to cope with the emergent society of industrial growth and the exploitation of the frontier. Writers and thinkers strove to re-invest them with new significance by putting them to the test of what Whitman called "the simple separate person."

In broad terms, then, the identifying characteristics of the period were those of recovery, re-orientation, re-dedication. This spirit gradually took shape in the Seventies sufficiently to merit being called a "tradition" of American life and experience, a tradition which seems to me to have been unsatisfactorily defined and undervalued. It was a tradition which had, and still has, vitality. In the recent critical revaluation of the major writers of that generation the literary stature of De Forest, Howells, James, and Mark Twain has been greatly revised and their artistic aims more accurately understood. At the same time we have been restoring the portrait of the period. But their literary accomplishments and the age which formed the matrix of their work have not always been placed in clear relationship. Not many historians now would accept at face value the interpretation of an age which has depicted James's career as a "pilgrimage" or Mark Twain's as an "ordeal." Nor would they be willing to adopt without qualification the earlier definitions of such widely used terms as "gilded," "genteel," or "innocent."

A few words of acknowledgment and thanks. Of the various kinds of indebtedness one incurs in forming his ideas, I have tried to indicate the more specific and direct ones in the notes and in the text itself. As for less tangible and often more vital matters of point of view, method, or attitude, I am deeply conscious of the insights and researches of many scholars and critics more skillful than myself who have provided me with materials, ideas, and even language without which I would scarcely have been able to clarify and express my own understanding of the subject. Most immediately and personally, however, I am grateful for the support and encouraging counsel of Leon Howard, Norman Foerster, and to Jane Falk for direct assistance and constant assurance. They all kept me from listening too long to the siren voices that speak soft words of comfort and delay.

R. F.

Contents

I

GILT AND INNOCENCE:

Idols of the Tribe

'The Genteel Tradition.' This phrase has had too
long a run. It has been stretched in so many directions that it is as useless as old elastic.

VAN WYCK BROOKS

WHEN FRANCIS BACON addressed himself to the task of taking all knowledge to his province, he first carefully weighed the possibilities for error in the existing modes of pursuing the truth.[1] The race of men (Bacon called it "the tribe") was impelled by an inherited need for order and meaning in the world to create systems or dogmas designed to resolve nature into abstractions. His reference was primarily to science, or "natural philosophy," but his plea for true "induction" as the best remedy for avoiding such "idols" of the mind might well be heeded by historians or critics whose judgments are subject to the changing, elusive, and symbolic nature of language rather than to the more readily measurable truths of the laboratory. The problem of imposing some unity upon even the smallest segment of human history presents infinite complications and contradictions. A case in point in American literary and social history is the period immediately following the War between the States which has been especially vulnerable to a formidable array of Baconian "idols of the tribe." Critics and historians during the 1920's and 1930's succeeded in establishing by the skillful use of language and metaphor a system of attitudes toward that "Victorian" generation which has influenced much of our thinking about it ever since.

Few periods of American thought, taste, and literary expression have been subjected to such a parade of disparaging epithets and historical idols. In its social character, its art and architecture, its manners, morals and literature the period has been portrayed in many a colorful and pejorative term. Common to them all is the concept of decline. A levelling off from earlier standards, an "Indian Summer" of New England's Golden Day, a twilight of transcendentalism—such is the theme. Decadence, mediocrity, simulation, and artificiality have, among other qualities, been ascribed to the span of years now known as "The Gilded Age," "The Genteel Tradition" or "The Age of Innocence." For the later historians a "Chromo-civilization," paying lip-service to propriety, but inwardly materialistic and culturally moribund, took the place of the earlier, mid-century idealism. The period has been named a "Great Barbecue" of political deviation, an "Age of Accumulation," or an "Age of the

3

Protestant Ethic." Color-symbolism was called into service to depict the Seventies and Eighties in a variety of uncomplimentary hues. The post-war Victorians were condemned in pigmentation. The 1890's, for example, were a "Mauve Decade," suffused in an effeminate glow of lilac or violet tones, synthetic shades, for the most part, pastels and lush poly-chromes.[2] The spring bloom of the prewar time had given way to autumnal browns, dingy, drab, chocolate, or "sooty" merging into blacks.[3] Since about 1920 the period in which Henry James, Howells, Mark Twain, Henry Adams, De Forest, and others came of age had been the subject of a steady current of historical denigration so that it has become difficult to take a fresh look at the social and cultural manifestations of that time without falling into one or another of the Idols of the Tribe.

But the first anti-Victorians were Victorians. The earliest dissenting voices belonged to the generation which itself established the cultural tone of the time. These were voices of thoughtful and sensitive contemporaries who looked at themselves, as it were, from within, and who criticized their own society through a Victorian perspective. Their protests against the materialism and the "gentility" of their age set the tone for the muckrakers and nation-baiters of the 1920's who added new embellishments and ironic touches to the picture until they succeeded in creating a classic structure of condescension. In the often brilliant historical arrangements of such writers as Charles A. Beard, V. L. Parrington, Van Wyck Brooks, V. F. Calverton and certain spokesmen of The Higher Journalism, like H. L. Mencken and Sinclair Lewis, a thoroughly disparaging portrait of the period emerged. To understand how this came about, one needs to go back to 1870.

One of the first to give forceful expression to a denunciation of the lowered social and ethical tone of the late Sixties and early Seventies was Walt Whitman. In *Democratic Vistas* (1871) he sharply criticized the materialism and moral indifference of certain segments of the postwar society. Anticipating by a few years Twain and Warner's novel, he reproached the corruption, bribery, falsehood, and maladministration of public life and found equal fault with the small aims and "tepid amours" of the fashionably dressed vulgarians of private life. Whitman wrote, however, within a framework of idealism and his comments were not meant as a blanket indictment of the age or its future. His words struck a responsive chord among the early opponents of the railroad stock manipulators of the period—Thomas Nast, for instance, whose powerful lampoon-illustrations in *Harper's Weekly* were largely responsible for bringing the corruption of Boss Tweed, Oakes Ames, and others to public attention. Similarly, Charles Francis and Henry Adams struck at the Erie Railroad scandals in the *North American Review*, and satiric novels such as De Forest's *Honest John Vane* and *Playing the Mischief* and Rebecca Davis's *John Andross* exposed stock manipulation and congressional lobbying in Washington.

4

Literary columns of eastern periodicals, at the same time, lamented the uncertain moral tone of native fiction and noted the diluting effect on literary production of the increasingly large, unlettered class constantly being transformed into readers of books. One of the keenest observers of such social tendencies was E. L. Godkin of the *Nation* who editorialized in 1874 that the sensational court trial between the radical feminist Theodore Tilton and Henry Ward Beecher over the estranged affections of Mrs. Tilton was an affair symptomatic of the moral condition of American society generally. Under the skillful heading, "Chromo-civilization," Godkin asserted that a superficial culture had grown up among a large body of persons "under the influence of the common schools, magazines, newspapers, and the rapid acquisition of wealth." A society of ignoramuses had arisen, he said, "who firmly believed that they have reached, in the matter of social, mental, or moral culture, all that is attainable or desirable by anybody." The result is "a kind of mental and moral chaos, in which many of the fundamental rules of living, which have been worked out painfully by thousands of years of bitter human experience, seem in imminent risk of disappearing totally."

Thus generalizing from one notorious incident, Godkin felt he could detect a widespread shift of standards. For him the action of the Plymouth Church in sending flowers to decorate the courtroom on the day Beecher came to trial was a symbolic breach of taste—like placing wreaths about the open manhole of a sewer! Similarly, he inveighed against the attitude of certain newspapers which supported Blaine in his candidacy for president in 1876. These newspapers were spokesmen of the society as a whole, he thought, and only a "Chromo-civilization" could have produced that blunting of the moral sense which could not see that Blaine's dubious transactions in the matter of the $64,000 Little Rock and Fort Smith Railroad bonds were to his discredit. The papers praised his "smartness" in the affair, saying: "that is just the smart man we want." One can scarcely quarrel with Godkin's interpretation of these incidents, but his colorful title helped later historians to castigate the age and to exaggerate its faults out of proportion to the whole.[4]

Even more influential was the complex of ideas and attitudes transferred to later critics by Mark Twain and Charles Dudley Warner's political satire, *The Gilded Age*. Van Wyck Brooks, for example, in *The Ordeal of Mark Twain* (1920) extended the implications of their title into a full-blown condemnation of the materialism of the 1870's and, by extension, of the business mind of America from the Civil War into the present century. Clemens and Warner had touched with acrimony and satire certain of the social hypocrisies and malpractices of political Washington, but it is open to question whether the intention of the book, written in the light-hearted period of Twain's career, was as serious as Brooks implied.

It was the epoch of industrial pioneering, the Gilded Age, as Mark Twain called it in the title of his only novel, the age when presidents were business men and generals were business men, when the whole psychic energy of the American people was absorbed in the exploitation and organization of the material resources of the continent. . . .

In Philip Sterling's search for a coal mine Brooks discerned a parable on the religious character of business in "The Gilded Age." All idealism, he said, ran into the channel of money-making. The American dream of unlimited wealth, a folk-odyssey epitomized by the cloud castles of Colonel Sellers, gave to the pursuit of money a sacred quality which, merging with the illusion of progress and manifest destiny, conspired against the creative spirit.[5]

All this was an early statement of what later was to become an elaborate structure of historical theory, built upon the title of a novel which was half romance and half humorous satire. Other historians, Charles and Mary Beard, for example, added rhetorical flourishes to the structure, building it into an economic thesis of far-reaching proportions. Their summary of Twain and Warner's book sounds like a Spenglerian prophecy of the doom of western civilization:

> In the guise of fiction [Mark Twain and Warner] displayed the new plutocrats, ignorant in mind and vulgar of tongue, assuming the airs of the grand style; a raw, rough, uncouth nation obsessed by the acquisitive passion; a scrawny country of villages striving to rival New York and Chicago with the aid of congressional plunder; corrupt politicians, municipal, state and national, given to high-sounding verbalism and low pillage; the roaring mobs of great cities fed on murder and scandal by a sensational press—an unlovely mess without beauty and prospect of taste.[6]

In dramatic blacks and whites the Beards described social relations in "The Gilded Age" as characterized by "the cash nexus, pure and simple." Then with sweeping vision the Seventies suddenly became the dividing line between feudalism and capitalism: "the feudal nexus had been dissolved; the cash nexus substituted." Such yawning antitheses now seem a compound of highly colored language, Marxist history, and Teutonic gloom.

Granville Hicks used *The Gilded Age* as a text for pro-Marxist ideas. Clemens and Warner, he said, had described a "debauch" which was nothing less than the demoralization of a nation. He was somewhat more realistic when he admitted that the authors were probably not sure just what lay behind such a spectacle of corruption. But he went on to imply that the authors were unable to see the full meaning of their exposé of the speculative spirit which was manifest in the comic excesses of Sellers, the

6

hypocritical dishonesty of Senator Dilworthy, and the unscrupulousness of Laura Hawkins. And he strongly hinted that this was the class struggle which they gropingly sought to reveal in their satire on greed and dishonesty in Washington politics.[7]

To V. L. Parrington "The Gilded Age" became a capsule portrait of a generation. He called the era of Jim Fisk and Oakes Ames a "Great Barbecue" of triumphant and unabashed vulgarity, a raw and uncouth generation peopled by such figures of earth as "the-public-be-damned" Commodore Vanderbilt, Jim Fisk, prince of barbarians, and shrewd and enterprising rascals like Jay Gould and Roscoe Conkling. Parrington's portrait is in many ways the most impressive in sheer skill of word-painting of all the economic-portraitists of the Twenties. He described with brilliance the political leaders of the time—fat, grasping, oily, their mutton-chop whiskers greasy with the spoils of economic opportunism feeding at the public trough. He sketched them as an unlovely, ungainly, irreverent crew "moving through pools of tobacco juice." Such was the "ripe fruit of Jacksonian levelling," he said, which gave to "The Gilded Age" its tone of picturesque vulgarity.[8]

It is beyond the limits of this chapter to attempt to trace all of the complex historical and intellectual origins of this portrait of "The Gilded Age." Some part of it derived from native agrarian protest against the rapid development of urban life and industrial society. Another source lay in the tradition of European intellectual dissent beginning around 1890 in the work of such forecasters of the decline of western civilization as Max Weber and Oswald Spengler. Thorstein Veblen contributed the idea of "conspicuous waste" to this stream of historical interpretation in 1899, but it was not until the 1930's that the full impact of the work of these critics reached the American cultural and literary historians. Weber's *The Protestant Ethic and the Spirit of Capitalism*, written and published in Germany in 1904, was not translated into English until 1930.[9] His study of the way in which the Calvinist zeal for signs of God's favor had slowly evolved into a sense of property and money seemed to American critics of business a perfect historical explanation for the Gospel of Wealth in "The Gilded Age." Both Weber and Veblen were early spokesmen of an economic-determinist theory of history. Disciples like Matthew Josephson in *The Robber Barons* (1934) applied these ideas to the social and cultural character of the late Victorian decades following the Civil War.

The critics of "The Gilded Age" concentrated upon political deviation and economic inequality, and they founded their "idols" upon the political protests of the Agrarians and the Populists of the Nineties. A second school of anti-Victorians, focusing more directly upon matters of taste and morals, drew their support from such critics of "innocence" and "gentility" as Henry James, Henry Adams, Mark Twain and other Victorian Americans. This school rallied primarily around George Santayana

7

who named "The Genteel Tradition" and Edith Wharton who called it an "Age of Innocence." It went back into the Puritan heritage to enforce its conclusions and became, finally, a thorough devaluation of the American experience. In order to comprehend the extent of this "Ungenteel Tradition" of historical idol-makers let us condense their opinions into a paragraph of caricature.

> The two or three decades of American life after 1870 were 'genteel' (that is, *not* 'gentle') and innocent (that is, hypocritically 'pure'). In this 'Age of Innocence' affairs were controlled by the twin gospels of business and false Puritanism. Imitativeness and bad taste prevailed in the realm of architecture and decoration. Effeminacy established a rule of censorship in book and magazine publishing. During those years society in general was 'the most ill-mannered that has probably ever existed.' It was disgustingly pure, because it was 'violently sex-conscious.' It was afraid of vulgarity because it was so 'immitigably vulgar.' It emasculated its literature, painted pantalets on piano legs, brought up its wives and daughters to a tradition of factitious purity, and shielded them from the facts of life. The 'polite mind' of the age paid lip-service to Puritan high-mindedness and transcendental idealism without believing in either. Intellectuals preached an inherited set of moral absolutes no longer relevant to the American scene. An orthodoxy of the soft and squeamish, drawn from spinsterish aunts and long-dead grandmothers drew a curtain of false delicacy across the nation.

The historians whose convictions are thus paraphrased sought in European manners and taste a standard of reference for the American. They were professedly humanistic, though their conclusions were antipathetic to literary and intellectual aspiration. They were disillusioned with Victorian 'idealism' and found fault with the American character as a whole. Mostly, they blamed the milieu for its sterilizing and vitiating effect upon literature and thought. In the Twenties and Thirties the words 'genteel' and 'innocent', in their critical meaning, became passwords to sophistication and cosmopolitanism, demonstrating the revolt of the intellectuals of the new generation from the patterns and ideals of the old.

After 1870 Europe became something more than a cultural barometer. It threatened to become a bone of contention. The image of the romantic artist—Longfellow, Irving, Hawthorne—seeking literary nourishment and inspiration in a *wanderjahr* on the continent, began to give way to the wealthy American tourist hunting comfort, luxury, or *objets d'art* in towns, hotels, and spas. A sense of cultural inferiority mingled with that of political and economic self-assurance. 'Culture' became an increasingly self-conscious word. The contrast between Old World and New began to penetrate a different class of society, further removed in time and place

8

from the earlier generation. Mark Twain illustrated something of this ambivalence, implying that American innocents abroad were not so innocent, and European grandeur somewhat less than grand. There was challenge as well as brashness in his preface to *Innocents Abroad*—"to suggest to the reader how *he* would be likely to see Europe and the East if he looked at them with his own eyes instead of the eyes of those who travelled in those countries before him." And in the Seventies Henry James, the grandfather of expatriatism, was busy balancing off the two sides of the Atlantic in endless fictional musings, establishing a reputation among some of his countrymen for deracination and Anglophilic tendencies.

But it was another expatriate (this time in reverse) who gave to later critics of American Victorianism the ambivalent phrase, "The Genteel Tradition." In his address at Berkeley, California, in 1911 George Santayana defined the term which has been used in so many different senses ever since as to lose most of its original force. Santayana sought to describe the genteel mentality of his adopted country, in which he was never, during his forty years residence, content, as a fundamental mediocrity and orthodoxy of mind stemming from a decadent Calvinism. His attitude was one of kindly condescension toward American people whom he viewed as rich and benevolent, but culturally backward like those of "many a barbarous land of the past." In his analysis of the complacency and timidity of the 'genteel mind' he became its first psychiatrist. He spoke of "the division of mind" which had produced, on the one hand, the material energy symbolized by the skyscraper and, on the other, the intellectual lag and traditionalism of the academic mind.[10]

To Santayana the essence of gentility was an ebbing Calvinism, strained through Emersonian idealism, leaving only a kind of aimless optimism which merged with the national good will. It was a "protestant ethic" which had not yet been wed to capitalism. He viewed the American ethos through the academic perspective of a Harvard philosopher, seeing the tradition as a type of wishful ideality lying like a protective fog around academy and university shutting them off from the realities of American life. His wording was skillful, but the general tone of his remarks was ironic if not critical and patronizing. His suggestive phrase, "Genteel Tradition," remained to influence a generation of critics who used it to express their own rebellion against Puritanism, materialism, and all forms of Victorian morality. It became a useful epithet, too, for those whose ideas were influenced by what Ludwig Lewisohn called "the venerated name of Sigmund Freud."

Santayana's down-grading of the French *gentil* (i.e. having the habits of a gentleman) had behind it, of course, the authority of English usage. The term had begun to take on, about 1850, a sarcastic coloring when used in such phrases as 'shabby genteel,' 'faded gentility,' or 'genteel poverty.'

The bias was in either of two opposite social directions—a slur from above on social climbers ambitious for the status of gentlemen, or a sneer from below at the aristocracy which retained the marks but not the income of gentlemen. More commonly, it referred to the pseudo-gentleman who, in the general levelling attendant upon the industrial revolution, attached undue importance to the outward signs of status. Bringing to bear the somewhat defensive mind of an outsider in the America of his residence (1870-1910), Santayana seized upon a word of satirical coloring and made it into a powerful instrument of intellectual criticism. Himself, above all, an intellectual, he characterized the cultural climate of nineteenth-century America in disparaging, even cynical, terms.

It was his suggestion of a split in American life and his discovery of the source of "The Genteel Tradition" in Puritanism which were echoed in succeeding decades of historical interpretation. Van Wyck Brooks, in one of his early volumes, *America's Coming of Age* (1915), broadened the implications of Santayana's criticism by adding a more pronounced Freudian dimension. He discovered a basic schizophrenia in the American mind, stemming from Calvinism, which he expressed as a conflict between "highbrow-ism" and "lowbrow-ism." At one extreme was the "highbrow" intellectual like Jonathan Edwards—solemn, frozen, and inflexible. At the other, the "lowbrow" like Franklin—practical, Philistine, moralistic. Brooks thus expressed a thesis similar to that of Max Weber that the protestant ethic was a marriage of Puritan godliness with capitalistic economics. But he did not go that far, preferring to hold with a position which simply condemned both extremes, the super-ego (Edwards) and the id (Franklin), as an insoluble compound affecting adversely the nineteenth-century mind.[11]

Thus Puritanism, a loosely-defined "idol," was wedded to gentility, and the offspring of their union was the "Victorian mind." Describing "The Reign of the Genteel," V. L. Parrington found its essence to be "a refined ethicism that professed to discover the highest virtue in shutting one's eyes to disagreeable fact" and this refinement amounted to a "Victorianism of a more maidenly purity than the English strain" because it had been so carefully filtered through the "puritan mesh." While he applied this formula at first to the Brahmin mind of New England— to such writers as Longfellow, Prescott, and Parkman—he extended his metaphor to include the generation which reached maturity after the War and which he discussed under the title "Victorian Realism." Henry James and William Dean Howells were specially designated in a chapter of *Main Currents in American Thought* which generalized as follows:

> To most Victorians realism meant Zola, sex, and the exploitation of the animal, and all the pruderies of the Age of Innocence rose up in protest against defiling letters with such themes.[12]

Following Parrington, V. F. Calverton regarded American literature of that time as in need of "liberation" from a dying Calvinism.

> The pruderies and reticences in our literature developed after Puritanism as a living force was dead. They came with the rise of the new philosophy of the upper bourgeoisie, that of respectability, which candied over everything real with the surface of decency. The puritanic philosophy of fortitude broke down, in the crucible of respectability, into the philosophy of sweetness and light.[13]

Similarly, Bernard Smith held that gentility had its origin in the principle of moral utility, "but as time went on became increasingly divorced from didacticism." By the late nineteenth century this principle had become a habit, hardening into an orthodoxy of the soft, the squeamish, and the mentally inert. "In the plainest words, then, gentility is conservatism," Smith concluded. "It is the moral and social orthodoxy of the bourgeois who has, so to speak, been 'refined.' "[14]

In 1930 the disparagement of gentility was given still further impetus when Sinclair Lewis entered the fray with his acceptance speech for the Nobel Prize in Stockholm. He delivered a tirade against American cultural and literary standards under the title "The American Fear of Literature." Lewis's speech was double-edged—aimed personally at Henry van Dyke who had ventured to express disapproval at the choice of Lewis by the committee, and more generally at the Victorian tone and "Howellsian timidity" of American letters which, he felt, had brought about a divorce "from all authentic standards of importance and reality." Furthermore, Lewis had in mind the Academy of Arts and Letters and the New Humanist Group, both of which he regarded as official organs of literary conservatism and belated revivals of the Puritan-genteel spirit, cut off from "the really harsh and magnificent reality of contemporary life."

Lewis spoke of the pale negations and chilly enthusiasms of the academic tradition and lamented the influence of Howells who "had the code of a pious old maid whose greatest delight was to have tea at the vicarage." He echoed Van Wyck Brooks in discrediting the work of Howells whose conception of art, he felt, was "essentially passive and feminine" and who had separated himself from "those drastic imaginative reconstructions of life and society that are of the essence of all masculine fiction." Lewis went on to praise Dreiser, Mencken, O'Neill, Wolfe, and other of the younger writers who had put aside "the old and lovely dreams of the eternal romantics." His conclusion was a prophecy: "We are coming out, I believe, of the stuffiness of safe, sane, and incredibly dull provincialism."[15]

While Lewis, Mencken and others were championing the realists in literature, a revival of certain of the Victorian standards of criticism developed around the New Humanists, notably Irving Babbitt and Paul Elmer More. The New Humanism was partly a philosophy and partly a literary attitude. As a philosophy Babbitt sought to define "Humanism" as a position somewhere between the older Christian supernaturalism and modern science in which an ethical "inner check" (formed somehow from the Christian tradition, but controlled by the intellect) became the distinctively *human* quality which preserved man from a purely scientific naturalism.[16] He was immediately challenged from both sides, those like T. S. Eliot and Santayana who saw Humanism as a compromise with an earlier Christian absolutism, and those of the modern school of scientism who regarded it as a late and unwelcome rebirth, in the universities, of an outmoded transcendentalism.

Eliot, in "The Humanism of Irving Babbitt" and "Second Thoughts on Humanism," objected that the New Humanism was attempting to make an ethical principle do the work of religion and that Babbitt was "trying to build a Catholic platform out of Protestant planks."[17] Santayana, in *The Genteel Tradition at Bay* (1931) saw it as a last dying gasp of the nineteenth century which showed signs of returning to the source from which the "genteel" had originally sprung—Calvinism. But the new humanists did not go far enough, he thought. If they wished to return to some form of supernaturalism they should seek to restore a genuine Christian theocracy rather than a vague, classical tradition. They should re-establish their moral sentiments on foundations more solid than tradition or gentility.[18]

As a literary attitude Humanism played a more influential role in the late Twenties than as a philosophy. Its taste was conservative, its point of view historical, and its scene of activity, the universities. Because of its scholarly, semi-clerical tone its spokesmen did not get the hearing they deserved, but such of its exponents as Paul Elmer More, Norman Foerster, Stuart Sherman, G. R. Elliott, and Robert Shafer succeeded at least temporarily in challenging liberal criticism which called for a new and vital realism based on science. The humanists championed a different school of writers, Frost, Cather, Glasgow, Wilder, E. A. Robinson, and they spoke disparagingly of the naturalists. They hoped to restore some of the older values, a sense of the past, and an element of dignity, restraint, and good taste which had been lost in the cry for fact-facing in literature. To the realists and Freudians, however, they represented only a belated revival of genteel taste and "Victorian" reticence.

Ludwig Lewisohn's *Expression in America* (1932) was the most thoroughgoing disparagement of the genteel outlook, up to that time, written from the point of view of a disciple of Freud. He discovered the roots of gentility in colonial writers like Irving and Paulding who sought to escape from the brawling equalitarianism of their day by emphasizing the values of propriety, refinement, and respectability which belonged to the eighteenth-century gentleman. After the Civil War, however, the "polite" tradition took complete possession of the field of letters. Such poets, said Lewisohn, as Aldrich, Sill, Stedman, Stoddard, and Richard Watson Gilder turned away from the turbulent and expanding America of their time to "write hymn tunes on a parlor melodeon." Lewisohn maintained that the attitude of the Victorian novelist toward love and marriage indicated a repressed consciousness of sex and a view of the marital relationship which was "revolting to every generous instinct." It placed wives upon a false, chivalric pinnacle of moral purity and at the same time relegated them to the limbo of "cooking stoves and diapers" with "a quiet but relentless sadism." In the work of James and Howells Lewisohn discerned a painful consciousness of sex in their very skirting of the subject—a paradox to be explained, apparently, by the Freudian theory of ambivalence toward social taboos. But the fundamental source of the "Genteel Tradition" Lewisohn found in the Puritan mind with its consciousness of sin; the type of polite writer he defined as somewhere between Longfellow and Brander Matthews; and the debilitating influence of gentility on literature, which reached well into the twentieth century, he regarded as owing to a separation of art and experience.[19]

In 1936 Malcolm Cowley undertook to summarize the meaning of the genteel outlook as it affected American letters. His introduction to *After the Genteel Tradition* set forth its chief characteristics, of which he listed five: (1) Puritanism, (2) the division of practical life from the life of the mind, (3) an innocently hopeful spirit of optimism bred by the speculative, frontier spirit, (4) the "bloodless" refinement of culture, and (5) an attitude of imitative provincialism toward the intellectual shrines of London and Oxford. American Victorianism, Cowley said, resembled its counterpart in England, but its outlines were made harsher by the Puritan insistence upon moral evil and the contrary optimism of American real estate developments and frontier speculation. After the Civil War, he felt, this "genteel" mind merged with the new American bourgeois philosophy of wealth and "refinement" to produce the polite tradition, regnant in literary circles until the revolt of Lewis, Mencken, and other writers of the 1920's.[20]

Cowley's was the most systematic effort to define a phrase which had already been too loosely applied. It had come to mean everything from Puritan morality to feminine reticence and from provincialism in taste to economic individualism. It was attributed to writers as far apart as Longfellow and Barrett Wendell and as unlike as Paulding, Aldrich, Gilder, and Henry James. Its roots were variously discovered in Puritanism, colonialism, Federalism, transcendentalism, the frontier, and finance capitalism. By the end of the Thirties, however, with the menace of a war in Europe and the changed outlook toward the American past and present, this "anti-genteel tradition" of historical interpretation had lost much of its earlier force. The spirit of flagellation lessened and with it the attack upon the Victorian mind. Only echoes were heard during the Forties serving to emphasize the fragmentary and eclectic elements which had gradually come together to form an orthodoxy. H. B. Parkes in *The American Experience* (1947) discussed "the cultural collapse" following the Civil War in terms of the acquisitive spirit of the financial barons and the failure of intellectuals to resist materialism—a failure caused by the lack of a spiritual affirmation and the absence of a dynamic social philosophy. Intellectuals, adrift in a world of outward expansion, turned for guidance, said Parkes, to the British class tradition.

> They interpreted American history in conservative terms, glorifying Puritanism, the Constitution, and the Federalists, vilifying Jefferson and the agrarians, and denying the radical elements in the American past; and they preached social and aesthetic standards of gentility and decorum that had no relevance to the American scene. This revival of Federalism became known as the 'Genteel Tradition.' It was exemplified most completely in the writings of certain Bostonians, such as Barrett Wendell, Charles Eliot Norton, and James Russell Lowell, who inherited the attitude from Federalist and Unitarian forbears.[21]

To this blanket indictment of gentility one is tempted to apply Dr. Johnson's description of the metaphysical poets—that "the most heterogeneous ideas are yoked by violence together."

In attempting to reinterpret the cultural tone and literary accomplishment of the 1870's and 1880's, we are strongly subject to the preconceptions of this mass of historical evidence and opinion. Nevertheless, one must create his own system and write his own stage-play, naming the actors and writing the script. Nor can a fresh attempt to evaluate the age afford to be simply another attack upon the Victorian mind. Neither can it become, contrarily, a Victorian melodrama with the critical tribe of the 1920's in the role of villains. But a changing climate of ideas since 1940 helps provide a more sympathetic interpretation of that generation. Distance and perspective are in our favor. We are no longer impelled to disparage the past in order to justify the deficiencies of the present. It is possible to review the Victorian period without falling into the well-worn grooves of dissent. "Don't forget to speak scornfully of the Victorian Age. There will be a time for meekness when you seek to better it." Thus James M. Barrie, in 1922, defended his own generation against the attacks of the younger one.[22] And we may come a little further toward the prophecy made as far back as 1876 by Ernest Renan: "When this poor nineteenth-century which we abuse so much is gone," he said, "it will be eagerly looked into, and much one day will be forgiven it."[23] By 1940 the anti-Victorian orthodoxy had already begun to show signs of wear. So many different kinds of meaning had been attached to it as to leave it largely meaningless. It had become a baroque structure and a critical anachronism. Even Van Wyck Brooks, one of its erstwhile truculent spokesmen, recanted when in *The Opinions of Oliver Allston* (1941) he wrote:

> 'The Genteel Tradition.' This phrase has had too long a run. It has been stretched in so many directions that it is as useless as old elastic. One cannot bear too heavily on suggestive phrases, and one grows heartily sick of such phrases as this when they have been used three times.[24]

A climate of forgiveness toward that age has been evident since 1940 in a steady current of revisionist scholarship. Biographies, collections of letters, new editions, and critical studies centering mainly around the major literary figures of the post-Civil War period have contributed to this newer dispensation. Its effect has been corrective. For one thing, literary and intellectual patterns, as opposed to the more demonstrable social and economic indicators, have weighed more heavily in these latter judgments. The total portrait has been retouched, familiar landmarks removed or altered, values revised and adjusted. It is more likely now that the negative implications of gentility and innocence can be modified. Certain positive values have attached themselves to the two terms least subject to pejorative connotation—"Realism" and "Victorianism." The first forms the literary center of the period we are here concerned with, and the second describes, in both positive and negative ways, the environmental setting. A combination of the two can be applied to the climate of ideas and the social tone which formed the background for the major literary accomplishments of the 1865-1885 period. Some homogeneity of thought, more harmonious than has been described by the historians, provided the matrix for the work of Henry James, Howells, Mark Twain, Henry Adams, De Forest, and others.

By proceeding historically and chronologically, with Bacon's inductive method in mind, it is possible to trace a tradition of literary expression which has been called "realism" as the central intellectual pattern during that twenty-year period. It is also possible to regard the "Victorian" element as a shaping, if not a determining force. It is, of course, the separate work of art and the individual writer which lend force and direction to an otherwise vaguely defined literary tradition. Previous interpretations of the period, however, have been concerned to explore the sources of disparity between the literary accomplishments and the social background of that era. The present study undertakes to discover certain elements of unity within it. One of its central purposes has been to show that the period from the end of the Civil War to about 1885 does comprise a recognizable literary "period" with certain conscious aspirations which had, and still have, value. It attempts to avoid the error of judging the past largely through the standards of the present and aims to look at the Victorian age as nearly as possible through Victorian eyes. "Realism" is the key word, though not in the sense given it in the twentieth century. It was a "vision" of the Victorian mind in its quest for reality. Like other such phenomena of literary history the Victorian mode was slow to become articulate. At first it was tentative and experimental. Later it found a period of realization and full expression, somewhere about the middle 1880's, and then gave way to a different literary program. After 1890 one can see clearly diverging tendencies which marked the end of Victorian realism. This cycle constituted the rhythm and inner logic of the period, and a new effort to understand it may help to restore to some favor an overly maligned phase of the national history.

II

THE SEVENTIES:
A Decade of Hesitation and
Literary Experiment

It's all tears and laughter as I look back upon that admirable time, in which nothing was so romantic as our intense vision of the real.

HENRY JAMES

MORE THAN ANY OTHER DECADE between the Civil War and the twentieth century the 1870's was a period of hesitation and uncertainty, a curious blend of the old and the new elements in American society and thought. The long conflict over slavery was a second American Revolution in a far wider sense than the first had been. As Charles Dudley Warner wrote in *The Gilded Age:*

> The eight years in America from 1860-1868 uprooted institutions that were centuries old, changed the politics of a people, transformed the social life of half the country, and wrought so profoundly upon the entire national character that the influence cannot be measured short of two or three generations.[1]

The Seventies comprised an epoch of intellectual cleavage, religious doubt, and swift social change. The new generation faced a disillusioning set of realities in the raw, emergent industrialism of the postwar years, and for the moment it was without an adequate social or intellectual philosophy with which to confront this situation. As later historians looked back on the 1870's, it seemed a period of maladjustment between the intellectual American and his environment. Such men as Clarence King, Henry Adams, Henry James, Howells, and Mark Twain turned away from the harsher realities of "The Gilded Age," or seemed unaware of the drift of affairs. "The old culture had broken down," wrote Van Wyck Brooks, "the old causes were dead and forgotten, and no new ideal had arisen to rally the minds of the younger men." These young men, Brooks said, were frustrated and confused by a mushrooming urban civilization which had "lost the sanitary influences of rural life," and in which Lincoln's stature had shrunk to Grant's.[2]

The political scene, indeed, presented a spectacle of scandal and guilt in high places. In 1869 Gould and Fisk were involved in a conspiracy to corner gold and force exorbitant rates from merchants compelled to have gold for the custom-house. Wall Street and Grant himself fell into the shadow of this unsavory episode. In 1872 came *Credit Mobilier,* an elaborate stock swindle of the Union Pacific Railroad in which it was

19

discovered that Oakes Ames had distributed a quantity of stock among influential members of the House including the Vice-President. In 1873 Grant was again implicated in the fall of the House of Cooke as the nation felt the weight of a sharp economic depression. The national Greenback Party formed a temporary coalition with the Grange to fight eastern business interests and freight hikes. The Knights of Labor gained adherents from various segments of the disaffected and struck repeatedly, though without much gain, against the corporations. The year 1875 witnessed a climax of degradation and scandal with the impeachment of Secretary Belknap and the involvement of the beautiful Mrs. Belknap; the Emma Mine affair which brought disgrace to the American Minister to Great Britain, R. C. Schenck; the disclosure of the whiskey racket in St. Louis where close friends of the president had been discovered remitting whiskey taxes in return for rich remuneration; and finally the stirring drama in the House, nine days before the political convention of 1876, during which the reputation of Blaine was involved in the sale of the bonds of the Little Rock and Fort Smith Railroad. All this, ironically coming to a climax in the very year of the centennial celebration for the signing of the Declaration of Independence, was played against the background of reconstruction politics. The "Great Barbecue" of American political opportunism was one part of the panorama of life in the decade of the Seventies.

But it was not the whole picture. Only if we grant that political lobbyism can determine the intellectual tone and decisively affect the higher aspirations of a people, can we agree with the social historians that "The Gilded Age" was mired in a morass of corrupt politics. Intellectuals in the Seventies looked both before and after to discover sources of cohesion and unity. The older idealism, for instance, provided some assurance that the golden day of American literary hopes had not really disappeared from the scene. Thoughtful men and women sought to redefine the heritage of transcendental thought and to counter the outward expansion of "The Gilded Age" with a new inner vision of ideality. The panacea, they felt, did not lie in a negative program of social criticism, however badly that was needed. Instead, it should be sought in an intellectual effort to harmonize the earlier democratic gospel with the new realities of the postwar decade.

No easy task, to be sure, and the voice of intellectual America during the tragic era may have sounded strident and a bit shrill. Those who, like Whitman, placed their hopes in the democratic idea found disturbing doubts in the social spectacle of the 1870's. Whitman restated his faith in *Democratic Vistas* in 1871, yet this reaffirmation seemed founded more in hope than in confidence, and the millenium appeared to beckon him mockingly from the future. Nevertheless, he rallied himself to a new and strengthened dream of the ultimate triumph of democracy. His volunteer nursing of the soldiers of both sides was itself a symbolic act, a sign that the breach between North and South would not be permanent, but in 1872 his health was broken and, like the nation itself, this break was long in healing. He came to realize that the "four years' war" was pivotal to the entire scheme of *Leaves of Grass*. His idealism was shaken if not diminished by the experience, and the realization of his hopes seemed more remote. "His war biography," wrote Henry S. Canby, "is a story of a rebirth of idealism, and the sublimation of one of the most powerful egoisms in literary history."[3]

In one way, the aftermath of Bull Run and Gettysburg was a fresh stimulus to patriotic motives, perfectabilian hopes, and faith in the progress of the nation. De Forest described the Northern view in noble words when he wrote in *Miss Ravenel's Conversion*:

> The twenty loyal millions of the North shuddered with rage at the insolent wickedness of those conspirators who, merely that they might perpetuate human bondage and their own political supremacy, proposed to destroy the grandest human fabric that Liberty ever built, the city of refuge for oppressed races, the hope of nations.[4]

De Forest understood that Northern hands were not free of guilt. He knew at first hand the realities of war, defeat, cowardice, political preferment, and questionable motives. But in his two best books, written in the immediate postwar years, he held to his faith in American principles.

One of the characteristic things about the Seventies was its response to the bustling feminist movement of the times. Constance Rourke in *Trumpets of Jubilee* has given us a vivid picture of the age and of the ways in which the long and turbulent history of feminism in America found new, colorful partisans in the social spectacle of "The Age of Innocence." From *Charlotte Temple* to *The Female Poets of America* in the delicate Forties the eternal feminine had clung closely to the literary fashions of the moment. At first, feminism had been associated with *Lady's Book* sentiment and obtrusive morality. In the rise of transcendental aspirations, however, it became colored with the tinge of liberalism, Margaret Fullerism, Fourierism, and freedom; it strode like Zenobia with a challenging rose in its hair. Out of the famous "conversations" at Boston and the anti-slavery sentiment of the Forties came the 1848 declaration of women's independence drawn up under the aegis of Elizabeth Cady Stanton. After the Civil War, suffrage for women was not the only aspect of the movement which entered the arena of "Gilded Age" society and politics with a new and vigorous force. Outwardly its aims were phrased by Wendell Phillips who, in 1850, flung the challenge: "After the slave, then the woman!"

About 1870 the Feminists split into conservative and radical wings of the party, and, as the slogans, manifestoes, speeches, and meetings gradually articulated the aims of the parties, there emerged in the background the spectre of further emancipations. "Freedom they proposed to have," says Constance Rourke, "and something more besides." The opprobrious term, free love, attached itself to the radical wing of the party.[5]

> The left wing of the feminist movement of which Mrs. Stanton and Miss Anthony were leaders was not concerned with the ballot alone, but with an entire reconstruction of the social and democratic position of women; candor on the problems of marriage and divorce was reaching astonishing lengths.[6]

The Civil War had given them a freedom they proposed not to relinquish. And now in the phantasmagoria of the "Dreadful Decade," the movement caught up some strange figures of earth: George Francis Train, described as "a crack-brained harlequin and semi-lunatic—with money"; Theodore Tilton, a dashing editorial Apollo, abolitionist, radical feminist, and follower of causes, whose wife was involved with Henry Ward Beecher in a notorious front-page scandal of the Seventies. Victoria Claflin Woodhull and her sister, Tennessee Claflin, who founded a weekly newssheet in 1871 on the principles of feminism, pantarchy, and universalism: "The organ of the most advanced Thought and Purpose in the World . . . the organ of Cardinary News. . . . News of the Aspiration and Progression of Mankind toward Millenial Perfection." Mrs. Woodhull, who became the first woman candidate for President in 1872, bespoke a philosophy of "Integralism, peace, love, truth, progress, purpose, and aspiration." She wore a flower at her throat and spoke with a beguiling femininity, boldly asserting the doctrine of free love.

Women in politics, women in education, women in the novel, women in the marriage relation, the problem of divorce, feminism and anti-feminism, the Bloomer girl, the symbolic *Lily*, a feminist publication— every possible variety of the subject found expression in and out of politics and society in the Seventies. As someone has put it, the proper study of mankind, in these years, was *woman*. Womanism in America had always associated itself with flowing gowns and poetry, with *Lady's Book* sentiment. It had always been regarded as eccentric and slightly neurotic, and not quite "nice." Now, however, in an age of politics and science, in the dawn of a new realism the movement became colored with different tones. A decade which vacillated between such intellectual extremes as the hard-boiled philosophy of survival-of-the-fittest and a lush Victorian sentimentalism over women could touch most of the notes in between. William Graham Sumner, one of the most tough-minded of the social Darwinists, combined the extremes in a single phrase. The two chief things with which government has to deal, he said, were "the property of men and the honor of women. These it has to defend against crime."[7] Rarely did the feminism of the Seventies remain unmixed with esoteric doctrines of free love, the religion of science, spiritualism, and universal progress. In New York five seances were operating at a profit four or five times a week in which dead lovers and relatives returned to caress the attending members for a dollar a sitting. In 1875 Madame Blavatsky and other feminists founded the Theosophical Society, and Mary Baker Eddy in the same year published *Science and Health,* a kind of transcendental approach to disease and mental healing. Walt Whitman had proclaimed the complete equality of the sexes and had spoken in his *Democratic Vistas* (1871) of the great need for women, the mothers of men. The self-consciousness of "The Age of Innocence" pronounced his *Leaves of Grass* immoral, yet the prevailing idealism toward women could be shared by writers as different as Whitman and Sidney Lanier. The voice of Lanier from the South cried out for a return to chivalry in the attitude toward women who, he felt, had redeemed the time. The period he described as "the epoch of Victorian women" and he regretted that the tendency of the time had been to dethrone her from the heights on which the Elizabethan poets had placed her.

Realism toward the woman question came usually from women; idealism from men, with some noteworthy exceptions, of course, like Henry James's *The Bostonians* or De Forest's *Miss Ravenel's Conversion* and *Kate Beaumont.* It was argued that men's brains were heavier than women's, that women were rash and impetuous, that they should not have the suffrage. Nonsense outweighed common sense in these forum discussions which literally filled the periodicals with articles and the public rostrums with speech. In the fiction of the Seventies, however, the accent began to shift from idolatry of women toward a more realistic presentation and likewise toward a scientific investigation of the springs of feminine conduct. It was the stimulus of the new evolutionary psychology, the essay of John Stuart Mill in 1869 on "The Subjection of Women," and Harriet Beecher Stowe's "Lady Byron Vindicated" (*Atlantic Monthly*, 1869) which touched off the postwar controversy about the new American woman. Henry Adams, a disciple of Mill, gave his lecture on "The Primitive Rights of Women" in Boston in 1876 with the professed aim of proving that women in primitive societies had not been in subjection, but rather were free members of the clan. He named the Church as the chief instrument in the dethronement of woman from her primal equality in society by its elimination of her from the Trinity. Adams represented the feminist position of the enlightened conservative. Parkman entered the lists on the side of reaction with an article unsympathetic to suffrage and equality. T. W. Higginson published his

Common Sense About Women in 1879. Articles in the *Atlantic, Harper's*, and the *North American Review* explored the subject in all its fascinating variety and suggestion.

Realism about women derived from two distinct, quite different sources, science and literature. In 1863 Rebecca Harding Davis wrote in "Paul Bleeker": "I chose a bilious, morbid woman to talk to you of, because American women are bilious and morbid. Men all cling desperately to the old book type of women, delicate, sunny, helpless . . . but how many of them do you meet on the street?" The new evolutionary psychology helped turn Howells, James, De Forest, Weir Mitchell and others toward soberer methods of analysis in the treatment of women characters in fiction. While Darwinists like Chauncey Wright were investigating the naturalistic origins of mental activity, other Americans went to the German behaviorists for new light on psychology. G. Stanley Hall was one of the leaders in this, bringing the studies of Wundt, Herman Lotze, Helmholtz, Fechner, Zeller and other German founders of psychology to the pages of the scientific journals, stimulating the study of psychic states as a means of understanding the mind. Holmes had approached character from a part medical, part theological point of view in *Elsie Venner* and *The Guardian Angel* in the Sixties, and as the growing interest in psychology and sociology began to affect the treatment of character in fiction, the brave hero and the virtuous heroine slowly receded from the scene. They had belonged, it became clear, to a pre-Darwinian psychology in which the origins of the mind were regarded as supernatural. Now, however, the study of growth and change under environmental conditions led novelists to discover and depict the "complex" character and especially the young American woman as a product of peculiarly national social conditions.

In literary circles in the Seventies some voices bespoke a renewed hope for a wave of nationalism in American letters. Horace Bushnell predicted a new and mighty literature, comparable to that of the Elizabethan period, with America as its theme. Henry James, years later, looked back upon the postwar years as a homogeneous experience in the national life. The war had given him a sense of awakening in which "America would be given . . . to a tune altogether fresh, so that to hear this tune played out might become on the spot an inspiring privilege."[8] And Thomas S. Perry, one of the most brilliant and balanced minds of the newer generation, voiced the temper of intellectual America turning from the despondency of conflict to face the challenge of evolutionary science, business acquisitiveness, and loose political morality:

> We ourselves know that even out of Civil War there may arise a grander comprehension of patriotism, fuller national growth, a broader view of the nation's duties and responsibilities.[9]

24

In the *Atlantic Monthly* for 1871 appeared the first installments of De Forest's *Kate Beaumont*, Howells's *Their Wedding Journey*, Henry James's *A Passionate Pilgrim;* three of Bret Harte's California stories; essays by John Fiske, John Hay, E.P. Whipple, Higginson, and Stedman. The same year saw the publication in *Hearth and Home* of *The Hoosier Schoolmaster*. *Roughing It* came in 1872, and in September of that year Howells wrote enthusiastically to James: "What do you intend to do for literature in '73?—a year destined to be famous."[10] The newly appointed editor had achieved the heights of his ambition at a young age and was anxiously in search of new material. His optimism reflected the spirit of a coming group of writers. *The Gilded Age* appeared in that year and Henry James finished such fine early stories as "The Madonna of the Future" and "Madame de Mauves." Howells himself completed *A Chance Acquaintance*, the first of a series of delicate penetrations into the psychology of the new American woman. A great question glowed in literary circles: what was to be the nature of the new literature?

Amidst the social desperations of "The Gilded Age" there was taking place a stir of intellectual activity borne in part upon the wings of evolutionary science and signalized by the appearance in 1871 of Darwin's *Descent of Man*. The *Atlantic* under Howells expanded quickly into the rich fields and new pastures of art, music, politics, and especially of the new science. While its literary section echoed to the names of Balzac, Turgenev, Taine, Sainte-Beuve, Dickens, Flaubert, Thackeray, in science the *Atlantic Monthly*, a symbol at once of new thought and respectability, moved steadily away from its classical moorings into, among other things, the uncharted waters of the Darwinian controversy. The success of the indefatigable popularizers of Spencer, Huxley, and Darwin in America —especially E.L. Youmans and John Fiske—and the influence of such new scientific periodicals as *Popular Science* and *Appleton's Journal* impelled the staunch literary magazines like the *North American Review*, the *Nation, Harper's, Scribner's* and the *Atlantic* to open their pages to natural selection, social Darwinism, and the scientific spirit. "The truth is," wrote E.C. Stedman in 1875, "that our school girls and spinsters wander down the lanes with Darwin and Huxley and Spencer under their arms; or if they carry Tennyson, Longfellow, and Morris, read them in the light of spectrum analysis."[11] The older and more narrowly literary approach to knowledge had indeed suffered some severe shocks. Huxley described poetry as "sensual caterwauling," and Turgenev's sceptical Bazarov (*Fathers and Sons*) opined that "a good chemist is twenty-times as useful as any poet."

Nevertheless the American mind of the Seventies was more sail than anchor. The heavy ballast of materialism and scepticism emanating from the pursuit of the dollar and from the naturalistic implications of evolutionary science could not altogether impair its buoyancy. The ideals of the Enlightenment and human perfectibility were firmly rooted in it; scientific doubts about the supernatural origin of mankind might unsettle it, but could scarcely warp it from its own orbit. The new science, instead, was swept into the optimistic view of evolution and lent its weight to the postwar idealism. A new phoenix was to rise over the ashes of Appomattox and Gettysburg. John Fiske, John W. Draper, and Youmans—philosopher-scientists—carried the torch of the new Positivism from Herbert Spencer to eager audiences of intellectuals in Boston and New York. The law of natural selection, the atomic theory, the physics of energy-conservation, and the mechanical theory of the universe—all ideas which later led to determinism and despair—now seemed to point to a new vision of reality in which only the forms, not the essence, of Christian teleology would be discarded. Henry Adams, much interested in Darwin and the historical idealism of Comte, saw only unity and certainty in the ideas of natural selection. Writing in his autobiography of the geology of Lyell, he said:

> Natural Selection led back to Natural Evolution and at last to Natural Uniformity. This was a vast stride. Unbroken Evolution under uniform conditions pleased every one—except curates and bishops; it was the very best substitute for religion; a safe, conservative, practical, thoroughly Common-Law deity.[12]

"Unity and uniformity," he felt, "were the whole motive of philosophy." It made little difference whether Biblical orthodoxy or scientific evolution was the way which led to unity. "Any road was good that arrived."[13]

The old romanticism was dead. Long live the new! Young men and women of the Seventies had intellectual interests and aesthetic aspirations, often vaguely defined, but deeply felt. They found excitement in the art classes of William Morris Hunt, the religious murals of La Farge, the portraits of J. F. Millet and the landscapes of Corot. They read the novels of George Eliot, Reade, Trollope, and Bulwer-Lytton, languishing over the inordinate delays of serialized fiction. They were too "sophisticated" for "The Idylls of the King," preferring "Ulysses" or "The Lotus Eaters." They drove to the opera in broughams and landaus and brown coupes to hear the music of Gounod, formed Browning societies, heard Fiske's lectures on the cosmic philosophy, studied the pre-Raphaelite vogue, and perused the latest English and American periodicals. For the *avant-garde* there were the lemon-covered volumes of the French *Revue des deux mondes* which led Henry James into ecstasies. It would be hard to find a period in American history when Art (with a capital) was taken more seriously or when the aesthetic ache was stronger in the blood. These were the years of greatest prestige for the literary monthlies which drew their contributors from the best writers of fiction at home and abroad, unhampered by international copyright laws, and they addressed their wares to a general, largely feminine audience. The newest novels were widely reviewed, discussed, and analyzed, their authors berated, and their denouements prophecied before the appearance of the last installments. *Scribner's Monthly* made great contributions to the broadening of popular culture in the Seventies by its improvement in the wood engraving process and its encouragement of civil service reform, kindergarten instruction, tenement house development, and religious liberalism. The revival of the lyceum system under Redpath, the popularity of lecturers like Mark Twain and Thomas Nast, and the founding of the Chautauqua Movement in 1874 helped stir the public mind. As Allan Nevins described it, "half a dozen years after the war it was evident that a new literature, displacing sentimentalism by realism and overthrowing a narrow eastern regionalism by its democratic breadth, was coming in like an irresistible tide."[14]

Much of the intellectual activity of the Seventies revolved about two opposite poles, the West and Europe. But these were antithetical symbols of two universal needs, the need for innocence and the need for experience. Their ideals shaken by the struggle over slavery and the lowering of public morals in "The Gilded Age," sensitive individuals turned toward the older voices of Europe seeking a new inspiration in the faded splendor of Old-World capitals. James and Howells created the self-conscious international novel. Artists travelled to Italy and Paris to absorb Bohemian freedoms and glory in the treasures of antiquity. On the other hand, they distrusted the darker shades of European society and like true innocents abroad they felt that a more genuine source of vitality, the real right thing, was after all an American secret. Europe held the key to the past, art, culture, decor, tradition, experience; America had found the *open sesame* to the future—democracy, youth, hope, freedom, progress, innocence. Which way should a writer turn? Should he search for reality in the national scene, a "daring Americanism of subject," which, as Thomas Wentworth Higginson pointed out, had brought such success to Cooper and Mrs. Stowe?[15] Or should he avoid the dangers of a too exclusive nativism and direct himself to the universal motives of mankind? "By insisting above all things on the novel being American," said T. S. Perry, "we mistake the means for the end."[16] Americanism must be subordinated to larger ideals, facts to general principles, realism to idealism. Should the novelist model himself after the fashion of the French realists, Balzac, Flaubert, Zola, the Goncourts? Yet this path was an affront to morality and false to the "higher decencies" of American life. The choice was a difficult one, for behind it lay the old, old conflict between the dreams of innocence and the songs of experience. Edith Wharton later was to dramatize this conflict in the figures of May Welland and Ellen Olenska, symbols of American "innocence" and continental experience sparring for the affection of the confused but enlightened intellectual, Newland Archer.

It is not easy to discover regional patterns in the thought and expression of the Seventies, but certain generalizations can be made. In New England, Unitarian liberals like O. B. Frothingham and Moncure Conway carried on the individualistic idealism of Emerson. Sociological criticism seemed contrary to the basic American faith in the primacy of the individual, and novelists like Howells and James felt that everything came at last to focus upon character. But the earlier transcendental exaltation of the individual soul was giving way to an increasingly critical and analytical approach to character with more than a hint of determinism. Fatalistic elements, for instance, are strongly written into the character of Isabel Archer in James's *The Portrait of a Lady*. As one critic has said, "In portraying her character and her fate, James was also writing an essay on the interplay of free will and determinism. . . . James knew how little she was free, other than to follow to an impulsive extreme everything she had been made by her environment and her background."[17] In his other books of the Seventies, James strove to paint the American soul in such generic types as Roderick Hudson, Christopher Newman, or Daisy Miller. Howells, too, discovered vitality in the individual, especially the young American girl, rather than in the group. When Charles Dudley Warner urged him to try a large canvas, he replied:

> I find I do not care for society, and that I do care intensely for people. I suppose, therefore, my tendency would always be to get my characters away from their belongings, and let four or five people act upon each other.[18]

On the Middle Border, however, the prewar spirit of individualism was gradually altered, under economic stress, by a tendency toward cooperative social activity and an interest in political reform of eastern freight hikes and high tariffs. In philosophy such westerners as Brokmeyer, Denton Snider, and W.T. Harris countered the eastern preference for individualism with a democratic idealism, derived from Hegel, in which "brittle individualism" was supplanted by a broader, nationalistic creed showing affinities with the earlier frontier equalitarianism. Western literary methods likewise showed a closer allegiance to the land and to native social conditions. Eggleston, for instance, studied rural schools, circuit-riding ministers, Methodism, real estate booms, and other social phenomena on the Middle Border in terms of the race-place determinism of Taine. Twain and Warner had satirized land speculation and Washington politics in *The Gilded Age*, the only novel of the decade which had successfully combined social criticism and satire with lasting literary merit. Bret Harte fathered the local color story in his Dickens-like mingling of satire and sentiment along the Pacific slopes. He burst into tremendous popular favor, then gradually settled into mannerism. In the South a more sentimentalized form of ideality survived as a compensation for the ravages of war. The vogue of Scott, as Mark Twain lamented, persisted there and the voice of Lanier was heard crying out for a return to the age of chivalry and decorum.

The wind was blowing in two directions during these years. Would the great American novel, when it was written, be a sweeping panoramic account of a social condition, slavery for instance, or would it be a profound psychological study of an individual? Writers were uncertain as to which was to be the prevailing current, but the temper of the Seventies was still largely individualistic. Social criticism was slow to take hold, though a collectivistic sentiment gradually developed in response to the economic depressions and political corruption of the period. The interest in social problems, which was to quicken the Eighties and reach a peak after 1887, had its literary beginnings in the 1870's. Lanier attacked the debilitating effects of trade in "The Symphony," Melville commented bitterly upon the malpractices of "The Gilded Age" in "Clarel," and Lowell in his "Ode for 1876" lamented the bovine comfort, inert prosperity, and the public scandal which endangered the heritage of freedom. In 1872 Whitelaw Reid urged Dartmouth graduates not to reject politics as a career: "The course and current of men in masses," he said, "that is the most exalted of human studies." It was recognized by a few observers that political ideas were, after all, the source and fountain of American originality. Western humorists had long used politics as a subject for indigenous literary treatment of western scenes and people. In 1866 Arthur Sedgwick urged the editors of comic magazines "to use politics as much as possible; it is the great chord of harmony that runs through the country."[19] The novel, too, responded with increasing tempo to sociological trends, though fiction could not approach the virility of treatment witnessed in the pictorial cartoons of Thomas Nast from *Harper's Weekly*. Elizabeth Stuart Phelps touched on the evils of the factory system in *The Silent Partner* (1871), Rebecca Davis described life in the iron mills with a missionary feeling of social injustice and dealt with political log-rolling in *John Andross*. J. G. Holland moralized in *Sevenoaks* over the career of a rich railway speculator who followed the path of the late Jim Fisk, Jr. Of De Forest's two political novels of the decade, *Honest John Vane* and *Playing the Mischief* a reviewer said: "You have but to change the names and dates a very little and you have the Congressional Washington of 1874-75"[20] Henry and Charles Francis Adams raised their voices against corporate greed and chicanery in the pages of the *North American Review* and Whitman spoke more broadly but no less earnestly on corruption in the *Galaxy* and later in *Democratic Vistas*.

Critical opinion, however, during the 1870's was inclined to turn away from social criticism, especially when it invaded the realm of art. Reviewers admitted the truth of the spectacle of social degradation, but hesitated over its value as literary material. Realism, literalism, factual reporting all were felt by the literary mind of the period to be beneath the level of true art. The characters of a work of fiction must "move on an ideal plane," wrote an *Atlantic* contributor, "parallel with yet above the real. . . . It is in this respect that his work differs from that of the photographer and the newspaper reporter."[21] John Burroughs represented the twilight of romantic thought in criticism in his comment on a work of J. T. Trowbridge which he found to be "almost too faithful . . . too literal, too near the truth, too photographic to charm the imagination."

> For however real and truthful your story or how faithful to contemporary events and characters, it must be bathed and flooded with that light that never was on sea or land to satisfy the best readers.[22]

T. S. Perry echoed these sentiments: "The idealizing novelist will be the real novelist," he said. "All truth does not lie in facts."[23]

The generation of the Seventies, not unlike other generations in American history, was confronted by conflicting and discordant social forces. It faced an ever-widening disparity between inherited ways of looking at the world and a new and harsh set of realities. It was a decade of hesitation and query, marked by intellectual stock-taking and soul-searching: whether to go on as though the war had not intervened to disrupt old dreams, or whether to move forward with science and progress toward a new democratic millenium; how to integrate tradition and actuality, science and religion, the individual and the group, literature and society, reality and idealism; which direction led forward toward vitality, Europe and Old-World cultural standards, with their taint of decadence, or America and the West, with its uncouth manners and its ethical innocence?

The story of the new generation's search to discover some pattern and harmony amidst the social problems and intellectual antitheses of the postwar decade is the plot material for the historian; the success of this effort, the denouement. In the world of letters, critics and novelists, sensitive alike to the older idealistic ways of thought and the new methods of science and pragmatism, earnestly sought for a renewed stabilization. The passage of years slowly assuaged the bitterness of sectional rivalry, and forward-looking leaders voiced a growing sentiment for reunion and national peace. The period was not wholly one of division and corruption and moral degradation. Social Darwinism provided the rationale for an economy of free enterprise and opened the door for opportunism and exploitation, yet increasingly there was heard in labor and agrarian circles a collectivist protest against the gospel of wealth and unrestricted economic individualism. Out of such opposing views, a political and social compromise emerged. In religion and philosophy, the materialistic implications of scientific thought threatened the fortress of orthodoxy and traditional faiths, but intellectuals found a new teleology in the evolutionary idealism of Spencer. A potential adjustment was in the making amidst the various pressures and warring elements of "The Gilded Age." America in the Seventies was redolent of a rank civilization, idle, rural, pastoral, the city streets often unpaved and muddy, plied by horse and buggy, dimly lit by gaslights in heavily ornate fixtures. New and old, country and city, uncouth and refined, poor and rich—a multiplication of paradoxes, yet the mood of the period was hopeful. There was promise of something better to come, and if we turn to the leading literary figures of the period, we may see the beginning of an aesthetic tradition from which developed the novel of Victorian realism.

It is not primarily to the first popular successes of Mark Twain in the late Sixties, nor even to the early short fiction and travel literature of Howells or James that one must turn for early signs of a growing American novel. Nor is it to the fiction of local color of Edward Eggleston or Bret Harte. Rather it is the remarkable and long-underrated novel of John De Forest, *Miss Ravenel's Conversion from Secession to Loyalty* (1867) which is the starting point of the Victorian American novel of realism and a standard of reference for much of the best fiction in the succeeding two decades. Almost twenty years after De Forest's book appeared Henry James wrote *The Bostonians*, his best wholly "American" novel, which in its different way of handling national life and manners, juxtaposing North and South, and treating the American scene from a European perspective, bears many interesting parallels to De Forest's book. In the following chapters it will be our purpose to delineate the course of Victorian realism in fiction and critical theory, a course which began with *Miss Ravenel* and closed with *The Bostonians*. Between these two dates, 1867 and 1885, was contained much of the essence of that vision of reality which constituted a native literary tradition in the Victorian mode.

1.

John W. De Forest: The Panoramic
Novel of Realism

The first American realist, a pioneer, and a gifted writer of war fiction, De Forest never found a public in his own time and his work has been greatly neglected down to the present. He has been described as a novelist at least potentially comparable to Tolstoi and Stendhal, yet it has been impossible until very recently to obtain any of his novels except *Miss Ravenel's Conversion from Secession to Loyalty* (1867). The latter alone has survived its inept title and certain mid-Victorian mannerisms to become an acknowledged masterpiece of the Civil War, superior in certain scenes to *The Red Badge of Courage* and at least as authentic in the depiction of battlefield and camp life as *A Farewell to Arms*. *Kate Beaumont* (1872) was equally successful as a treatment of Southern life and character and led William Dean Howells, who sought for thirty years to gain for De Forest the appreciation he deserved, to describe his talent as sufficient "to make the fortune of a dozen ordinary writers."[1] A *Harper's* reviewer called *Miss Ravenel* "the best American novel to be published in many a year" and compared it favorably with the books of Thackeray and Trollope.[2] De Forest lived for six years of his formative career in the Near East, France, and Italy. He knew both Italian and French well and had read widely in the fiction of Thackeray, George Eliot, Dickens, Balzac and Stendhal, a preparation which qualified him to write about the American scene during and after the War over Slavery with a cosmopolitan perspective and within the mainstream of European fiction. Howells wrote of De Forest in 1872: "we are not so much lacking in an American novelist as in a public to recognize him,"[3] and it has become apparent to perceptive readers by now that he cannot be dismissed as the author of a single realistic novel on the Civil War or one belonging to an outdated age because he quite naturally used certain of the stylistic devices of nineteenth-century fiction.

Twentieth-century scholarship and criticism has been slow to acknowledge De Forest's work and to accept fully Howells's judgment of it. Of his twelve novels, only one has been generally available, and though his war diary and autobiographical journals of reconstruction have been published, they have received only passing critical attention.[4] Dozens of his short stories and articles still lie buried in the magazines where they first appeared. The first and only attempt to collect a complete bibliography of De Forest was in 1956.[5] In the first sixty years of the present century only two articles on his work have appeared in scholarly periodicals.[6] During the 1920's in the literary histories of Parrington, Blankenship, Lewisohn, Calverton and others anxious to expose the gentility and fear of reality in "The Gilded Age," De Forest is unmentioned. The first to treat his work in any detail was Arthur H. Quinn in *American Fiction* (1936). Van Wyck Brooks discussed him favorably in *New England: Indian Summer* (1940), placing his emphasis negatively on the inadequacy of the milieu and the audience which ignored De Forest's work. Like Howells he blamed the reception upon feminine readers with "narrow horizons," though giving due credit to his skill in characterization, his irony and masculine style, and his broad national interests. Even after 1948 when *The Literary History of the United States* described De Forest as "the first American writer to deserve the name of realist," all but one of his novels remained inaccessible. A reprint of *Miss Ravenel*, edited by Gordon Haight in 1955, gave generous evaluation to that book and helped define the special quality of his work as a whole. Still, his relative obscurity down to the present time provides one of the unaccountable mysteries of our literary history and a bleak chapter in the record of American taste and opinion.

What was the particular nature of De Forest's accomplishment in the immediate postwar years and how did his novels contribute to the growth of realism? The answer must rest largely on his two best books, *Miss Ravenel* and *Kate Beaumont*, and it should likewise take account of his pioneering in social satire and the fiction of muckraking. But for Howells's continued championship of De Forest he might be even less known than he now is. His review of *Miss Ravenel* in 1867 touched on matters of characterization and dialogue, but it was in the war scenes where he particularly felt the force of De Forest's realism. Tired of seeing the war treated in fiction by women "fighting the campaigns over again as young ladies would have fought them," Howells recognized at once that De Forest "was the first to treat the war really and artistically."[7] He spoke of the bold, masculine quality of the De Forest style and "the stamp of verity" in the characters. Some portions of *Miss Ravenel*, however, were too strong medicine for the still untried young editor of the *Atlantic*, highly conscious of his female readers. He bridled, for instance, at "the highly colored and strongly flavored parlance of the camps" (De Forest had already permitted this, in a letter to his publisher, to be bowdlerised), and he was squeamish over the frank handling of the intrigue between Mrs. Larue and Colonel Carter. Mrs. Larue, described by a recent writer as "the first profligate woman to escape retribution in an American novel,"[8] was portrayed by De Forest objectively and even sympathetically as a refined and cultivated woman of Creole origin who bears comparison with Becky Sharpe or perhaps with James's Christina Light. She is as amoral as she is attractive, "as malicious as Mephistopheles," educated enough to quote Balzac and Dumas "le Jeune," talk enticingly of *le sainte passion de l'amour* and coolly enter into an adulterous affair with the husband of her close friend and relative to whom she remains loyal, amiable, kind, and even remorseful. American fiction has seldom approached the complexity of this portrait. Howells never extricated himself sufficiently from the canons of propriety to accomplish it, nor was Henry James quite prepared to match the outspoken candor of De Forest's pen.

Colonel Carter and Doctor Ravenel are male types which no American writer of the time but De Forest could have drawn with such a close mingling of sympathy, satire, and penetration. His insight into Southern manners and his equally careful observation of the New England, Puritan character, combined with his first-hand experience of army life and his detached European outlook upon both sections, produced these two antipodal portraits. They illuminate each other and the young hero, Colburne, as well, in a brilliant contrast of Northern and Southern attitudes and prejudices. Dr. Ravenel is a bit stiff in his moral righteousness and strong abolitionist sentiments, yet altogether human in his relations with his daughter, Lillie, and in the warmth and geniality deriving from his Southern temperament. But it is Carter who stands as the most completely realized character in the novel, and it may not be excessive to say that he is unsurpassed for fullness and virility in any fiction of the Civil War, then or now. He is more authentic than James's Southerner, Basil Ransom, in *The Bostonians* and he combines in himself extremes as remote as Rhett Butler and Colonel Sartoris. In his destiny are written volumes of psychology beyond the ken of De Forest's contemporaries in realism. His mixture of Latin blood and gallantry, his West Point training, his gentlemanly principles, and his weakness for alcohol and women make him a convincing product of two divergent cultures.

Howells regarded *Kate Beaumont* as De Forest's "shapeliest" novel, though he remained loyal to his first admiring opinion of *Miss Ravenel's Conversion* in later judgments when he compared De Forest to Balzac, Thackeray, and Tolstoi. In *Kate Beaumont,* he recognized "the first full and perfect picture of Southern life and society of the times before the war." De Forest's superiority in the treatment of Southern character, Howells observed, lay in "his refusal to deal with slavery except as a social fact," thus showing his people as men and women rather than as social phenomena.[9] The theme of a family feud handled in terms of the Romeo-Juliet "course of true love" is comparable to other American literary reworkings of Shakespearean or classical themes—Melville's use of Shakespeare in *Moby Dick,* for instance, or O'Neill's transposition of the Agamemnon story into nineteenth-century New England. De Forest sentimentalized his story, Victorian fashion, by the conventional romantic triumph of innocent love over social evil as he had done in *Miss Ravenel's Conversion*. When the mincing peace-maker Major Lawson senses the parallel between Shakespeare's plot and the healing of a Southern feud by a love match between the McAlister and Beaumont clans, he gurgles with delight: "What a romance! Why not? Romeo and Juliet in the South . . . with a happy ending." Frank McAlister reminds him, "You forget the fate of Romeo and Juliet," but the Major is too carried away with the "charming" thought, a subject "to decorate all over with flowers from Shakespeare." It is interesting to speculate on the ultimate reputation of *Kate Beaumont*, had De Forest chosen to write a tragedy, but his concession to "romance" was not only a bid for an audience but an indication that even the best writers in 1870 could not avoid the conventions of the romantic novel.

As in *Miss Ravenel*, however, the love theme does not obscure De Forest's authenticity of characterization, his range and versatility, and what Van Wyck Brooks called "his panoramic eye for American manners." A certain coherence and a balanced proportion of theme and character gave *Kate Beaumont* a structural unity which its predecessor did not achieve. As a study in tribal customs and codes of the Old South it is entirely convincing. His portrait of the martyred patriarch of the tribe, Old Colonel Kershaw, an idealized figure of a passing age, is one of his most appealing characters. Peyton Beaumont, the hard-drinking, hot-tempered clansman is much more than a caricature of a Southern plantation aristocrat. He is lifelike in his alternate blustering and tenderness and in his wavering loyalty to the feudal code while dimly sensing that a more enlightened age was making it a relic of the past. Another of the male characters is Randolph Armitage, the handsome and dissipated husband of Nellie Beaumont, who along with Colonel Carter may have influenced Howells's characterization of Bartley Hubbard of *A Modern Instance*.[10] His drunkenness and brutality toward his wife show De Forest's temperance principles and his tendency to preach, but he likewise provides the occasion for one of the most vigorously naturalistic scenes in the novel—a "Cracker" dance in a dilapidated log cabin belonging to two "poor white" women.

De Forest treats this episode with all the meticulous realism of the social historian. It belongs in the tradition of American grotesque humor extending from Longstreet and G. W. Harris to Faulkner and Caldwell. In its detail and honesty, it helps preserve the tone of actuality in the book. The setting is described as follows:

> The one room of the cabin, eighteen feet or so by twenty-five, was crammed. In the centre eight couples were jostling and elbowing through a sort of country dance. Squeezing up close to them and

squeezing against the log walls, and filling the two doorways, and covering the shaky stairways which led to the loft, was a mass of young men and girls, applauding, yelling, chattering, laughing, or staring with vacant eyes and mouth.

The scene, writes De Forest, was "nauseously" interesting. Armitage attends the dance in the company of Redhead Saxon, a Sut Lovingood type—a "coarse, long-legged, hideous desperado and sycophant in homespun" who calls his gentleman-companion "Square." Randolph's attentions to Sally Huggs result in a fight with her lover, a pugnacious mountaineer, but the incident ends without tragedy when Armitage loses consciousness in a drunken stupor, after exchanging shots with his rival, and is deposited on his doorstep by his servant and the loyal "Red" Saxon. De Forest's realism of low life shows itself in such an episode, as it does in the sinking of the *Mersey* early in the novel or in the Van Zandt scenes in *Miss Ravenel's Conversion*.

Howells's explanation for the public neglect of De Forest's work rested upon the fact that his "scornful bluntness" in handling female duplicity incurred the vengeance of women readers who could not appreciate his masculinity and his "inexorable veracity."[11] Yet Howells himself contributed to this result (if such was the case) in his own genteel demurring over Mrs. Larue, whose "lurid" career made him shudder, and in his apologetic comments on "the simply selfish and disagreeable Mrs. Chester," the aging coquette and the meddlesome aunt of Kate Beaumont.[12] Howells felt, in both these cases, that De Forest insisted too much upon "unpleasant" characteristics and that the vanity of woman was too openly and contemptuously revealed. His own treatment of a *femme fatale* in Mrs. Farrell of *Private Theatricals* was considerably less bold, but it is hard to believe that feminine readers in the Seventies were as sensitive as Howells assumed or that De Forest's Mrs. Larue, Mrs. Chester, Jenny Devine, or Olympia Vane were portrayed in too satiric terms, especially when they were counterbalanced by his many other idealized men and women characters. Mrs. Chester as a portrait of widowed vanity with a pathological mania for "young fellows" may be compared to James's Aunt Penniman of *Washington Square*. James's character is superior in the larger degree of amused detachment of the author. De Forest, for all his honesty and verity, loses something by his impatience and moral righteousness—a tendency, as Howells put it, toward "the New England ethicism so fatal to fiction."[13]

The judgement must rest ultimately, not upon De Forest's unkind treatment of certain women in his fiction, but upon the skill of his satire. Contemporary comment on his satiric tone used such adjectives as coarse, strong, rough, blunt, honest, masculine, and vulgar. One critic described him as "Hogarth with a pen."[14] Delicacy was not his forte, though in

Mrs. Larue he was able to maintain the proper balance between condemnation and tolerance by revealing her partly through the eyes of Dr. Ravenel, whose prejudices help mitigate the irony of the portrait. Both James and Howells spoke of De Forest's over-directness of style. Mrs. Chester is a case in point. She is almost a humor-character out of Jonsonian comedy or Restoration drama, except for the author's tendency to let his own indignation show through. Satire at its best requires moral indignation and even reform behind it, but the surface should be tranquil and unruffled. With Mrs. Chester he allows himself to become increasingly contemptuous as the story unfolds until he finally disposes of her with a curt indication that she died of "softening of the brain." Nevertheless, satire of De Forest's direct, honest sort was rare in the 1870's and its influence as a counterforce to sentimentalism was significant. Two separate strands of literary realism combined to form his style—native humor elements and the satiric detachment he found in Balzac or Michelet.

The American reading public in the Seventies vacillated in its taste between conventionally idealized Victorian "romance" and an eager, somewhat self-conscious curiosity to see itself and its national scenes realistically depicted. De Forest achieved both aims in his best two novels, but when he failed to find an audience he sought in such novels as *Overland* (1871) to appeal to the interest in western scenes and adventure or in mystery and regionalism as in *The Wetherell Affair* (1873). These books contain many passages of skilled description and interesting portraits of regional types, but one must turn to his political satire for some of his most pungent and advanced realism in the handling of native materials. Major Gazaway in *Miss Ravenel* was his first detailed study of political corruption. The episode of a hulking former prizefighter turned saloon-keeper who exchanges his influence as political boss of a small town for a commission in the regiment of the Tenth Barataria carries an air of conviction so vivid as to suggest that it was a thinly veiled transcription from De Forest's own experience. In fact, De Forest's own failure to gain a colonelcy in 1862, despite letters sent from influential friends to Governor Buckingham of Connecticut, is probably the personal background for his account of the cowardly Gazaway who is "whitewashed" and promoted by the Governor of "Barataria" over Carter's vigorous protests.[15] Political intrigue was to be the most vulnerable target of De Forest's satiric pen.

In 1872 he published a short story entitled "An Inspired Lobbyist," containing a caricature-portrait of one Ananias Pullwool, "the most successful and famous lobbyist in Washington," whose fat fingers were constantly in the pockets of congressmen and voters with an impudence which amounted to inspiration.[16] Pullwool is shown as a barefaced swindler into whose obese and disagreeable physiognomy the devil himself has entered. The story contained more bite and righteous wrath than subtlety, closing with a strong plea for extirpating such parasites from the halls of Congress. "The subject is too vast for the human pen," he concluded. "It requires the literary ability of a recording angel." Pullwool was an egregious emblem of corruption possibly inspired by Thomas Nast's lampoons of *Credit Mobilier* and the Tweed Ring. In the following year *Honest John Vane* began appearing serially in the *Atlantic,* a more extended satire on lobbyist activities in Washington and a piece of critical realism generally agreed to be the most successful political novel of the decade.

"Honest" John Vane is the victim of circumstances. He is well-disposed but weak, and the pressures upon him of his society-minded wife, Olympia, the high cost of living in Washington, and the system of privileges and dispensations all conspire to corrupt him. The major villain of the story, however, is Darius Dorman, De Forest's picture of the devil incarnate. He is described as "charged with some dark, pulverous substance," his features haggard and ghastly, with griping claws. He resembled some goblin from the "lower regions," a being from "a subterranean region with a highly heated history." There is even a suggestion of a tail hidden beneath his coat skirts, a stroke which led Henry James, reviewing the novel, to guess shrewdly that De Forest might have been reading Hawthorne. Through Dorman and a certain oily Senator Sharp, based closely upon one of the legislators of the Erie Railroad affair of 1871-72, Vane is persuaded to buy stock in a pure swindle called the Subfluvial Tunnel Road under the Mississippi River, uniting Lake Superior with the Gulf of Mexico! Sharp urges Vane to enter the field of "finance" or "special legislation" and to abandon his pet idea of legislation on abuses in the franking system.

De Forest was here simply transposing into a novel the events which followed the exposure of *Credit Mobilier* as published in the form of letters in the *New York Sun* from September to December, 1872. John Vane was a composite of several of the less guilty senators who had seen their mistake in purchasing the stock and returned it before the Luke Poland Investigation brought the whole Union Pacific Railroad affair into the open. Oakes Ames, the representative from Massachusetts, and James Brooks of New York were the two primarily censured and their expulsion from the House of Representatives was recommended. A reviewer of *Honest John Vane* suggested that the incidents of 1871-72 were thinly disguised by De Forest, and it does not take much imagination to recognize in such characters as the socially prominent party leader Senator Ironman ("Pig Iron" Kelley was one of the exonerated senators), the wily Sharp, and "Weathercock Vane" himself certain of the suspect, if not openly guilty, group which surrounded Ames. One of them, John A. Logan, came from De Forest's own state of Connecticut. Like Vane he had subscribed for shares, but had not paid for them, Ames covering for him (as does Dorman for Vane in the novel) out of dividends and giving Logan (like Vane) only a small cash balance.[17]

Again De Forest is compelled to close with a plea for decency:

> Can we not withdraw altogether from Congress the power of aiding corporations and schemers out of an income which is contributed by all for the equal benefit of all? . . . Nothing in the future is more certain than that if this huge "special legislation" machine for bribery is not broken up, our Congress will surely become, what some sad souls claim it already is, a den of thieves.

Honest John Vane and its immediate successor *Playing the Mischief* (the latter vying with Twain and Warner's *The Gilded Age* by portraying a woman lobbyist in Washington) were eye-openers in the Seventies and have been praised for their realistic exposure of malpractices in the Grant administrations. An *Atlantic* reviewer concluded that De Forest had written the best political satire yet in American fiction and said of his characters: "Whether they are pleasant people or not is quite beside the purpose. One feels them to be true and that is enough."[18] Howells praised De Forest's "masterly handling of the flabby material of our ordinary political virtue." As art, however, *Honest John Vane* showed more vigor than finesse, and it was the young Henry James who made this point. Reviewing the book in the *Nation* he compared De Forest to Charles Reade in a certain similar want of delicacy. He called the novel "wholesome" and its cause worthwhile, but he felt about the events an aroma of "vulgarity." The material De Forest handled dictated this tone, he admitted, because the author intended to "overwhelm the reader with the evil odor of lobbyism."[19] James could not conceal his own tenderness toward such themes as political corruption and vulgarity as subjects of fiction, but he touched accurately upon a characteristic of De Forest's fiction. Howells, too, had complained of his "bluntness," and Van Wyck Brooks echoed him by speaking of "the impalpably masculine character" of his work. At a time when New England was ready for realism, Brooks said, De Forest "showed the kind that New England was *not* ready for."[20]

As a novelist, even as a realist in the best sense, De Forest's reputation will rest eventually upon *Miss Ravenel's Conversion* and *Kate Beaumont*. In these and in his political satires he set a standard for a forthright kind of realism and demonstrated a range and variety of experience in American life and character which was not equalled by any of his contemporaries. The realities of the battlefield have never been surpassed in Civil War fiction, even by the brilliant journalistic colorings of Stephen Crane, who was probably indebted to De Forest in some of his war scenes, but was not his equal in professional military knowledge or in the sense of immediacy communicated in the battle scenes.[21] De Forest drew upon his war journal and his letters home while actually under fire for his descriptions of the agonies of wounded or dying soldiers, the grim sights of a field hospital, the noise and confusion and shock of battle, and his use of military language and profanity. When these journals were published in 1946, the source of many of the details in the novel came to light, though anyone who had taken the trouble to read his articles in *Harper's* during the years when De Forest was writing *Miss Ravenel* would have discovered similar material in his accounts of "The First Time Under Fire" and "Port Hudson."

Howells's theory of feminine-reader "vengeance" may explain some part of the indifference to De Forest's books in his own time, but it cannot account for the continued neglect of his reputation nor explain why he has not been accorded a more important place in literary history. One reason may be that De Forest, unlike Howells, never attempted to formulate a defense of his methods or a rationale for the novel of realism. His sole essay on the state of fiction in America was concerned with international copyright, a cause for which he argued throughout his career. His observations on "The Great American Novel" were brief and negative. He wondered in 1868 if it were not too early for it to be written and felt that insufficient talent existed in America. In practice he emulated the methods of Thackeray and Balzac, but he was silent about the techniques they used, and his reputation has suffered somewhat from the want of standards by which to measure it. More direct and vigorous by nature than either Howells or James, he was unwilling or unable to reject the conventions of the "romance," and the realistic elements in his two best books remain as partially integrated episodes of war or Southern life and reconstruction, parallel to, but outside, the structure of the narrative.

De Forest himself blamed his poor reception upon a "female or very juvenile public" which preferred *Helen's Babies* or *That Husband of Mine* to the realities of war and reconstruction.[22] On the other hand, he partially compromised with the double standard which prohibited the actual language of soldiers and the moral ambiguities of Mrs. Larue from appearing in monthly magazines so as to be "proper for families."[23] He felt it necessary to explain in an "aside" to the reader that "by Jove" and "by this and that" were bowdlerized substitutions for the real language of Colonel Carter or Lt. Van Zandt. Frequently throughout *Miss Ravenel's Conversion* he stopped to inject such authorial remarks as: "This is not the way heroes or heroines meet on the boards in some romances," or, describing the savagery of some unwomanly Southern women, "No novelist would dare invent such characters. Nothing but real life could justify him in painting them." In retrospect, he felt that he had been unable to describe the whole truth about war. "I tried and told all that I dared and perhaps all that I could," he told Howells, "but did not dare state the extreme horror of battle and the anguish with which the bravest soldiers struggle through it."[24] Once, in 1887, he wrote to the press about the "colonialism" of American letters, blaming this upon the "drenching" of our youth "with English pictures of life, English ideas and preferences and prejudices." Yet this call for independence (again in terms of the need for a copyright law) came belatedly from a writer whose most advanced work had suffered somewhat from American provincialism of taste and outlook and whose own models had been English or continental fiction.

In the early Seventies, De Forest was the most promising novelist in America. Yet even his unique war experience and his ample talent were not enough to gain him a just reception, despite some favorable criticism of his best books. The fault lay partly in the audience and partly in De Forest's own failure to achieve a satisfying harmony of realistic subject matter and romantic plots. The temptation is strong to compare him with Stephen Crane. Crane, of course, discarded the romantic love plot, replacing it with the theme of the maturing of a green recruit under battle conditions. De Forest had done something of this sort, incidentally, with his hero, Colburne; in fact, the transformation of New England innocence and simplicity into hardened combativeness is central to his interpretation of the effects of war. But the contrast between De Forest and Crane is more marked in style. De Forest's realism tends to be one-dimensional, linear—a matter of authenticity and accuracy. To achieve his aim, he was mainly concerned with greater precision of statement. Crane, on the other hand, deals with effects, visions, states of mind, impressions. De Forest is objective and scientific; Crane is concerned with the consciousness of the observer. De Forest adopts the loose and baggy methods of the omniscient Victorian author, while Crane seeks a tight adherence to a single point of observance. The difference lies in two diverging conceptions of realistic fiction, both valid, but appealing to different tastes. De Forest is a historian, Crane a painter. De Forest draws clearer outlines and recognizable names, dates, places, details. He is closer to Mathew Brady's photography, while Crane views the war with imaginative coloring, leaving a hazy impression of the actual military maneuverings, plans of battle, and tides of conflict.

To read De Forest today, one has to make allowances for the tastes and conventions of the Victorian mid-century novel. The theme of reconciliation of North and South, employing the familiar pattern of lovers from opposite sides, was a concession to contemporary taste unprepared for authentic scenes of war. Almost fifteen years after *Miss Ravenel* appeared, he sought once more to apply this formula in *The Bloody Chasm*, a novel dealing theatrically with the marriage of a Northern officer and a Southern woman. This time, the plot was more factitious than before, and suffered from the absence of De Forest's realistic war descriptions. After an arranged marriage is terminated, the officer disguises himself, courts his own wife, and wins her! Arthur Sedgwick, reviewing this novel for the *Nation*, stated bluntly that the Civil War was no longer a subject for such romantic treatment and that De Forest had failed to recognize the changed atmosphere of 1880. Whether the review was the cause of his ceasing to write or not, De Forest abandoned fiction in the Eighties and devoted himself to a revision of *Miss Ravenel's Conversion* and to editing his war diaries for a prospective collected edition of his writings. For all his undoubted talent, something in his age and milieu conspired to prevent the fulfillment of his earlier promise as a novelist. He did not take the novel as an art seriously enough to study its methods and to attempt to alter his style with the changing times. The absence of a strong current of native criticism of the novel left him hesitating between his continental models and the American materials he knew from experience. In a later age, he might well have become a major novelist. In the decades just following the war, circumstances worked against him. Women readers may have been responsible in part, but the age which ignored Melville was not one to appreciate De Forest either. Howells sensed the unfortunate timing of De Forest's career when he said that "his work has in some respects not only not been surpassed, but not approached among us—a realist before realism was named."

2.

William Dean Howells: The Romance
of Real Life

The 1870's were the last period in American literary history when it could still be said that there was an official locale and a group of writers and critics who constituted the leadership of the national letters. Boston and Cambridge, after 1880, would remain the symbols, but not the active centers of authorship. The process of decentralization begun by Howells's move from Boston to New York during the mid-Eighties, altered the character of literature in America and began the trend toward separateness and isolation which has marked so much of the writing ever since. At some indeterminate point in the late years of the 19th century, American writers began to look to Europe, not simply for nourishment and enrichment of their careers, but for the sense of fellowship and mutually exchanged ideas which they missed at home. This gradual and subtle change of feeling, though not precisely datable, marks the Seventies with special historical significance in the growth of literary thought and expression in America. Howells, as editor of the *Atlantic Monthly* from 1871 to 1881, became the official spokesman and central figure of the new fiction. By some unaccountable genius of perception he managed to gain the personal confidence and friendship of the three or four men who would become the leading writers of their generation, so that later historians have spoken of Howells, James, and T. S. Perry as a "triumvirate" and of Howells and Twain as a literary team of mutually shared understanding and admiration. "Mr. Howells," wrote Perry in 1882, "has made over the American novel . . . and, with one predecessor and one or two contemporaries, given it a place in literature along with the best of modern work." This small group of contributors to the *Atlantic* comprised a national "school" of writers with a potential, if not a fully articulated, philosophy of letters. As editor, novelist, critic, friend of genius, and generous correspondent Howells possessed the equipment and the tact to carry out the role of guide, philosopher, and friend to the new fiction. His reviews of others' work, his own expressed aesthetic ideas, his successful fiction of the period (together with the reviews and opinions of his own writing) formed the nucleus of the earlier realism.

Thus, while it is generally true that Howells's artistic creed in that period was corrective rather than deeply original and that it was weakened by his compulsion to play the role of protector of genteel sensibilities, the importance of his position as the youthful "dean" of American letters makes a review of his theories of realism during the decade of hesitation a rewarding task for the historian. Critical attention has been directed more often toward the middle years of Howells's career when he became an embattled champion of social causes and a critical realist, but the special blend of romance and reality which characterized his aesthetic temper during the Seventies remained to modify and soften his literary and social creed even during his later career.

Scarcely a full-blown theory of the novel, this creed was, instead, a development of Howells's poetic temperament mingled with a strong, bookish solution of the English writers of the eighteenth and early nineteenth century. It was a loose compound of what he called "romance" and what he regarded somewhat sentimentally as "poor real life." The first held for Howells certain transcendental implications and poetic associations, while "real life" meant to him the outward show of contemporary places, events and the average people whose habits, dress, manners, expressions—all the minutiae of everyday living—escaped the notice of the casual observer. Howells did not, however, consciously apply the word "realism" to fiction in any significant sense until after 1880. During the Seventies he was content in his critical writing with phrases which were relatively neutral— phrases such as "truth to life," "authenticity," and "the stamp of verity." Realism as an aesthetic concept or a rationale for the novel was for him a very gradually understood term, at first quite uncongenial with his poetic temperament. It was not until 1884 that he first spoke of the prevalence of "realism" in the literary atmosphere and began to associate this idea with the growth of the novel as a form. Like many of his contemporaries of the Seventies, Howells preferred the term "romance," derived from Hawthorne, because it allowed a greater license for the writer to shape his material and provided a larger opportunity for him to indulge moods of fancy and sentiment, or attempt poetic flights of the imagination.

Nevertheless, from the beginning of his own fictional career, he strove for an air of reality and truthfulness. His sense for contemporaneity of effect and truthfulness of observation was evident in his early travelogues and character sketches. Nice touches of human nature and gentle satire lent a salty flavor to his early fiction. Goldoni-like domestic comedies maintained the ballast of reality in these books and preserved them from excessive "archness" and sentimentality, but it does not follow that Howells was prepared to accept the philosophical implications of critical realism or determinism which characterized the advanced school of novelists after about 1890. Instead, he emerged very slowly from his first literary role—that of poet and "romancer."

His early sketches abound in flights of descriptive fancy, and in the books he read he praised the qualities of the "picturesque," the charming, the quaint, and the imaginative. The true artist, he felt, would "shun the use even of real events if they are of an improbable character," and would prefer to look upon man "in his habitual moods of vacancy and tiresomeness" where he is "very precious," rather than in his occasionally heroic moments.[1] Details, ordinary traits of American life, little everyday things, dull places, bits of landscape, conventional people, simple incidents—such are the materials for the writer—but they must be heightened by the touch of the artist to whom they become significant and meaningful. Like Goldsmith, "the founder and master of the natural school of English fiction," and Goldoni, "the inventor of realistic Italian comedy,"[2] Howells sought an eighteenth-century flavor of simplicity and gentle understanding—average people, urbane satire, quiet morality, and 'pure' taste. This was the mood of *Their Wedding Journey* and *A Chance Acquaintance*. Added to these influences was the tone of Irving's sketches, Hawthorne's play of mystery and fancy, and George Eliot's charming commonplace. Like George Eliot who gladly turned away from angels, prophets, and heroic warriors "to an old woman bending over her flower pot" while the softened light through the leaves "just touches the rim of her spinning wheel and her stone jug, and all those common things which are the precious necessities of life to her,"[3]—so Howells in similar phrase found man in his natural and unaffected dullness to be "precious." The rare, estimable quality of truthfulness which George Eliot found in Dutch paintings, Howells shared in his early romances. Their tempo is slow and the author pauses long to linger over scenes and attitudes of ordinary people—peasant women with hats of felt and straw carrying baskets of onions, an Indian wedding, quaint and pathetic, "quiet gliding nuns with white hoods and downcast faces." The figures are small, remote, and picturesque, exuding the charm of Old-World romance, moving as though in pantomime and presenting to the eye of the author an artistic arrangement.

In his quest for material for the *Atlantic*, Howells was led to read the European masters of realism, especially Björnson and Turgenev, and to hold up their work as a standard for the American realists, along with that of Hawthorne, George Eliot, Dickens, and Thackeray. In his early reviews of the Norwegian writer he discovered the perfect mingling of the ideal and the real which he sought in his own early romances. "Simplicity," "reticence" (that is, the art of representation by a few delicate touches rather than by elaborate detail), and the democratic quality of describing "humble, but decent folk" were the characteristics he admired in Björnson's *Arne, The Happy Boy, The Fisher Maiden* and other tales. "From him we can learn," Howells wrote in 1870, "that fullness exists in brevity rather more than in prolixity; that the finest poetry is not ashamed of the plainest fact; that the lives of men and women, if they be honestly

45

studied, can, without surprising incident or advantageous circumstance, be made as interesting in literature as are the smallest private affairs of men and women in one's own neighborhood."[4] When he reviewed the work of American realists, such as Eggleston, he brought it to the test of Björnson's example and found *The Circuit Rider*, for example, faulty in its tendency to use authorial comment on the characters. Björnson's mood of rural simplicity and common experience struck a chord in the young editor whose Ohio boyhood had been composed of such simple fare. It was a quality he found in George Eliot, too, and in the genre painting of J. F. Millet and the Dutch school of painters. One has only to turn through an early edition of *Their Wedding Journey* or *A Chance Acquaintance* to see how the illustrations by Augustus Hoppin or William Sheppard pictorially suggest Howells's sense of landscape and figures. Scenes on the Hudson River night-boat, a pair of rural lovers exchanging the slang of the day, an Anglican curate stepping directly out of the pages of Anthony Trollope, the clamor of Venetian gondoliers, a group of ordinary people in a railroad car, Hebrews discussing merchandising in the rich dialect of their race—such transcriptions from Howells's notebooks and travel sketches indicate the particular atmosphere of the realism of the commonplace which Howells discovered in Björnson, in George Eliot, Trollope, and Reade. It was the charm of the ordinary, the heightening of the commonplace into the "picturesque" with the touch of the pen.

This was the right mood. But there remained another important factor —the technique, especially that of portraying character. Here Howells turned to the example of the Russian, Turgenev, whose work he had read in the Cambridge years, the late 1860's, and which he later termed "my most notable literary experience." In the mid-Seventies, when Turgenev's influence began to be widely recognized, Howells was writing his first novels of character and learning the method of dramatic portraiture. Turgenev's method, he felt, "was to the last degree dramatic. The persons are sparely described, and briefly accounted for, and then they are left to transact their affair, whatever it is, with the least possible comment or explanation from the author."[5] In a letter to Charles Dudley Warner in 1877 he called the Russian novelist "the man who has set the standard for the novel of the future" because he avoided the long, tedious narrative in favor of allowing a few people to act upon each other. It was Turgenev's example which encouraged Howells to avoid the excesses of romanticism, on the one hand, and the large canvas and broad naturalistic picture of conditions, on the other. Later, he would come to the larger canvas, but for the time being, as he wrote Warner, "isn't the real dramatic encounter always between two persons only? Or three or four at most?" Above all, it was Turgenev's technique of objectivity which Howells admired in such novels as *Liza* and *Dmitri Roudine*. "He seems the most self-forgetful of the story-telling tribe, and he is no more enamoured of his creatures than of himself; he pets none of them; he upbraids none, you like them or hate them for what they are; it does not seem to be his affair." Turgenev's portrayal of young women in his books may have been the inspiration for Howells's own discovery of the American girl, and his praise of the young girl Natalie in *Dmitri Roudine* "whose ignorant trust, courage, love, and adoration for Roudine, changing to doubt and scorn,— whose whole maidenly being,—are expressed in a few scenes and phrases"[6] was written in the same year, 1873, that Howells's first such characterization appeared in Kitty Ellison of *A Chance Acquaintance*. It was, therefore, not only as an editor interested in bringing the European realists to American readers, but as a practicing novelist that Howells studied Turgenev and learned from him methods of dramatic portrayal of people and even hints for similar types he had observed in his own experience.

One comes closer to the center of Howells's aesthetic temperament in his fiction of the 1870's than in his essays and reviews, but his criticism for the *Atlantic* provides ample evidence of his preference for the poetic mood above the realistic. Reviewing Boyesen's *Gunnar* he found he liked the book because "it was the work of a poet."[7] Eggleston's *Circuit Rider* he praised for its truthfulness to social conditions, but described it as a "romance." He enjoyed James's *A Passionate Pilgrim* despite the fact that its atmosphere was "at first that of a novel," because it gradually changed to "the finer air of romance" and was, on the whole, a poetic and highly imaginative tale.[8] Writing to James of his own *A Chance Acquaintance* he concluded that the book had prepared him "better than ever for the field of romance."[9] It was not until 1879 that Howells began to clarify in his mind the distinction between a romance and a novel. Reviewing W. H. Bishop's *Detmold: A Romance* he pointed out that the romance, like the poem, was "at once more elevated and a little more mechanical than the novel."[10] And in the same year he found fault with Henry James's *Hawthorne* because his friend had used the terms synonymously. "The romance and the novel," Howells now thought, "are as distinct as the poem and the novel."[11] In 1882 Howells was still uncertain as to his preference between these two different directions for prose fiction. In his controversial essay of that year on Henry James, he tried to describe and account for the reaction of *Atlantic* readers toward James's early work. It was not always sympathetic, he pointed out; they found the flavor strange. In an effort to defeat the growing indifference to James's work, Howells emphasized the romantic and ideal qualities which readers had overlooked. He pointed out the likeableness of certain of the personages—Newman, the Touchetts, Claire Bellegarde. Then, Howells said, James stood at the dividing ways between romance and the realistic novel. He regretted that James had since chosen the path of realism and the novel.

His best efforts seem to me those of romance; his best types have an
ideal development, like Isabel and Claire Bellegarde . . . perhaps the
romance is an outworn form and would not lend itself to the repro-
duction of even the ideality of modern life. I myself waver somewhat
in my preference. . . .[12]

But it was in 1884 in a review of Bellamy's *Miss Ludington's Sister* when
Howells began to recognize "the prevalence of realism in the artistic
atmosphere" of the early 1880's and to associate realism with the novel, a
form quite different, he felt, from his first love—romance. The propor-
tionate emphasis between the two sides of his aesthetic philosophy began
to alter, and he now felt that there was "nothing antagonistic in realism
from poetry and romance." The two can exist together and Bellamy's
novel had done "about the only thing left for the romancer to do in our
times, if he will be a part of its tendency: he has taken some of the crudest
and most sordid traits of our life, and has produced from them an effect
of the most delicate and airy romance."[13] Howells spoke of this new
literary atmosphere with a certain regret and with the air of a man resigned to adjust to new things while at the same time sighing for a lovelier,
bygone day.

If Howells's aesthetic temperament in the Seventies was touched with
nostalgia for the romantic past, one needs only to sample the reviews of
his work during that decade to realize that, paradoxically, he was regarded as a modernist. Brownell in the *Nation* recognized that his work
showed great technical gifts, but felt that there was "a lack of romantic
imagination." Despite Howells's avowed adherence to the principle of
"romance," Brownell felt that his society novels were "all death to romance." He accused him of trying to substitute photographic detail for
imaginative creation and described his methods as "too unromantic . . . to
deal adequately with the large and important elements of fiction."[14] Emily
Dickinson, too, felt that the realism of Howells and James was touched
with pessimism—"their relentless music," she wrote to Higginson, "dooms
as it redeems."[15] Even Hamlin Garland, later Howells's ardent admirer,
was at first repelled and irritated by what he called Howells's "modern-
ity." In 1879 the *Nation* summed up the case against him as follows:

Like Mr. James, Mr. Howells is a realist—he copies life; and realism
in literature, although not so plainly a disappointment as in art, is
quite as unsatisfactory. . . . What is valuable in literature is not the
miniature of life, but the illumination of life by the imagination. . . .
Our regret is that Mr. Howells has built in stones of the street when
he might have built in more durable and beautiful material.[16]

But Howells in the Seventies was hardly a "realist," nor did he attempt
to build in stones of the street. Instead of copying "life," he tried to avoid

literalism and newspaper factualism. Bartley Hubbard in *A Modern Instance* was such a reporter, and Howells's description of his methods helps to clarify his own concept of the writer's task. "He went to work with a motive as far as possible from the literary motive. . . . He did not attempt to give it form. . . . He set about getting all the facts he could." In 1885 Howells wrote Mark Twain, disclaiming his membership in the "analytical school."

> What people cannot see is that I analyze as little as possible; they go on talking about the analytical school, which I am supposed to belong to. . . .[17]

If this was true in the Eighties, it was even more the case in his writing in the previous decade. Yet criticism of Howells remained persistently obtuse. Certain critics, however, saw more clearly the strength and purpose of his early fiction. Among them was Henry James who recognized at once his original qualities and his most significant contribution to the development of the novel—his young American women characters. There were four portraits of this type, in Howells's writing of the Seventies, who belong in the permanent gallery of the fiction of realism—Kitty Ellison of *A Chance Acquaintance*, Florida Vervain of *A Foregone Conclusion*, Mrs. Farrell, the neurotic female of *Private Theatricals*, and Lydia Blood, the heroine of *The Lady of the Aroostook*. James himself was indebted to Howells for his discovery of the type, and in his own international tales he developed it in his own way. In 1875, he reviewed *A Foregone Conclusion* in the *Atlantic Monthly*, a book which "puts us for the moment, at least, in good humour with the American manner." But James felt that it was in his representation of "the delicate, nervous, emancipated young women begotten of our institutions and our climate, and equipped with a lovely face and an irritable moral consciousness" that Howells was at his best and most spontaneous self. His equipment for this, James pointed out, was his experience with the *Atlantic*. His young ladies were the actual ones who perused that magazine.[18]

Howells's feminine characterizations were delicate and careful studies, complimentary, for the most part, to the national pride. They formed at once a new generic type in fiction, and they commenced a tradition in the novel of temperamental American young women whose distinguishing traits can be traced from them through Daisy Miller down to Edith Wharton's Lily Bart and Sinclair Lewis's Carol Kennicot. They were unconventional and innocent types placed in the complications of a new society, though they did not, as Thomas S. Perry too sanguinely put it, "settle everything by their native judgment."[19] More often their innocence, different from the calculated false front of May Welland, for instance, in *The Age of Innocence*, made them unwitting causes or unin-

49

tended victims of social maladjustment. Howells dealt realistically and at the same time generously with the type, reflecting the self-conscious Americanism of the 1870's in an eager parade of the national character, the western young girl, and the mildly neurotic young woman. When viewed historically, in the initial phase of the novel of realism and within the limitations of Victorian taste and literary decorum, Howells's originality in this type was notable. And the barrage of "anti-genteel" criticism of his work among the journalistic critics of the 1920's was either willfully blind to this fact or historically naive.

Kitty Ellison and her priggish Bostonian lover in *A Chance Acquaintance* (1873) vastly tickled the fancy of readers and were quickly promoted to the distinction of types. Arbuton's repudiation of Kitty and her counter-rejection of him became the subject of lively conversation and animated literary controversy. Some readers were provoked at Kitty's impertinence and western spirit of independence. Others, displeased by Howells's unromantic conclusion, felt "cheated out of a marriage festival and that pleasurable emotion which one feels at the sight of a bride."[20] But the critical reaction was in the main a highly favorable one. The *Nation* noted the American quality of individuality in Kitty, "her innocence, her readiness to be pleased, her kindness toward Arbuton's foibles, her sensitive dignity, [and] her charming humor"—all of which traits went to the making of "a real human being."[21] Henry James complimented Howells on his unerring touch and his portrayal of a character "so real and complete, so true and charming." And some years later T. S. Perry described Kitty as the first of Howells's delicate penetrations into the feminine over-soul, an independent and generous western type whose character testified to the democratic belief that inborn merit will triumph over arbitrary standards of etiquette or caste.[22]

Two years later *A Foregone Conclusion* appeared and its heroine, Florida Vervain, whose deeper, almost fierce, temperament given to mercurial moods and sudden perversions was abundant evidence that the author had added a different and equally original creation to his gallery of nervous women. Howells, as James put it in 1875, was "one of the few writers who hold a key to feminine logic and detect a method in feminine madness."[23] James sensed the special excellence of the character when he pointed out that Howells had achieved a singular triumph in gaining the reader's sympathy for a girl "who is positively unsympathetic, and who has an appearance of chilling rigidity and even of almost sinister reserve." Florida, he felt, "just escapes being disagreeable to be fascinating"; she represented the opposite end of the pole from Kitty Ellison and thus indicated the versatility of Howells's imagination.[24] Don Ippolito was recognized as a triumph among Howells's characters and as good as anything in American or even in contemporary fiction. He is a tragic figure in his hopeless straining for a different life, and his presence in the novel gave it a depth and seriousness which contradicts somewhat the belief that Howells always preferred smiling aspects and sunny moods. The ending of the story, however, was not only a sop to the sensibilities of readers of the *Atlantic*, but an indication of Howells's own genteel proclivities. He seems to have regretted his carrying the narrative beyond the rejection of the priest's love by Florida into the account of his death. Then, to make all right in the end, he tacked on the marriage in New York of Florida and Ferris. Apparently he did not trust his original instinct, to follow out the deeper shadowings of the tale, and sought to make amends to his audience which could not stand a tragic ending.[25]

Like Don Ippolito, Mrs. Farrell of *Private Theatricals* was a figure of almost tragic proportions, and in her case Howells did not force the conclusion to a conventional ending. Mrs. Farrell is in the modern sense of the term a psychological study and a realistic portrait of a neurotic woman, an inspired flirt, a fatally attractive coquette unable to restrain her strong resentments and her self-centered vanities. Her beauty is pointedly physical, her fickleness of mood and changes of heart are swift and perplexing, and according to one critic she was Howells's only portrait of a bad woman. Like Beatrix Esmond or Hedda Gabler she was the unworthy cause of tragedies (though Howells smooths over the rift between the two men at the end). Brownell objected that Howells had shrunk from the tragic *denouement* demanded by her character and career and had explained away his weakness on the ground of her inbred "histrionism." Howells's avoidance of tragedy in *Private Theatricals*, according to Brownell, was caused by his realism, his belief that this is an "every-day" world, and his "lack of romantic imagination."[26] But the story deserves a higher place among Howells's work because of its psychological penetration into the character of an arch and mischievous flirt whose capricious moods are essentially those of the stage. With a different emphasis the book could have taken on the more serious proportions of Henry James's *The Tragic Muse*. Howells's own interest in dramatic dialogue, his reading of Shakespeare and use of Shakespearean titles, and his twenty-odd plays might have prepared him for a firmer handling of narrative in terms of tragic drama. But the limitations of his concept of realism in the Seventies, at any rate, together with the proprieties of his audience prevented him from detailing the sterner realities. He remembered in his reading of Shakespeare's histories and tragedies that the passages he most liked were those "where the alliance of the tragic and the comic was closest."[27]

The latter Seventies were the hey-day of the American *jeune fille* in fiction. Daisy Miller had captured the attention of readers on both sides of the Atlantic. She was compared with Lydia Blood of *The Lady of the Aroostook* and both were regarded as types of American innocence.[28] Criticism divided over the question of which author had handled the type with more interesting, or patriotic, results. Editorials analyzed, not always sympathetically, the American Girl. She was described by one writer as vain, superficial, and self-conscious with an innate inability to be frank. Society divided itself into Daisy Millerites and anti-Daisy Millerites with the nationalistically inclined leaning to Howells's girls rather than James's. Lydia Blood is the last of Howells's uncultivated ladies of the Seventies who triumph over their difficulties. She is an admirable portrait of the "Yankee Schoolmarm" with all her New England self-repressions and self-consciousness upon her head; yet she holds to her training and convictions with a tenacity which sets off the Old-World sophistications and corruptions of Venetian society. Higginson felt that Lydia was Howells's best portrait because he had left off depicting "disagreeable" characters and trusted himself to a "generous impulse." Some reviewers objected to "vulgar" elements in the book, such as the scenes showing the drunken Hicks aboard ship. The same critic complained that Howells took a depressing view of the South Bradfield Massachusetts milieu, from which his rose had sprung, and accused him of "an absence of genial sympathy with the bright side of things"—a statement which gives the full measure of the genteel reader.[29]

One of the noticeable changes which came over Howells's fiction after 1880 when he resigned his editorship of the *Atlantic* to devote himself to writing may be seen in his treatment of the love theme. The master passion, which he later felt was, among novelists, treated in a monstrous disproportion to other relations of life, controlled the structure of his early books. Not that Howells was primarily interested in the love theme in its romantic aspects. Rather he was interested in the springs of feminine conduct and manners, but his early fiction inevitably shaped itself into the romantic pattern of courtship thus attracting but also misleading his conventional-minded readers. It was this division of interest which was partly responsible for the tone of disparagement which runs through much of the contemporary criticism of his early books. The disciples of "romance" objected to his "disagreeable" characters and his lack of fervor or passion or romantic incident. His work was characterized as "having the peculiar charms of unromantic bleakness, of spiritual tenuity, of a thin gilding of the picturesqueness of the commonplace."[30] Reviewers chastised him for his "clinical" methods and his anti-romantic strokes. Even more acute and objective observers like Brownell found defects in Howells's treatment of women. He confessed in 1880 that these ladies did not seem "the important creations they are almost universally assumed to be," and that Howells's cleverness veiled the fact that they lacked genuine humanity. They were instead mere "machinery."[31]

Despite such comment, Howells's portraiture of the Young American Female in the 1870's was widely popular, and in the perspective of the growth of realistic fiction, it was a significant forward step. His instinct for the complexities and psychological shades of character was subtle, his ear for dialect was accurate, and his literary style masterly. If his early fiction lacked high drama and bold adventure, it was because he deliberately sought out the non-dramatic and the commonplace in a reaction against the passion and moving accidents of mid-century romantic fiction. His theory lagged somewhat behind his practice, for he clung to the concept of "romance" and to the poetic and imaginative associations this word had for him. Reticence later became for him a conscious part of his creed of realism, and it was decades after he formulated his ideas in defense of propriety and the smiling aspects that critics like Mencken began to belabor him as timid and spinsterish for his treatment of the master passion. Mencken, Lewis, Ludwig Lewisohn, and others charged Howells with a variety of evasions, including a painful consciousness of sex, but in *Criticism and Fiction* Howells rested his case squarely on the grounds of realism and fidelity to the common experience of his average people. Guilty intrigue, adultery, passion, and "the fetid explosions of the divorce trials," simply were not true to the American experience as he knew it. If "the profound dread and agony of life, the surge of passion and aspiration, the grand clash and glitter of things"[32] constituted reality to Mencken, they were the exception for Howells, and to devalue his work because he did not see life as they did in the Twenties (or as some did) is a point of view scarcely to be taken as serious criticism.

3.

Henry James: Aesthetic Theories and Critical Methods

Several sources of interest belong to the early critical writing of Henry James, a phase of his career which began in 1864 with reviews for the *Nation* and *North American Review* and achieved recognition and fulfillment with the appearance in 1878 and 1879 of the two volumes, *French Poets and Novelists* and *Hawthorne*. James's criticism has been closely studied in a number of excellent articles and books[1] from which three different points of emphasis have emerged. First, the criticism may be considered as a reflection of his youthful reading of English and French fiction, revealing the evolution of his tastes and the formation of some of his methods as a novelist. Second, the critical essays provide a more direct approach to James's ideas than does his fiction, where the ideas are rendered through character, scene, and incident. And third, there resides in this early work the discovery and development of a technique of literary portraiture which was to become James's signature as a critic and mark the finest development of his non-fictional writing. In a letter to his friend, T. S. Perry, in 1867 James expressed a timorous but yearning ambition to do for American letters what Sainte-Beuve and the best French critics had done for French literature. He spoke in a highly serious, dedicated way of such a mission at the thought of which he wrote, "my eyes fill with heavenly tears and my heart throbs with divine courage."[2] Thus, before his interests centered mainly upon fiction, James thought of himself as a critic, and if criticism became a secondary activity in his later years, it remained a significant corollary to his creative work and scarcely separable from it.

What was Sainte-Beuve's special genius in criticism? The young James had described it as "the unrivalled power of reproducing the physiognomy of a particular moment or of a particular figure of the past." It was the rare ability of selecting some obscure *litterateur* or "some forgotten king's mistress" and in twenty pages placing the person before you "as a complete human being, to be forever remembered, with a distinct personality, with a character, an expression, a face, a dress, habits, eccentricities."[3] Criticism of James's criticism has been directed either toward admiration for the skill with which he accomplished this ideal of literary portrayal or

54

else to analysis of the principles and theories upon which his aesthetic philosophy rested. Even setting aside the famous late Prefaces, it is still quite reasonable to accept Morris Roberts's opinion that "taken as a whole his best criticism cannot be matched in English for certain qualities of style, or for the just and vivid communication of literary quality."[4]

There has been from the beginning a division of mind about James's criticism evident in the first reviews of *French Poets and Novelists* in 1878. Some opinions, like that of Brander Matthews, were ready to accept without question the obvious superiority of language and insight which marked his first volume.

> It is not too much to say that this book is by far the finest collection of purely literary criticism which has been published either in this country or in England since the appearance of Mr. Lowell's last volume of essays.[5]

Matthews ranked James, after Arnold and Lowell, "the foremost literary critic of our language." Others, unfortunately more typical of the general level of taste in the magazines, were disturbed by James's "anxiously impartial" method of balancing off favorable and unfavorable judgments. An *Atlantic* contributor called the volume "the most perversely uncertain book of criticism I have ever read" because its author loses a total effect among his many lesser observations. Howells, as editor and friend of James, took a mediating position. He paid high compliment to James's "brilliancy of style," but found fault with his "exasperating inconclusiveness" and a certain "nervousness" to reveal all sides of a question for fear of not seeming liberal enough. The tone of Howells's review, despite some generous praise, was tactfully patronizing. He was concerned about the numerous paradoxical (even when sympathetic) judgments in James's book. Like his contributor Howells preferred a kind of systematic criticism which "works out a problem to some conclusion on one side or the other" rather than a mass of keenly analytic impressions which "approach as nearly as possible to an equation of conflicting views."[6]

He recognized at once, however, James's resemblance to Sainte-Beuve. More of a *causeur* even than his master, the author of the famous *Causeries*, James was less of a pure critic. His criticism, Howells said, especially in the chapters on Turgenev and Alfred de Musset, is that of a "highly suggestive, charming talker," but even the "splendid" essay on Balzac is marred by a mixture of frank admiration and "brutal snubbing."[7] Howells's opinion did less than justice to the method of literary portraiture which informs the best chapters of the book, but it pretty much established the line of division which has existed toward James's criticism ever since. It is interesting to compare it, for example, to the statements of T. S. Eliot in the *Little Review* in 1918. Eliot remarked bluntly that

James's criticism of books and writers was "feeble" and that he was "emphatically *not* a successful *literary* critic." Where Howells objected to James's elusiveness from accepted canons of criticism, however, Eliot found this quality to be the source of James's great strength. "He was a critic who preyed not upon ideas, but upon living beings. It is a criticism which is in a very high sense creative." From this, Eliot proceeded to an even more curiously anti-intellectual position, namely, that James's "critical genius comes out most tellingly in his mastery over, his baffling escape from, Ideas; a mastery and an escape which are perhaps the last test of a superior intelligence."[8]

"Mastery and escape,"—a strange pair of synonyms. Eliot's paradoxical aphorism—that James "had a mind so fine that no idea could violate it"—perhaps described a quality he held in common with James, but it says, in the end, more about himself than about James who, for all his impressionism, never quite discarded the intellectual framework and the aesthetic ideas of late-nineteenth-century criticism. Recent opinion has tended to deny Eliot's view insofar as it defined the nature of James's criticism. René Wellek finds that the critical writing as a whole contains a "well-defined theory and a point of view" involving much of the paraphernalia of the organic concept of art—unity of form and content, a moral standard of reference, an inner harmony of means and ends—and furthermore that its roots were those of "organistic aesthetics," that is, "asking the artist to create a world which is somehow like life and to create it on the analogy of nature in order to support man in the belief in the moral and social order of the universe."[9] Another commentator, speaking largely in terms of James's early criticism, says: "It would be a mistake not to emphasize James's stress upon the value of ideas, his receptibility to them, nay his quest for them."[10]

James's earliest conception of the function of criticism allied it closely to philosophy. His opening sentence in a review of George Eliot's collected works defined the duty of the critic as that of seeking out some "key" to the author's method, "some utterance of his literary convictions, some indication of his ruling theory."[11] The metaphysical tendency of his mind derived from his inheritance of romantic and Coleridgean principles of criticism. He struggled, not always successfully, to resolve such dualities as the relation between idealism and reality, imagination and actuality, subject matter and artistic "effect," morality and truth. As his interests centered upon the novel, he added to this list certain other critical alternatives of the period—the novel versus the romance, novels of incident and novels of character, literalism versus selection and other similarly contradictory concepts. One of his earliest essays drew a distinction between "great" and "small" criticism, the mark of the former being that it touched "more or less" upon philosophy. From the beginning he drew upon Goethe and Arnold, but he was soon studying the French critics, Taine, Sainte-Beuve, and Scherer. Gradually, he began to shift his allegiance from philosophical to historical models and to move toward a greater precision of language and independence of thought.

In a youthful and rather cloudy passage James sought to resolve certain contradictions regarding the nature of criticism. Writing of Arnold, Scherer, and Sainte-Beuve the twenty-two-year-old reviewer took a long step in the direction of impressionism when he admired Arnold and Scherer for their rejection of doctrinaire theories. Scherer's strength lay, he wrote, in the fact that "he has no doctrines." The mark of a liberal mind was that it refused to commit itself. Of all men who deal with ideas, the critic is the least independent. His position depends upon that of the author. "It behooves him, therefore (James felt), to claim the utmost possible incidental or extrinsic freedom," and he should renounce all servitude to outside dogmas, principles, or theories. He should cultivate "his natural and proper servitude to his subject." Edmond Scherer was such a critic—undogmatic, unencumbered by theories, possessing "truly devout patience" in reserving judgment. Critic and philosopher thus far diverged:

> The philosopher's function is to compare a work with an abstract principle of truth; the critic's is to compare a work with itself, with its own concrete standard of truth. The critic deals, therefore, with parts, the philosopher with wholes.[12]

On the other hand, James recognized a fundamental unity and consistency in Scherer's mind, a "moral sense" or a "delicate spiritual force"—even a religious conviction—which lay behind his criticism animating, coordinating, and harmonizing the mass of brief opinions which constituted his work.

Impressionism, yes, and literary portraiture, but not at the sacrifice of unity and consistency. Such was the earliest theory of the youthful critic. Stoutly he held to the principle of the "moral sense," and the burden of much of his early criticism was an effort to clarify his mind upon this abstraction. Discussing Turgenev in *French Poets and Novelists* he makes it the very mark of the Russian writer's genius that he possessed "an ideal of delicacy," and "an ideal of joy." Flaubert lacked this quality— "the something else, beneath and behind" which gives art and life its meaning. Words like "picturesque," "charming," "ideal beauty," and "delicate spiritual force" are used to assist James in his search for an aesthetic ideal containing elements of ethical and metaphysical truth. Morris Roberts suggested that this indefinable quality became at times nothing more than a rationale of the New England conscience, "a genteel distaste for the uglier facts of life," especially when James employed it as an antidote to the excesses of French realism and sensuality.[13] But his critical theory in the Sixties and Seventies strongly suggests the infusion of an attenuated transcendental idealism—James's inheritance from mid-century Emersonian and Swedenborgian thought. And his vacillation was characteristic of the fluctuating taste of the 1870's.

In his early reviews for the *Nation*, the *North American Review*, and the *Atlantic* the direction of James's thinking was steadily toward a greater precision of thought. At first this took the form of a progressive refinement upon the critical alternatives which confronted him, and central to his search for a synthesis of opposing views was the conflict between an idealistic and a realistic ideology. His natural predilection for the moral wholesomeness of an Anglo-Saxon "conscience" was at odds with his need for French honesty and reality. But within each of these areas of thought much depended upon execution. James was instinctively repelled by the native school of mid-century romantic novelists along with the shallower forms of domestic realism as he read more of the fiction of George Eliot, Thackeray, Flaubert, and Balzac. He referred in 1865 to "the famous realistic system which has asserted itself so largely in fictitious writing in the last few years."[14] Balzac, he thought, belonged at the head of the "great names in the realist line" because he presented objects as they are. One of his youthful reviews urges Harriet Prescott to renounce her "ideal-descriptive" style and "diligently study the canons of the so-called realist school."

To understand James's use of the term realism in his apprentice years, one must take account of the qualifications he placed upon it. Far from recommending it, he felt, "on the contrary we would gladly see the vulgar realism which governs the imagination leavened by a little old-fashioned idealism."[15] Nonetheless, in the work of Balzac, Flaubert, Turgenev, and others of the French school, he sensed a healthy antidote to the cloyingly Tennysonian manner of Miss Prescott's *Azarian* or the narrow actuality of *The Wide Wide World*. He equally distrusted "the fidelity to minute social truths" of the indefatigable Trollope. Nor does James approve at all of the "injudicious striving after realistic effects" which characterized Rebecca Harding Davis's stories of common life and people or the "evil odor of lobbyism" in De Forest's novels of Washington politics.[16]

Closely related to the ideal-real conflict (James sometimes resorted to verbal gymnastics as when he remarked of Browning's language that it was "too real for the ideal and too ideal for the real") was the question of morality and "truth." He shied away from George Eliot's didactic tendency, much as he admired her work, because "her colors are a little too bright, and her shadows of too mild a gray." In all her novels he could not recall a single instance of "gross misery." Nor could he find vice, poverty, or squalor. "There are no rags, no gin, no brutal passions."[17] This call for an advanced realism by the young reviewer should, however, be placed beside his more conventional repudiation of Baudelaire a decade later expressing a Victorian distaste for the "rags, bad smells, and unclean furniture" of the Gallic mind. At opposite extremes, both statements sprang from James's unwillingness to accept the philosophical position of either George Eliot's moralism or Baudelaire's truth. The young James once precociously recognized the role of critic as essentially one of "opposition." "He is in the nature of his function *opposed* to his author," James wrote, "and his position, therefore, depends upon that which the author has taken."[18] But he was not prepared himself for such servitude, and his response was to differ with the author under consideration—in George Eliot a difference as to the degree of wholesomeness, in Baudelaire the degree of unwholesomeness.

Out of such ambivalences James sought a middle ground. In the conclusion to the admirable essay on Balzac in *French Poets and Novelists* he discovered the French writer's serious fault to be that, unlike Shakespeare, Thackeray, or George Eliot, "he had no natural sense of morality." Whatever this quality was, he believed, it should not be obtrusive, but should only make itself felt. It should be "sensed" as a kind of "essential perfume."[19] But if it was George Eliot's fault that she excluded misery from her sunny landscapes, James could (contrarily) acclaim Turgenev's truth to life because " 'life' in his pages is very far from meaning a dreary liability to sordid accidents." He valued most those realists who had an "ideal of delicacy" and those elegists who had an "ideal of joy." Alone among the continental novelists, Turgenev satisfied James's "puritan habit" without violating his need for aesthetic honesty and truth. He combined the method of a searching realist with a certain brooding tenderness and, while inclined to pessimism and melancholy, his view of life was for James "more impartial, more unreservedly intelligent than that of any novelist we know."[20]

French Poets and Novelists originated in a suggestion of William James who wrote Henry in Paris in 1873 expressing enthusiasm for his article on Gautier and urging him to try his hand in the same way on Turgenev, Balzac, George Sand and others. "Collected, they would make a standard book," William wrote. Read today the book is an impressive display of James's saturation in the French literature of the period and of his rare talent for gathering together material of both lasting and merely passing interest and weaving it into a smooth flow of narrative-criticism. It is a series of literary portraits each stamped with medallion-like clarity. The chapters range from the authoritative and definitive essays on Gautier, Balzac, Turgenev, and George Sand to reviews of individual books such as Paul de Musset's biography of his poet-brother, the correspondence of the Ampères, father and son, or the letters of Madame de Sabran to her husband. Those in the first group seek to render a comprehensive interpretation of the writings combined with a delicately discriminating portrait of the personality behind the work—"to fix a face and figure, to seize a literary character and transfer it to the canvas of the critic," as James once described the method.[21] The second group consists of intimate, personal sketches or memoirs of now obscure men and women of letters whose lives belonged to the half-realms of French literary gossip and social history. These chapters show James's skill in transforming love letters or journal entries into the very stuff of French court life of the First and Second Empires. Some of these literary courtships and marriages such as the relationship between Alfred de Musset and George Sand or that of Jean-Jacques Ampère and Madame Recamier or the touching and bashful courting of Juliet Carron by André Ampère are skillfully delineated narrative portraits. A few of the more ephemeral pieces such as the long essay on the Théâtre Français and the letters of Prosper Mérimée are lesser journalism and discuss matters remote from poetry and the novel.

The chapters on the minor figures have been little appreciated and have been unjustly neglected, while opinion has centered on the more familiar and controversial essays, those on Flaubert, Baudelaire and Turgenev. When James allowed the critical faculty to intrude too strongly, as in his unsympathetic and even obtuse treatment of Baudelaire, he was least successful. Here, and in certain statements about Flaubert, he deserted his own finely stated ideal of sympathy and identity of the critic with his subject—the generous talent "to catch a talent in the fact, follow its line, and put a finger on its essence."[22] The occasional lapse into taking "sides" and indulging in debatable issues with a "heated party air" stemmed in part from his doubts and uncertainties in the mid-Seventies over the decision, gradually formed in his mind, "to get abroad again and remain for years." It was a decision not lightly made, despite the off-hand way he referred to it as "my little plan," and it involved a central intellectual conflict—the conflict between his allegiance to the Anglo-Saxon moral world and his strong attraction to the French seriousness and devotion to letters. The ambivalence of Lambert Strether in the late novel *The Ambassadors* toward culturally rich and morally sensual Paris was already implicit in the young James's attitude toward French fiction in the 1870's. He made his choice, not without misgivings, to live in the Old World and to begin by establishing residence in Paris in November of the year 1875.[23]

Of the twelve chapters in *French Poets and Novelists* only five could have been written after his arrival in France, and of these only one, the essay on Flaubert, could have been affected by his personal contacts with the circle of French writers he met that winter—Flaubert, Turgenev, Maupassant, the Goncourts, and Zola. With Turgenev, "the beautiful genius," James always felt a temperamental affinity even before he came to know him intimately. The element of difference in Turgenev from the French realists was owing in part to his Slavic character. His example aided James in his early effort to define the perfect combination of the novelist. The chapter on Turgenev described the Russian writer's special quality as a commingling of realism and idealism, a middle zone between "moral meaning" and "art for art." Turgenev's pessimism and morbidity James discovered to be his major fault "for we hold to the good old belief that the presumption in life is in favour of the brighter side."[24] Nonetheless, when he was able to judge Turgenev through a personal as well as a literary acquaintance, he sensed the depth of his character, its simplicity, modesty, gentleness, and "sweetness"—qualities which reflected similar ones in James himself and which answered his need for something beyond mere realism. He recognized, too, something of his own complexity of mind in the Russian novelist who "felt and understood the opposite sides of life; he was imaginative, speculative, anything but literal."[25]

With Flaubert, however, the case differed. James admired him personally in Paris when he was an occasional visitor to the "little *coterie* of young realists in fiction." He praised *Madame Bovary*, even going so far as to proclaim it a highly moral book, but its didactic character derived from the fact that "every out-and-out realist who provokes serious meditation may claim that he is a moralist."[26] The relative failure of Flaubert's other work, however, led James to feel that the success of *Madame Bovary* was an accident. Left out of Flaubert's nature were the very qualities James recognized in Turgenev. A certain "dryness and coldness" of mind prevented him from realizing his potential—"the great machinery of erudition" he possessed. James meant quite sincerely to commend Flaubert when he spoke of realism having said its last word in *Madame Bovary*, but unlike Turgenev, the Frenchman was too much the artist in his passion for perfection of form and not enough the spokesman of an idealized view of life. James wrote his father, at the time he was forming an opinion of Flaubert: "In poor old Flaubert there is something almost tragic," and although he admired him more and more, he felt he could easily "see all round him intellectually."[27] James's discussion of him in *French Poets and Novelists* is a miracle of baffling contradictions and brilliantly counterpointed epithets.

The English Men of Letters Series *Hawthorne* presented quite a different problem for James. He found himself on peculiarly sensitive international ground, writing about an American author already considered a classic and accepted as a national monument, yet still untouched by serious criticism. He was bound to offend American readers by taking the detached, critical line. Nor could he risk the danger of a nationalistic overrating of Hawthorne to the English audience. The details of Hawthorne's life were too well known to permit the sort of personality portrayal he employed with the French poets. Within these limitations the book seems a remarkably judicious distribution of applause and discrimination, reflecting James's sense of a close blood-relationship with his subject and at the same time a firm adherence to international standards of judgment. In the same year, 1879, that he had outraged some American readers with his portrait of Daisy Miller, he offended nativist critics by emphasizing the provincial New England background which formed the matrix of Hawthorne's fiction. Again it was Howells who rose to Hawthorne's defense, though he did so with his accustomed grace and genuine regard for James's genius. He foresaw that James would be "in some quarters" accused of "high treason." For himself, he wrote, "we will be content with saying that the provinciality strikes us as somewhat over-insisted upon." He argued persuasively that it was no more "provincial" for an American to be American than for an Englishman to be English or a Frenchman to be French, and he differed with James's contention that the emptiness in the American scene of sovereigns, courts, cathedrals, abbeys, museums, and all such aristocratic traditions and usages seriously impoverished the novelist. Even leaving out all these things, Howells contended, "we have the whole of human life remaining, and a social structure presenting the only fresh and novel opportunities left to fiction." But James's book, broadly considered, Howells called "a miracle of tact and self-respect, which the author need not fear to trust to the best of either of his publics."[28] And in a letter to James at this time Howells amusingly described the horde of *Atlantic* readers, clamoring for James's scalp, and the "contributing bloodhounds" whom he was holding at bay from publishing their ruffled feelings in the pages of the magazine.

James in a long letter of rebuttal replied to Howells's opinions with more fervor than he was accustomed to allow himself in such matters. His sensitivities were aroused not so much by Howells's review, but by other unfavorable opinions such as those of T. W. Higginson and of the "bespattering" of the decent public periodically, with "my gore." He did not agree with Howells "at all" on the question of the provinciality of national types. He held that "certain national types are essentially and intrinsically provincial," including (presumably) the American, but apparently excluding English and French. And he sympathized "even less" with Howells's protest against the view that it takes an old civilization to set a writer in motion. Established manners, customs, and usages, James felt, "are the very stuff his work is made of." Of Howells's most doctrinaire objection, however, that James ignored the "radical difference between a romance and a novel" by using the terms interchangeably, James said nothing, but it is clear that by 1880 he had begun to tire of such distinctions as old-fashioned and irrelevant to the main concern of the novelist.[29]

James's *Hawthorne* has survived these strictures to be considered a classic of its kind, a persuasive portrait, and a mellow critical work. New

England has mellowed, too, enough to accept more readily his European view of its innocence and its wintry mental weather. Of the contemporary opinions, that of W. C. Brownell in the *Nation* was a welcome counter to the criticisms of Howells and Higginson. He spoke of James's book as "saturated with the essence of literary criticism"—a careful, conscientious, and vivid literary portrait.

> We venture to think . . . that Mr. James has made an important contribution to the literature of criticism in America, and that the fact will one day be recognized with the most effusiveness by the same persons who may now be nourishing irritation at his audacity in venturing to describe the features, instead of being content to worship at the shrine, of so august a divinity as Hawthorne.[30]

James seemed to have reversed himself in his discussion of realism since *French Poets and Novelists* where he had criticized Baudelaire, Flaubert, and Balzac for their sacrifice of "charm" and "the pictorial side of life" in the interests of sordid and dreary fact. Taking the opposite tack, he charged Hawthorne with a "want of reality," regretted his lack of "paraphernalia" and his abuse of symbolism and "the fanciful element" in *The Scarlet Letter*. He indicated a preference for *The House of the Seven Gables* because it was pervaded by "the whole multitudinous life of man which is the real sign of a great work of fiction."[31]

These two volumes, marking the end of his apprenticeship in criticism, are revealing of the different directions which his philosophical theorizings and his literary practice were taking him. In one sense the division of his mind is indicated by the title of the first book with its separation of "poets" and "novelists." The dreamy, speculative, youthful reviewer and the busy, cosmopolitan critic and traveller of the middle 1870's were never quite reconciled in his early criticism. The words "charm," "pictorial quality," "richness," and "picturesque" run like a refrain through his comments to describe the essential inspiration of a work of art, its imaginative content. "That a novel should have a certain charm," he wrote of Flaubert, "seems to us the most rudimentary of principles."[32] Balzac, too, lacked this elusive but vital element, this "southern slope of the mind." Whatever it was, it blended on one side with James's sense of propriety, his penchant for certain Victorian furbelows and embellishments; on the other, it sought to express his carry-over of an attenuated transcendental idealism—a moral quality. Of the novelists, Turgenev alone possessed it. The poets possessed it, too, but with an excessive romanticism which failed to satisfy the realistic side of James's aesthetic sense.

In the reverse context stood the proponents of art-for-art for whom everything was execution. James admired the artistic devotion to form of the French school, but he was repelled by their "ferocious pessimism and handling of unclean things." Scenes of low life, poverty, vice, sex, and violence belonged to the extremes of realism, which annoyed and fascinated him at the same time. "Vulgar," "sordid," "dreary," "ugly," and "repulsive" were frequent adjectives revealing his distaste for this side of French fiction. In his effort to resolve the conflict, James leaned toward critical impressionism and relied upon the method of literary portraiture. He spoke often in distrust of doctrinaire theories, hewing to the line of technique and asserting that on such ground alone could criticism be justified. The result might be called a kind of eclecticism, or a marshalling of contrapuntal opinions which fairly bristle with paradox. Often, James's criticism seems to reflect the fluctuation of taste and vacillation of mind which characterized the literary temper of the Seventies. Yet he never accepted, even in the late Prefaces, a thorough-going relativism. Ideas remained as a kind of shadowy framework for his most impressionistic writing, and we will find him much later in life discussing in the Preface to *The American* the two antipodal requirements of the artist—the romantic and the real.

In his later years, looking back upon the awkward age of the 1870's with its climate of social and intellectual fluctuation, its eager provincialism and its premature cosmopolitanism, James described the period with gentle irony and a subtle symbolism.

> It's all tears and laughter as I look back upon that admirable time, in which nothing was so romantic as our intense vision of the real. No fool's paradise ever rustled to such a cradle song. It was anything but Bohemia—it was the very temple of Mrs. Grundy. We knew we were too critical, and that made us sublimely indulgent; we believed we did our duty or wanted to, and that made us free to dream. But we dreamed over the multiplication table; we were nothing if not practical.[33]

This portrait of the Seventies, pointedly satirical, yet not without a certain nostalgic feeling for the past, contains within it a clue to and understanding of the intellectual aspirations of the Victorian mind in America during the early phase of realism. This "romantic vision of the real" was a synthesis toward which that generation strove in art and letters, and in the work of James and a few of his contemporaries there was envisioned an ideal which could encompass the best elements of the old and the new. It has been called a Victorian compromise. Yet in a more generous mood one might well see it as expressive of the highest aims of young and ambitious writers and critics of the 1870's, searching amid the conflicting pressures of "The Gilded Age" for a satisfying harmony and an artistic pattern. James was a leader in this effort to carry the older idealism into a new period of science and pragmatism. The direction of his thought and method, as revealed in his early stories and his criticism, was toward just such a synthesis, and in his best work of the Seventies he achieved a harmony that was decades ahead of most of his contemporaries.

In criticism, he stood apart from the age in the skill of his expression and the breadth of his interests. If he wavered in judgment, he did so from a larger frame of reference, making the task of synthesis more difficult. The strongly critical and metaphysical bent of his mind, his serious conception of the function of criticism, and his vast curiosity to discover techniques to apply it raised his work beyond the level of those, like Howells, who looked for fixed standards and "pure" criticism. James's restless search for a greater precision of language led him into subtle paradoxes and verbal juxtapositions which puzzled and irritated some of his contemporaries, but which have come to be identified with the complexities of our time. Eliot perhaps overstated the "mastery and escape" from ideas he felt in James's mind—at least as his words refer to the critical writing. And they apply even less to the early period. But a twentieth-century novelist, F. Scott Fitzgerald, another admirer of James, described the case more accurately than Eliot in a context quite remote from fiction or criticism. "The test of a first rate intelligence," he wrote "is the ability to hold two opposed ideas in the mind at the same time, and still retain the ability to function."[34]

James's romantic vision of the real was such a balance even though in practice he could not hold to it steadily. In a few essays like those on Turgenev or Balzac, and in perceptive passages on George Sand, Gautier, or Alfred de Musset he closely approximated the ideal. Much of the book on Hawthorne likewise fulfilled this lofty aim. Regarded as an intellectual quest James's criticism sought to reconcile the extremes of thought in aesthetics and criticism as they impinged on his horizon in the 1870's. He never quite abandoned his faith that he could hold to the "Anglo-Saxon faith," the figure in the carpet, or the "ideal of delicacy," without at the same time rejecting naturalism, science, and the sense of reality. He could do so because, unlike Howells and many of his contemporaries, he was capable of accepting uncertainty, of resting with doubt and inconsistency —satisfied (in Keats's phrase) with a "Negative Capability." For James the ultimate test of the literary imagination was a willingness to defer decisions which demanded an "irritable reaching after fact and reason."[35]

But the final thing which must be said of his early critical writing is that the direction he was following took him away from ideas toward the less controversial ground of history, biography, and literary portraiture. Goethe and Arnold yielded as his models to the French critics, Taine, Sainte-Beuve, Scherer, and Brunetière. Art, especially that of the portrait, supplanted history and conventional biography as methods of criticism, and James came to distrust the yardsticks of contemporary reviewing because they smothered "the exquisite art of criticism" by a harsh application of extrinsic judgments. He never, even in the late Prefaces, quite discarded the Coleridgean language of antithesis, but his critical writing, both early and late, flowed with the greatest ease and spontaneity when he assumed the role of creative journalist or literary portraitist—when the critic in him became, as he wrote, "a reader who prints his impressions."

4.

James's Studio Stories: The Disinherited of Art

The metaphysical tendency of Henry James's mind in the apprentice years, as indicated by his youthful critical formulations, became less insistent when he submitted himself to the demands of fiction. The narrative discipline required that ideas be embodied in character, incident, and scene. Furthermore, it forced him to search more widely and more deeply into his own experience for material which, in his critical writing, the books and ideas of the authors under discussion could provide. In his handling of such concepts as the "ideal" and the "real" he had followed the method of setting up alternatives and weighing opposed values. The ruling theme in his work of the Seventies was the international one—the values of Europe versus those of America. He had treated it in theoretical terms in his essays discoursing over the differences between Anglo-Saxon and French literary methods. In fiction, however, what had been part of an abstract problem became increasingly personal, and the choice of Europe or America as a place to live and write gradually formed itself as a predominating and crucial issue. In the Preface to Volume XIII of the New York edition of his work, he grouped three of his early international stories, those he regarded the best, as expressions of this pressing alternative—the Old World and the New. The conflict had begun to claim his attention in 1869 when he embarked upon his first independent trip to Europe. The three stories most revealing of this experience were "A Passionate Pilgrim" (1871), "The Madonna of the Future," (1873), and "Madame de Mauves" (1874). They were all inspired by what he called the "nostalgic poison" instilled into him by his early glimpses of the European scene. Thus, James himself became the first "Jamesian" commentator to describe these tales as self-portraiture, "in the highest degree documentary to myself," recovered from the past (he reminisced, more than thirty years later) for their "consolatory use."[1]

He was, in the early Seventies, only slowly beginning to prepare himself for the role of alienated artist. For the time being he would remain the observer, standing apart from involvement, exploring the possibilities, and measuring the middle ground. Stephen Spender has described the psychology of this early period aptly: "The problem that faced James was to absorb the tradition of Europe and the tradition of English and French literature, without losing his own individuality as an American."[2] James likewise recognized this, writing of his early international stories: "As American as possible, and even to the pitch of fondly coaxing it, I then desired my ground-stuff to remain."[3] Each of the three tales he selected to stand as monuments to this transitional period represented a different international experience of the young traveller. Italy, England, and France made separate impressions upon his mind, and in each case the impressions were handled in terms of general, as well as personal, experience. Contrasts were contained within contrasts. In each story the mood of ecstasy and delight, which marked James's personal discovery of Europe, was counterpointed by a critical note to preserve the equilibrium between romance and reality. And the framework of these stories revealed more subtle and complex ties than the word "international" implies. There was an English situation, an Italian experience, and a French experience.

James described the three stories as "sops instinctively thrown to the international Cerberus." Cerberus functioned to his imagination, he said, as "keeper of the international 'books.' " As a group, the tales of three countries comprised his defense against the prospect of becoming a realist or local colorist of the American scene. Cerberus was, he said, "my prime view of the telling effect with which the business man would be dodged." In other words, James wanted to preserve his identity as an American without becoming a novelist of the conditions of business or commercial life. The "international Cerberus" became for him a guiding spirit keeping "a disengaged eye upon my sneaking attempts to substitute the American romantic for the American real."[4] Like Spencer Brydon in the late ghost-story, "The Jolly Corner," he was abhorred by the spectre of playing the role of the American man of action, either for himself or for the male heroes of his stories. Ambivalence was at the root of this complex frame of mind, and his international tales were framed in terms of differing kinds of contrast.

Of the three countries, Italy made the most romantic impression upon the young tourist. It stirred his aesthetic being deeply, and at the same time it impressed him with a sense of decay. "Italy is a delightful place to dip into, but no more, . . ." he wrote his sister in 1873. "The weight of the past world here is fatal. . . . The ancients did things by doing the business of their own day, not by gaping at their grandfather's tombs,—and the normal man of today will do likewise."[5] His early letters home record the two moods of enthusiasm and disappointment with nearly equal conviction. From Rome: "My dearest William. . . . Here I am in the eternal city. From midday to dusk I have been roaming the streets. *Que vous en dirai-je?* At last—for the first time—I live!" And a few months later: "I'm sick unto death of priests and churches. Their 'picturesqueness' ends by making me want to go strongly into political economy or the New England school system. I conceived at Naples a tenfold deeper loathing than ever of the hideous heritage of the past. . . ."[6]

"The Madonna of the Future" was written in a period of such sharply fluctuating moods. Its locale was Florence where the young traveller revelled in the rich setting of the galleries of the Uffizi, the Palazzo Vecchio, and the sculptured piazzas and winding streets of the old city. It was the first of the studio stories, concerned with artists and models, of which *Roderick Hudson* (1876) and "The Real Thing" (1890) were logical successors. The first two, however, belonged to James's early international phase in Italy, and they present a complicated mingling of the author's personal reception of Florence and Rome, with his intellectual speculation on theories of art. An emotional excitement underlay his narrative accounts of alienated American artists in the studio world, and James's primary concern with the workings of the artistic imagination was sometimes obscured by the intrusion of his personal moods as a traveller. It will be helpful, therefore, before discussing the early Italian studio tales, to see how James at a later date worked out a similar intellectual theme in "The Real Thing" where the subject is treated without the hovering international Cerberus to complicate the atmosphere, and where the literary influences of Hawthorne, Balzac, Dumas *fils*, and others were not as evident in his work as they inevitably were to the younger writer of the 1870's.

Ironic contrast is at the heart of this tale of the studio. The question posed is that of the proper source material for the artist. Is literal reality an adequate substitute for the shaping and selecting mind? Behind this question lies the true heart of the matter for the artist. By what mystery does he successfully establish the illusion of reality so that, as James once put it, "the way things don't happen may be artfully made to pass for the way things do"? The intellectual framework of the story, however, is so gracefully and impressionistically shaded by the surface action involving a shabby-genteel couple looking for employment as artist's models that its point comes through only by indirection—though it does so all the more forcefully for that. James balances off illusion and reality in the contrast between the professional models and the Monarchs who represent "the real thing." At the same time he softens the quality of the narrator's distrust of the Monarchs as suitable models for his illustrations of upper-class society by his equally sympathetic regard for their poverty and their pride.

In 1872, when James wrote "The Madonna of the Future," the question of illusion and reality in art was handled in more romantic terms. The extremes are farther apart, more allegorically considered, and his youthful mood of ecstatic feeling for Italy intruded so strongly as to become almost a dominating factor. "It relates to my youth, and to Italy: two fine things!" Thus James's narrator begins the strange tale of an American artist in Florence who dreamed of painting a great Madonna. For the youthful aspirant to fiction, the challenge lay in this: how to give narrative form and symbolic content to his aesthetic emotions and his tourist delights? The story took shape in terms of the same counterpointed debate which had informed much of James's early critical theories, particularly the alternate values of "romance" and "reality." It became a distillation into fiction of his speculation on the problems and the aims of art. It was concerned with a painter and his model, but it was meant to extend its meaning from the artist's studio to the writer's desk. Both "The Madonna of the Future" and its companion piece, "The Sweetheart of M. Briseux," were suggested to James by Balzac's *Le Chef d'Oeuvre Inconnu* which narrates an incident from the career of Nicholas Poussin. In this tale a painter has convinced himself that his portrait of the ideal woman is more alluring than flesh and blood. Confusing fancy with reality, he has fallen in love with it. Poussin, his young disciple, permits his fiancée to pose undraped for the finishing touches of the portrait, but in the final scene, acting from mingled feelings of sexual and professional jealousy, he disillusions the artist by pointing out that his masterpiece is nothing but a jumble of incoherent scratches and daubs.

James appropriated these ingredients, preserving some of the provocative elements, but altering them in the direction of a parable on opposed theories of art. His version of Balzac's story became a study of the contrast between a visionary and a utilitarian attitude. A letter from his father, just prior to the appearance of the tale in the *Atlantic Monthly*, indicates, however, that there was much more of the suggestive quality of Balzac in the original version than Howells allowed to be printed, a fact which may have influenced later critical readings of the story. Alfred de Musset's *Lorenzaccio*, it has been pointed out, may have provided James with the name of his central character, Theobald, and with certain passages in which he deprecates his artistic failure and his loneliness.[7] Something, too, of the failure of the American artist, W. W. Story, may be reflected in Theobald's case, but the actual original for this disinherited American painter seems to be suggested in a letter from James to his mother in 1869 describing his own homesickness on his first visit to Florence.[8] He met one of his compatriots, he wrote, "a seedy and sickly American" who "seemed to be doing the gallery [the Uffizi] with an awful minuteness." They fell into conversation and arranged to meet again, as do the narrator and Theobald in James's story. The man did not impress James greatly, and if he is the germ of Theobald he is vastly transformed in the tale. For Theobald becomes the passionate pilgrim and displaced artist who lectures wildly to the narrator about art. In one of his perorations he describes the "two moods" in which one may walk through the galleries, "the critical and the ideal." The critical, oddly, is the more generous mood; the ideal takes such high ground of taste that even Raphael cannot be entirely swallowed. This provides James with one of his ironic critical antitheses, but more central to the theme is the problem of the alienated artist. Theobald tells his young listener:

We are the disinherited of Art! We are condemned to be superficial!
. . . The soil of American perception is a poor little barren, artificial
deposit. . . . Our crude and garish climate, our silent past, our deafen-
ing present, the constant pressure about us of unlovely circumstance
are . . . void of all that nourishes and prompts and inspires the artist. . . .

The story gains its symbolic dimension from the way in which the
narrator scrutinizes, without quite committing himself to either one, two
conflicting attitudes toward art and toward life. In the person of Theobald, whose canvas grows cracked and discolored with time while the
Madonna of whom he dreams remains a pathetic ideal of his imagination,
James measures the limitations of aspiration without talent. In the fine
sketch of the vulgar modeller of the cats and the monkeys, Theobald's
rival for the decaying charms of the middle-aged Serafina, he surveys the
empty success of the commercial artist and worldling. In the admirably
conceived scene at the apartment of the model, where the narrator comes
to inform her of Theobald's illness, the theme of the story is sharply revealed. "Cats and monkeys,—monkeys and cats,—all human life is there!"
says the jaunty Juvenal of the chimney piece. "Human life, of course, I
mean, viewed with the eye of the satirist!" Theobald has been pathetic
in his hopeless worship of perfection, but his satirical rival is even worse
—cynical, vulgar, and commercial. Theobald's idealized devotion for the
commonplace Serafina is weighed against the possessive attitude of the
modeller of clay figures, just as the painter's idealism is doomed to fail
while his rival's realism is a vulgar success.

The account of Howells's bowdlerizing of the tale is given in a letter
from Henry Sr. to his son, dated January 14, 1873.[9] After reporting the
high opinion of the story in the family council in Cambridge, father James
went on to report that Howells could not provide enough pages of the
magazine to print it in its full length. "And besides he had a decided
shrinking from one episode—that in which Theobald tells of his love for,
and visit from, the Titian-ic beauty and his subsequent disgust of her
worthlessness, as being risky for the magazine; and then, moreover, he
objected to the interview at the end between the writer and the old
English neighbor, as rubbing into the reader what was sufficiently evident
without it." Father James admitted to Henry that he regarded Howells as
"*in general* too timid," but had to agree with William, Alice, and Mother
that there was ground for his timidity in this case. "I went to Howells accordingly this morning," he continued, "and told him that if he would
consent to publish the whole tale in one piece, I would take upon me the
responsibility of striking out the two episodes. He agreed, and he has made
the connection of the parts perfect, so that no one would ever dream of
anything stricken out." The pieces were then returned to James with the
suggestion that he restore them in his forthcoming volume "which
Howells says ought to be published forthwith." James did not restore

them, nor is there any record of his reaction to Howells's review of the story which objected that the reiteration at the end of the "cats and monkeys" philosophy introduced a "jarring note" and a needless affront to the reader's sensibilities.

It seems clear, however, that James intended the two episodes to provide some part of the suggestive flavor in Balzac's tale in order to counteract the excessive pathos and the symbolic suggestion in the story of the disillusioned painter. The metaphysical tendency, he may have felt, required a fleshly underpinning, and the Hawthorne element needed the worldliness of Balzac to restore the proper balance. If the aesthetic "lesson" of the story was James's sense of the artist's duty, at all costs, to *represent* without prostituting his work by vulgar commercialism or cynicism—then James erred in distributing unequally the sympathy for the two "artists" in their human roles. Perhaps, with the stricken episodes restored, the story might approach more closely to this intended counterpoint, though Theobald would still easily outstrip the modeller of clay figures in any bid for readers' esteem.

James was fascinated by the possibilities inherent in the study of the artist as personality, the strange and puzzling contradictions involved in genius confronted with the ordinary workaday world. In his earliest tales of artists and in later brilliantly ironic barbs at the literary life of the Yellow Nineties, he explored every facet of the artistic experience. Taken together, these stories form his portrait of the profession, touching every note in the scale from the earlier philosophical and critical tales to the later grimly realistic or satiric ones. They are concerned with everything from serious and gifted artists or writers to dowdy composers of popular trash. There is a clear shift of emphasis, however, from the Seventies, when James was absorbed with the pictorial and the plastic arts, a theme deriving from his youthful travels abroad and his many art reviews and notices to the Eighties and Nineties when he dealt more specifically with the artist as novelist. The later stories were concerned with dramatic and literary art, and back of them all was his lifelong faith in the essential unity of the arts. As a small boy and reader in the James family library he had been fascinated by book illustrations. "My small 'interest in art,'" as he put it, "that is, my bent for gaping at illustrations and exhibitions, was absorbing and genuine."[10] His primary education in the visual arts was climaxed by the vivid nightmare he described as a small boy in the Gallerie d'Apollon of the Louvre impressing him somehow with the intellectual experience of great painting and even a "sense of glory" to be found in it. In 1860 William James was studying under William Morris Hunt in his Newport studio. Henry has recorded in *Notes of a Son and Brother* the deep impressions which this experience with Hunt and John La Farge made upon his growing concern for art and "the dawning perception that the arts were after all essentially one and that even with canvas and brush whisked out of my grasp I still needn't feel disinherited."[11]

The recurrence of the term "portrait" in his titles and the many metaphorical parallels between the arts of painting and fiction which permeate James's critical vocabulary from the early period to the late Prefaces are testimony to his feeling that "there is no essential difference between the painting of a picture and the writing of a novel."[12] He admired the work of Frank Duveneck, for example, an early American realist of the Munich school, and he came to know and appreciate such contemporary portraitists as Eakins, Homer, Sargent, Du Maurier, and Edwin Abbey. James's effort in writing to achieve "complete pictorial fusion" brought the methods of the picture and the novel, as he conceived them, closely together and puzzled readers and critics who found his technique difficult. It has required many separate studies and special investigations to clarify the means by which he blended in theory and, more intricately, in fiction the disciplines of the visual arts. On the simplest level, the analogy provided him with subject matter and characters for his fiction. Furthermore, pictorial art was a subject so close to his heart that he could see his own psychological frustrations adumbrated in the problems of the alienated artists and painters he described. When he began to invent complex, psychological characters and new methods to depict them, James rejected the overstrained adventure and action of the popular romance for the novel of character analysis. Point of view became his primary aim, and the "reflector" or "central consciousness" supplied the painter's eye for his arrangements of scene and incident. He developed the need for "composition" and he was led away from the moralistic novel of Meredith or Thackeray. Instead he substituted the slower tempo and pictorial arrangements of his brother of the brush, especially the portrait painter for whom the supreme interest is the illumination of character. For what, he rhetorically asked himself, "is either a picture or a novel that is not of character?"[13]

Roderick Hudson was James's first full-length novel, a long fiction with a complicated subject and a romantic setting in the studio world of Rome. It was his only full-length portrait of the artist as American, a young and talented sculptor corrupted by the sensuous wealth of Italy and by his fatal passion for a *femme du monde*. Again it was James himself who anticipated later criticism of the novel by pointing out the division of interest between Roderick's romantic tragedy and Rowland Mallet's conscious reflection of the action. He came to feel, thirty years after, that the book had been misnamed, that Roderick's adventure was only "indirectly" his subject, and that it was Rowland's view and experience of Roderick which contained the essence of the book. Roderick's "large capacity for ruin," James thought, was not convincingly portrayed. It had happened too fast and without sufficient preparation, and

73

too much weight had been placed upon Christina Light as "well-nigh sole agent of his catastrophe." He traced much of the trouble to the inadequate time-scheme which moved too rapidly and which made Roderick's disintegration scarcely convincing. The novel was saved from failure, however, by his dawning realization (one guesses that James was here arguing after the fact) that the subject was essentially that of Rowland's center of consciousness, and it was this which provided the novel with its "principle of composition." In other words, James virtually admitted that he had begun his story with one intention and finished with another.

Technically the book was an experiment. As James said in his Preface to the New York edition, his aim was an artistic arrangement, a pictorial fusion, in which the central intelligence was to be placed in Rowland Mallet's consciousness. Everything was to focus there, "and the drama is the very drama of that consciousness." In his emulation of the painter of portraits James followed a method which ran counter to the narrative continuity of the conventional Victorian novel. As Joseph Warren Beach described the technique:

> It is an arrangement of objects (that is, of persons and incidents involved)—by likeness and opposition, by balance and cross-reference, with all regard to emphasis and proportion,—corresponding to the arrangement of figures, of background and foreground, of masses and lines, in a painting.[14]

Meaning in the novel springs as much from such relations of character to character as from the normal ingredients of developing incident, chronology of event, or implicit moral content. The crowded canvas of *Roderick Hudson* might well be named, in place of its given title, simply and allegorically "Art." In the center stand Roderick and Rowland Mallet, each representing one side of the artist's nature—Roderick possessing genius in the romantic sense—volatile, unstable, emotional—and Rowland having the will and means, the staying power, balance, and necessary detachment, but lacking the capacity to create. Together they form the complete artist. This interpretation has been given the novel by more than one commentator citing as evidence Rowland's self-analysis early in the novel: "Do you know I sometimes think I am a man of genius, half-finished? The genius has been left out, the faculty of expression is wanting" and Roderick's similar remark about his patron: "The poor fellow is incomplete. . . ."

What gives further credence to such a reading is the earlier example, both in James's criticism and his short fiction, of the method of symbolism through a juxtaposition of opposing ideals. This is carried out among the minor characters as well, grouped as they are around the central figures in various arrangements of sympathy or antipathy. Mary Garland represents the New England aspect and plays a supporting role to Rowland who is "the restrained, suppressed American in James, all decorous caution and New England conscience."[15] Mrs. Hudson becomes a secondary figure in this group in her feeble and despairing maternity. Christina Light, brilliant and tempting to Roderick's passionate nature, admiring and moody by turns and still unaccountably respectful of Rowland's conservative judgment, hovers over both like an evil angel. The other artists in Rome—Gloriani, Singleton, and Miss Blanchard—each represent a different philosophy of art and of life. They are foils for each other and, as a group, they illuminate the strong and weak side of Roderick. Each of the characters and groups has a kind of compositional unity, revolving about its own particular sun, and each system throws light upon the central subject, Art.

Behind these arranged characters James has etched the background, also in symmetry and opposition. Northampton versus Rome, symbols of New England cultural barrenness and Italian richness and moral obliquity. He felt later that he had failed to "do" Northampton as his master Balzac would have done in such a case of a *ville de province* because he had not equalled Balzac's "systematic closeness." Lawyer Striker belongs in the Northampton setting while Mrs. Light and the Cavaliere represent the native Roman world. Madame Grandoni is a ministering figure and a bar of judgment with her European experience and in her role as mediator *sans* sentiment. All of the contrasts which confronted James in his critical speculations during the Seventies are heightened and transposed into pictorial groupings containing allegorical content. Yet the allegory is admirably shaded off into convincing international personages. The international theme is paramount, but other conflicts appear throughout in the witty dialogue or in the advancement of the central debate between art and passion, romance and reality, art versus morality, Boston versus Bohemia, genius vis-a-vis talent. As such, the novel is a summation of James's thought about art in the fervid and formative years of the Seventies.

Like "The Madonna of the Future" *Roderick Hudson* is part of James's intellectual autobiography. He is questioning the wisdom of his decision to leave America, searching for a philosophy of art, measuring the range of his own powers. Roderick in his alternating moods of hope and despair, but dependent upon flashes of inspiration, becomes an emblem of the Victorian morality of art: genius alone is not enough. He needs Rowland's calming hand and Mary's wholesome, if colorless, ethic. Gloriani's cleverness and calculating opportunism, despite his intelligence, is likewise insufficient. His statues were "florid and meretricious; they looked like magnified goldsmith's work . . . but they had no charm for Rowland." Completing this microcosm of the studios there is the slender talent of the patient and plodding Singleton and the slight work of the pretty Miss

Blanchard who "did backs very well," but was "a little weak in faces." James did not force the obvious symbolism of these portraits. Even Roderick's suicide is prevented from becoming an admonishing commentary on the romantic agony. Too much the realist and too wary of absolutes James would have included in his ideal artist something of all these types—Roderick's genius, Rowland's moral fibre, Gloriani's intelligence, Singleton's patience, and Miss Blanchard's "backs." It was such versatility of mind that distinguished his work from that of his contemporaries in American fiction and criticism.

His ability to sustain all points of view and to rest in inquiry disappointed readers and puzzled reviewers of *Roderick Hudson*. An undertone of dissatisfaction was apparent in these reviews, and a fretting over the elusiveness of his meaning.

> Is it a novel at all, in the common acceptance of that word? [asked a writer describing himself as a 'semi-disappointed admirer of Mr. James'] Instead of being a dramatic and diverting tale to take the reader captive by the strange charm of improvisation, and instruct or elevate him while under the influence of that spell,—is it not rather a biography, a curious psychological struggle based on types . . . ?[16]

Others expressed a genteel distaste for James's "coldness" of treatment and his "chilliness" of effect, his "lack of sympathy" for his characters. A few objected to the analytical method, the over-elaboration of detail, and the "offensive want of compression." Only the *Nation* observed James's use of indirect portraiture through Rowland's consciousness, but it remarked that the device resulted in an "outside view" of Roderick because Rowland does not fully understand him and the character was therefore less successful than if he had been more "boldly" revealed. Critical dissatisfaction with James's fiction in the Seventies is a measure of the distance he had travelled beyond accepted canons of opinion. Very few reviewers understood his purpose in restricting the point of view or his artistic impartiality which forced readers to think. Generally, it was admitted that James showed superior skill, and the discerning recognized that he was "a unique and versatile writer of acute power and great brilliancy of performance."[17] Such power, the critics felt, was misdirected when it was bestowed upon "unpleasant" people—Lawyer Striker and Mr. Leavenworth were cited as cases in point. Readers wanted to be instructed or elevated and, if they were not, they felt "defrauded."

From these early reviews until the present time *Roderick Hudson* has been the subject of controversial opinion. On one point only has there been general agreement—that the book revealed an unusual literary talent having originality, power, range, and variety. As a novel it has called forth extremes of admiration and adverse judgment. Turgenev wrote James in

1876 his opinion that certain scenes were written "with the hand of a master."[18] And there has been general consensus ever since that it is a rewarding book, challenging the reader's participation, and that as a first novel it has few equals. On the other hand, Beach felt that it failed to make its point.[19] T. S. Eliot spoke of James's "failure to create a situation" and charged him with the cardinal sin of having failed to "detect" one of his main characters.[20] F. W. Dupee called it "not much more than a museum piece to the present-day reader."[21] Its "faults" have been amply aired and confidently demonstrated, yet somehow the discussions of them do not greatly elucidate the essential mystery of its meaning. This is because *Roderick Hudson* is an apprentice work, not technically mature, as James quite candidly pointed out in his late Preface. Furthermore, it cannot be said to have an intended "theme," though much effort has been expended to give it one. More correctly understood, it is a book with an autobiographical orientation and several strands of interest which might be called its *raison d'etre*. Roderick and Rowland may be the artist as split personality and also the two sides of Henry James measuring in the mid-Seventies his capacities for success in fiction and debating with himself the wisdom of separation from America and the possibilities of Italy as a place of residence and source of material for an alienated writer.[22]

To attempt to describe the novel by most recognizable canons of criticism is to do it a certain injustice. It has been considered as a romantic tragedy and it has been called a "comic melodrama."[23] Is Roderick the tragic protagonist or is Rowland the center of consciousness in whom (as James himself said) the interest primarily resides? Or are both to be paired as different sides of the artistic personality? Does romantic allegory of the Hawthorne sort prevail or is Balzac's realism and sense of place the fundamental influence? In his own re-assessment of the book, James said that Balzac was his technical master, but he was unaccountably silent about the definite Hawthorne strain and equally so regarding the influence of Turgenev and George Sand. It was Hawthorne's influence, no doubt, which counterbalanced, and perhaps restricted, his emulation of Balzac's realism and sense of locale. And there was an approximately equal distribution in the novel of Turgenev's restrictive method and George Sand's romantic expansiveness.

It is as injudicious to interpret the novel according to its implied symbolism as it is to ignore the symbols. The novel is not "an object lesson in the danger of converting artistic genius into a mere flair for adventurous living,"[24] because James has been careful to comment critically upon Roderick's extravagant temper and his excessive romanticism. Rowland, on the other hand, serves the author as spokesman for sense and sobriety, but he is also a mirror of the chilly negations of New England morality. *Roderick Hudson* is not a failure, even partially, nor a book "dead at the center."[25] Its center was alive with James's own immediate experience of

Rome and with his enthusiasms for the artistic world of Italy. If anything it is *too* full of life and *too* fertile in its anxiety to represent all sides of the picture and all degrees of the studio world in Rome. Such unity as it has is only suggested and unfulfilled. Its center is an abstraction toward which multiple illustrations point, but do not arrive. As F. W. Dupee put it, it is James's portrait of the artist as American and his portrait of the artist James did *not* wish to become.[26] Its "theme" hangs in the balance. It ranges somewhere in the indeterminate zone among several alternatives: art and passion versus loyalty and steadfast virtue, freedom versus self-control, America versus Europe—in short the broad theme which underlay much of James's thought in the Seventies, Art versus Worldliness. Its true subject is complexity. "It's a complex fate being an American," he wrote in a different context, "and one of the responsibilities it entails is fighting against a superstitious evaluation of Europe."[27]

Like Roderick Hudson, James had become one of the disinherited of art. He had separated himself from native sources of material and inspiration, and he was confronted with the new inheritance of Europe and of the rich traditions and unknown quantities it contained. He was not at once ready to accept this new inheritance with all of its implications, above all the unpredictable fate of a writer who has staked almost everything upon his own still untried talent. Out of his new situation came doubts and self-questionings and long, inner debates which are reflected in his early stories of artists and studio life in Italy. The form and method of these tales with their arrangements of values and their almost schematic juxtapositions of people and points of view was a reflection of this uncertainty.

5.

James as Passionate Pilgrim and Disappointed Observer

The two most important reviews of Henry James's first published book, *A Passionate Pilgrim, and Other Tales* (1875) were those of Howells and James Russell Lowell.[1] Both had become close literary and personal acquaintances of Henry James. Howells had assisted and encouraged him as early as 1866, when he accepted an early story for the *Atlantic*, and the association had ripened into a "suburban friendship" during their Boston and Cambridge period in the late Sixties. Lowell had met James in the autumn of 1872 in Paris where the two took long afternoon walks and attended the Théâtre Francais in the evenings. In his *Nation* review Lowell paid homage to the young writer's "air of good breeding," his "large capital of native endowment," and his "faculty of rapid observation." He emphasized the general qualities of distinction in James's book, the careful workmanship and the intellectual character of his mind. He spoke of James as a story-teller who dealt mainly with problems of character and psychology and as a stylist whose prose "often lacks only verse to make it poetry." Lowell took note of James's preference for French models and Old-World materials, admired his cosmopolitanism and his *obiter dicta* on the arts of painting, sculpture, and architecture. Above all, Lowell underlined the delicacy of James's method which allowed the reader "to do his share." The review was warmly written. It was an estimate, in broad terms, of James's fictional method but without specific discussion of individual stories in the volume.[2]

Howells, similarly, took the occasion to launch James into the world of letters with warm and generous, as well as judicious, criticism. His review began with a conscious effort to forestall anticipated complaints (which he had heard in his capacity as editor) that James was a disparager of America, that his characters were "unpleasant," his method "analytical," and his inspiration "French." He emphasized James's richness of style, the seriousness of his aim as an artist, and "the precision with which he fits the word to the thought." James was "not a mere admirer of Europe and contemner of America," Howells said, and "our best suffers no disparagement in his stories." Howells rated "A Passionate Pilgrim" the best of the tales because of the qualities of tenderness and "poetic passion" in the character of Clement Searle and the "air of romance" in James's descriptions of the English countryside. He was impressed by the strain of humor and sentiment in the story, but grumbled a bit over what he felt was a tone of scornfulness and condescension in the attitude of the narrator toward his American friend.

Despite certain reservations Howells's judgment of James's work was highly complimentary. He discussed each of the stories in some detail, ranked them in order of preference, and observed (here he was the first of a long line of Jamesian analysts) the effectiveness of the use of a narrator-observer whose function was both dramatic and critical. Howells faced bravely the central situation of "Madame de Mauves" in which the French Baron advises his American wife to take a lover, but he demurred to the extent of saying that only a French writer could make such an idea convincing. He emphasized, instead, the gracefully drawn portrait of Euphemia, calling her an "ideal" woman, "wholly of our civilization" in her purity, courage, and "inflexible high-mindedness." He either overlooked or chose to ignore the significant counter-thrust to James's characterization by which the irony is at least partly directed at the heroine's rigid morality, just as he underestimated in the title story the deliberate intention of James to counteract the "passionate" mood by introducing a more realistic episode of social criticism. James's characters, on the whole, Howells regarded as too cultivated and therefore narrow in their sympathies and emotions. Sometimes, he said, "even the ladies and gentlemen of Mr. James's stories are allowed a certain excess or violence in which the end to be achieved is not distinctly discernible, or the effect so reluctantly responds to the intention as to leave merely the sense of excess." He referred to the reiteration of the "cats and monkeys" philosophy at the close of "The Madonna of the Future," which seemed to bring a "jarring note" to that otherwise "pensive romance."[3]

The title story, "A Passionate Pilgrim" had first appeared in the *Atlantic* in 1871. It was reprinted several times thereafter during James's lifetime with many revisions, the last time when it was included in the New York edition of his work, where James grouped it with several of his early international tales. It was an expression, he wrote in the Preface, of his rediscovery of the "lost vision" of Europe after a long absence,[4] a symbol of its author's youthful passion for the Old World, and until about 1930 it was usually interpreted in autobiographical terms. Clement Searle, the defrauded American claimant to an English title, has been identified—in his fevered enthusiasm for England and disparagement of America—with the young traveller, Henry James.

But Searle's mood of nostalgic delight in the stately mansions and the beautiful countryside of England was only one side of the story. James intended it as a tale of an American adventurer in Europe in which both romantic and realistic reactions were to be recorded. It was planned as a balanced criticism of English life. The author shared with Searle and his narrator-companion much of the excitement and reverent feeling of discovery, but he likewise held certain reservations. A letter James wrote his father from England in March, 1870, at the time he was writing "A Passionate Pilgrim," contains a highly romantic description of his visit to the Worcester Cathedral and surrounding country,[5] a long passage which was transferred bodily into the text of the story where it is told by the narrator. The early paragraphs of the narrative in which James speaks of the "latent preparedness of the American mind for even the most delectable features of English life" likewise suggest the mood of a passionate pilgrim. The emotion felt by the American toward England is described as "more fatal and sacred than his enjoyment, say, of Italy or Spain." In James's late revision of the story, however, the world "delectable" was altered to "the most characteristic" and the "fatal and sacred" emotion of the American pilgrim became a "searching" one. Throughout the story James's alterations removed some of the "passion" from the pilgrim's utterances.

More significant of the intended (if latent) realism of this early international tale is evidence from a letter of 1869 in which James described a typical English hotel in terms quite the reverse of those used in the account of the picturesque Red Lion Inn of the story. He told his mother about Morley's Hotel in Trafalgar Square, a "terrible" place (like all English hotels) with a "musty bedroom" and a "stupid coffee room," quite different from the Red Lion of the story with its echoes of Dickens and Smollett and its "magnificent panelling of mahogany."[6] A recent commentator[7] on "A Passionate Pilgrim" has emphasized James's implied criticism of the British aristocratic system and the social results of the law of primogeniture as evidenced in the episode of Rawson, the shabby-genteel graduate of Oxford, who is reduced to pushing a bath-chair for the Americans to keep his family from starving. Searle, on his deathbed, wills his remaining few valuables to the indigent victim of this system and urges him to leave "this awful England" for a new chance in America. England is a country of tramps and privation as well as the scene of cathedrals, and it is clear that James's intention (though not always successful in the execution) was to reveal both sides with equal conviction.

In "Madame de Mauves" James shifted the scene of his American adventures from England to France and deepened the element of melodrama. At the same time he intensified the psychological reality of his international theme. The result was one of his most successful short stories of the 1870's. Neither England nor Italy had been able to inspire James to the brilliancy of statement, clarity of international contrast, or the fine delineation of moral conflict of this story of an American girl "born to be neither a slave nor a toy, marrying a Frenchman, who believes that a woman must be one or the other." The reasons for the superior artistry of this long story are not readily apparent. It seems likely that James had experienced moods of depression and disappointment in the summer of 1873 which may have added a deepening tone to the tale. One of the most homesick letters of his life was written to Howells in June of 1873, just a few weeks before he wrote "Madame de Mauves." In the letter he spoke of "this desolate exile" abroad and of the "dreary necessity of having to live month after month without our friends for the sake of this arrogant old Europe which so little befriends us."[8] He found less to capture his imagination in France than in either Italy or England and greater obstacles in the way of his attempts to establish some relationship with its culture or society. His two visits to France in 1872 and again in 1875-6 were disillusioning, and he was unable to depict French people in either "Madame de Mauves" or *The American* without recourse to a conventionally melodramatic symbol of moral obliquity and cynicism. Like his narrator, Longmore, in "Madame de Mauves" James was, toward things French, less the passionate pilgrim than the "disappointed observer."[9]

Despite his reservations toward France, however, the story has become a minor classic. Rarely has the theme of renounced love been so eloquently depicted in fiction as in the closing scenes when Euphemia de Mauves, urged by her husband and his sister to take Longmore as a lover, calls him in for a last "interview."

> She was standing close to him, with her dress touching him, her eyes fixed on his. As she went on her manner grew strangely intense, and she had the singular appearance of a woman preaching reason with a kind of passion. Longmore was confused, dazzled, almost bewildered. The intention of her words was all remonstrance, refusal, dismissal; but her presence there, so close, so urgent, so personal, seemed a distracting contradiction of it.

Longmore is momentarily overcome by the physical sense of her beauty and proximity, but in a sudden reversal of mind "this last suggestion of his desire" (James altered the words in a revision to "this last sophistry of his great desire for her") died away, and in its place came a sense of "something vague which was yet more beautiful than itself." He is touched with a kind of "awe" for the towering idealism and adherence to principle of Madame de Mauves who later, in a final twist of the story, drives even her cynical French husband to suicide.

The temptation is strong, without biographical evidence, to explain the tense and overwrought emotion in this episode to some personal attachment in James's experience followed by a dedication to a life of art and celibacy. The mystery is only heightened by James's unusual vagueness as to the origin of the story in his later Preface where he says he could not recapture "the dimmest responsive ghost of a traceable origin" for it, recalling only a "dark and dampish room" in Bad-Homburg, Germany, where he had gone for the cure and where he remembers being "visited by the gentle Euphemia" who "muffled her charming head in the lightest, finest, vaguest tissue of romance."[10] But the story portrays a woman scarcely "gentle" in her muscular conscience, nor does the theme of French profligacy and provocation bear out his recollection of the story as one of light romance. Its quality derived from James's ambivalence toward French character. The licentiousness and license of French morality, which he suspected, and the honesty and realism of its literature, which he admired, were subtly mingled in his mind. With these alternatives on one side, he placed New England moral discipline and his own idealism on the other and handled the oppositions in terms of subdued melodrama. The story cannot be termed "realistic" in its dialogue or its theme, but neither does "romance" adequately define its quality. What comes home most forcefully to the reader is the sharpness of the moral antitheses and the intensity of the undercurrents of feeling.

The critical dissatisfaction which runs through much of the commentary on James's international stories of the Seventies derived in part from his artistic impartiality which, as Howells pointed out, baffled readers of *The American* and *Daisy Miller*. They failed to see that his impartiality "comes at last to the same result as sympathy."[11] Even his brother William, always a bit edgy at "Harry's" much earlier fame, struggled to understand his restrictive method. He had to admit its success in some of the early stories, but he returned to his belief that "the thorough and passionate conception of a story is the highest" and urged his brother to return to it.[12] Christopher Newman, Daisy Miller, and the Wentworth family in *The Europeans* offended readers and critics whose national pride was affronted. Richard Grant White complained, for instance, that Newman was not "what Mr. James would like to have accepted as a fair representative of the social product of his country." And Daisy, he felt, was a "faithful" portrait of "a certain sort of American young woman who is unfortunately too common."[13] Almost without exception contemporary reviewers were disturbed by the unconventional endings of James's stories which seemed to violate the standards of romantic tragedy and at the same time failed to provide the wedding-bells-and-happy-couple expectation of popular romance.

A minor tempest of opinion stirred in the periodicals over the "disappointing" conclusion of *The American*. T. W. Higginson's perplexities typified the wavering opinion of the late Seventies between smiling aspects and frowning realities when he observed that "the very disappointment which the world felt at the close of *The American* was in some sense a tribute to its power." James, he noted, had conjured up characters who insist upon working out destinies of their own and this "defeat" was greater than a "victory." But Higginson's recognition of James's skill succumbed in the end to his sense of propriety, for his final words reflected the provincialism of contemporary taste. James, he concluded, should not have let his situation get out of hand because "the most complicated situations often settle themselves unseen, and the most promising tragedies are cheated out of their crises."[14] In this ingenious argument, Higginson brought realism to the defense of a romantic ending.

Howells, too, joined the chorus of dissent over James's tragic, or near-tragic, conclusion in a private letter to which James replied from Paris with less than his usual patience. His letter indicates the differences between the two men and the widening gulf between James and his feminine reading audience in America. "I quite understand," he wrote, "that as an editor you should go in for 'cheerful endings' but I am sorry that as a private reader you are not struck with the inevitability of *The American* denouement." The interest for him, James went on, lay in a situation which presented insuperable difficulties to the marriage of Claire and Christopher Newman "from which the only issue is by forfeiture—by losing something. . . . We are each the product of circumstances and there are tall stone walls which fatally divide us." To the Howells who had glossed over the tragic implications of his own novel, *A Foregone Conclusion,* in deference to the sensibilities of his readers, James made this challenging remark: "It is the tragedies in life that arrest my attention more than the other things and say more to my imagination."[15]

One anonymous writer in the Contributor's Club of the *Atlantic,* whose remarks Howells must have admitted to the magazine with some sacrifice to his own vanity, openly defended the conclusion of the novel against the general opinion. Newman, the writer held, acquired both interest and dignity by his sacrifice, and this "tragic sanction" was of greater aesthetic advantage than a happy ending which would have been "unsatisfactory to anyone save novel-readers whose taste has been corrupted by a low class of literature."[16]

Certain of the suggestive undercurrents of the story did not escape genteel reviewers, especially the relationship between Noemie and Valentin. The former was called "offensive" and the latter "gilded beyond his deserving" by the author. None of these comments, however, mentioned the ambiguous implications involved in the episode of Madame de Bellegarde's murder of her husband. Here James had apparently succeeded in concealing an even more "indecent" story from his more prudish detractors. By revealing the details through the eyes of the faithful Mrs. Bread, James managed to obscure the cause of the disagreement between Madame de Bellegarde and her husband over Claire's marriage. We learn only that a quarrel had taken place and that a long-standing animosity between M. de Bellegarde and his wife had flared up anew. This disagreement by itself seems scarcely adequate to explain his murder, and James must have made a choice between a more suggestive motive for Madame de Bellegarde's act (thereby risking the editorial blue pencil) or leaving much unsaid. He chose the more discreet alternative, straining the squeamish reader's credulity rather than offending his (or, more likely, *her*) moral sensibilities.

Nearly fifteen years later James produced his dramatic version of *The American* in London. Then he apparently felt no compunction to obscure the motive for the murder. In the play, Mrs. Bread informs Newman that her mistress had been carrying on an affair with M. de Cintre at the same time that she was planning to marry her daughter to him. "The Comte de Cintre had loved my lady—he was her lover still. My lady, in her day, went far, and her day was very long." Mrs. Bread adds that de Cintre knew things about Madame de Bellegarde and furthermore "she had money from him, and to the best of her ability she made it up to him in money's worth! But he taught her that her debt to him would hang over her till she had given him her helpless child." Madame de Bellegarde's dual role as adultress and panderess had been quite buried in the original novel, but James openly revealed her motivations in the play. The reasons for his change are not far to seek. The play did not need to be offered to an American editor dependent upon wide circulation and feminine readers; Ibsen's example had liberalized the English stage; and, finally, James was seeking a popular triumph, which had been denied him by the novel-reading public. In his anxiety for stage success, he felt he must submit at all costs to what he regarded as the necessities of the theater—sensation and vulgarization, "big knockdown effects."[17]

On the other hand, in his search for audience approval, he wrenched the conclusion of the story into a conventional stage ending. Newman and Claire ring down the curtain with an embrace while Madame de Bellegarde, like some villainous female Shylock, curses her daughter and burns the incriminating note from Mrs. Bread to Newman which the latter had used to bargain for Claire's hand. Even this conclusion seemed to actor Edward Compton to be too gloomy for the British audiences, with Valentin dead and the tone one of defeat until the last moment. James was asked to rewrite it so that Noemie could bring about a reconciliation between Valentin and Lord Deepmere. Against his finer artistic scruples James conceded the point and wrote a new fourth act in order, as he wrote to William, to "basely gratify their artless instincts and British thick wittedness."[18] The conclusion of tragic frustration and defeat which had so disturbed readers of *The American* in 1877 was now cynically altered to suit what James called "the vulgarity, the brutality, the baseness of the condition of the English-speaking theatre today."

As a work of art the play is clearly inferior to the novel because of James's deliberate decision to sacrifice subtlety and indirection for popular acclaim on the boards. He was, during the Nineties, depressed at the indifferent reception accorded his fiction and determined to win a public following in a medium which ran contrary to his own natural bent and his deepest convictions about art. His letters to William James at this time indicate the waverings, self-justifications, and the secretiveness of a man struggling to convince himself of something against his own deeper inclination. Seldom does one find among James's writings a more misguided optimism than his assertions to William James and to Robert Louis Stevenson in 1891 in which he seems to be trying to convince himself of the values of the scenic art. "I feel at last as if I had found my real form, which I am capable of carrying far, and for which the pale little art of fiction, as I have practised it, has been for me, but a limited and restricted substitute."[19] There is much irony in the fact that James, who constantly sought in the dramatic method a means to give form and direction to what he once termed (referring to the sprawling Russian novel) "the loose and baggy monster" of fiction, faltered when he came to write his own plays. He failed to realize the fact that it was not the drama, as such, but the novel with certain dramatic disciplines in which he was able to do his finest work. It is more than an accident that those works of his which have recently succeeded on the stage were not his plays, but dramatized versions of his fiction.

The dramatic form, together with his own mistaken notions of its fitness for him, combined to deprive James of the very qualities which have made his best fiction live—finesse, ambiguity, indirection. The "fig-leaf" of his style, his suggestive indefiniteness, his veiled hints and hesitations and overtones—these are what modern readers most value in his method. It is also interesting that insofar as writing to an audience shaped his work, the feminine reader of the *Atlantic Monthly* in 1877 was more congenial to his purpose than was the British "thick wittedness" of 1891. His own innate reserve together with the decorum of the age helped to produce an artistic method of unexampled skill, but when he tried to throw off his inhibitions in the interest of popular theater, he descended to melodrama and stage intrigue. In other words, James did not find himself entirely frustrated by the restrictions of public morality in "The Age of Innocence." On the contrary, these restraints combined with his own inner compulsions to produce what some readers have come to recognize as his strongest weapon—the undercurrent of meaning and suggestive quality of his work.

In his later Preface to *The American*, James made no reference to the play or to the motivation for the skeleton in the Bellegarde closet. Instead, he devoted himself to a philosophical discussion of the romantic elements in the novel which he felt had been too strongly marked. "I had been plotting arch-romance without knowing it." His conception of Paris as the scene of "bold bad treacheries" and the picture of the Bellegarde's

86

secret villainy and crime seemed to his mature mind consummately romantic and belonged to "the infancy of art." *The American* failed, he felt, to achieve a just proportion of opposed elements, that balanced commitment in both directions which is evident in the best work of Scott, Balzac, or Zola—a rich mixture of "the near and familiar" with the "far and strange." If he were to write it over again, he said, he would furl "the emblazoned flag of romance," set the scene in Boston or Cleveland, and emphasize the greed rather than the aristocratic pride of Newman's antagonists. He explained that his initial conception of Newman as a "beguiled and betrayed" and "cruelly wronged" compatriot had led him to impute to the Bellegardes an excessively romantic sense of pride in their rejection of him. Actually they would (like the more opportunistic Baron de Mauves, for instance) "positively have jumped" at the rich and easy American as a match for Claire, and their pretentious pride should more appropriately have been treated "in the light of comedy and irony."[20]

Comedy, irony, and a tone of contemporaneous realism replaced the seriousness of the earlier international tales in the group of stories written during the prolific year 1878-79. Beginning with *The Europeans*, a clever comedy of manners which James too readily dismissed from the New York edition as slight, he experimented with a series of *nouvelles*, set at least partly in resort towns or watering places such as Newport, Vevey, or Geneva where the atmosphere was less subject to moral or social conflict and where "manners" provided the major form of contrast. Certain gayer international types like Felix Young of *The Europeans*, Lord Lambeth of *An International Episode*, and even Winterbourne of *Daisy Miller*, a potential idler despite his stiffness, play important roles in these tales of the late Seventies. Differences turn on breaches of etiquette provoked by the "innocence" of young American girls of the Howells variety. Serious psychological divisions and social problems are avoided. Another important distinction between these stories and those preceding *The American* was pointed out by Christof Wegelin who demonstrated that the problem turned not on a conflict of the American girl with some alien form of conduct, but rather upon the provincialism of her compatriots.[21] Daisy Miller's real antagonists are not the Italians, but the transplanted American social snobs such as Mrs. Costello, who is a prude, or Winterbourne, who cannot make up his mind. It is a case of American innocence versus a new form of American experience—the self-conscious "sophistication" of the Europeanized social set.

It was somewhat inconsistent, then, with this change of mood that James subtitled *Daisy Miller* "A Study," suggesting that his purpose was to analyze closely a certain type of American womanhood. Noting this, newspaper critics and some readers declared his cast of thought to be French and deplored the shift in his work toward hard and brilliant character contrasts with the resulting loss of poetry and pathos. Not all reviewers, however, agreed with *Harper's* that Daisy was a caricature and a national insult. Several attested to the truth of the portrait and dismissed the "protests of the girls who belong to her own class and pronounce her a caricature."[22] In the perspective of his later Preface James explained that the subtitle was meant to take into account "a certain flatness in my poor little heroine's literal denomination" and to prevent readers from expecting melodrama or "stirring scenes." As between an analytical and a passionate intention James straddled the point. He confessed to an initially analytic aim to reveal "the measured and felt truth" about Daisy, but then went on to admit that in the course of developing her portrait he had yielded, subconsciously, to his "incurable prejudice in favour of grace," as well as "prettiness and pathos," and that the final effect of her character had been not realism, but "pure poetry."[23]

Despite the lighter tone and comic intention of these international stories, however, James was some years away from achieving the brilliant ironic level of his satires on the literary life of the Yellow Nineties, and one feels a certain disparity between the inner intention and outward action of *Daisy Miller, An International Episode,* or *The Pension Beaurepas.* The interplay between seriousness and irony was not always held in balance, and a certain disharmony resulted as illustrated by the unexpected ending of Daisy Miller in her death from the Roman fever. What gives that story its undercurrent of seriousness is not her death at the end, but the fact that James apparently conceived the story in terms of international intrigue and then proceeded to write it by playing down at every point the melodramatic implications. As in the case of *The American,* he dramatized the plot some years after the original fictional version. The play of *Daisy Miller* appeared in the *Atlantic Monthly* in 1883, but never actually reached the stage. A comparison of the two versions indicates that James had already begun to reconcile himself to a different standard of success in the theater. Where the *nouvelle* is poetic and psychological, the play is full of blunt contrasts and accidents. Where the story is subtle, the play is conventional. The story ends with a dying fall; the play closes with Daisy and Winterbourne happily anticipating wedlock while Giovanelli gnashes his teeth over his defeated hopes.

Furthermore, the play of *Daisy Miller* exploits certain of the improprieties which were only implicit in the story. When James had first submitted the original story to a Philadelphia publisher, he recalled that the editor had promptly returned the manuscript "with an absence of comment that struck me at the time as rather grim." When he related this to a friend, he was told that the story could only have passed with the Philadelphia critic for "an outrage on American girlhood."[24] Possibly the flurry of popularity which the book received emboldened the author to develop the undertones of suggestion into the more flagrant intrigue of the play. In the original tale, for example, Winterbourne is described as a Europeanized American "studying" at Geneva. Less sympathetic observers, however, hinted that

> . . . the reason of his spending so much time at Geneva was that he was extremely devoted to a lady who lived there—a foreign lady—a person older than himself. Very few Americans—indeed I think none—had ever seen this lady, about whom there were some singular stories.

The reason for this rather gratuitous side glance into Winterbourne's past seems obscure since his connections with the foreign lady are dropped at that point. But in the final paragraph of the story mention is made that, after Daisy's death, Winterbourne returned to Geneva "whence continue to come the most contradictory accounts of his motives of sojourn: a report that he is 'studying' hard—an intimation that he is much interested in a very clever foreign lady." James's sly dig at gossipy and provincial American visitors was noticed at once by brother William who wrote "Harry" objecting to the closing paragraph of the story. Henry replied that William's objection seemed a "queer and narrow one." He appealed to the license of the story-teller's art and brushed aside the suggestion that readers would wish the paragraph omitted. He apparently felt that William's remarks were of a piece with the narrow and prudish New England attitude.[25]

It seems clear, at any rate, that James meant to invest the rather colorless Winterbourne with a hint of the adventurer and thus, by indirection, throw a more suggestive flavor over Daisy's trip with him to the castle of Chillon. In the play, however, this guarded hint was developed into a full-blown intrigue whereby Eugenio, the courier, has become a blackmailer and Madame Katkoff, "the foreign lady," is amorously associated with Winterbourne, receiving him into her home as a "privileged visitor." Eugenio's plot to marry Daisy to Giovanelli and divide the inheritance fails when Madame Katkoff refuses to take part in the plan and confesses it all to Winterbourne. The curtain rings down when Winterbourne realizes his love for Daisy while Giovanelli and Eugenio are left planning another intrigue for the next heiress. The play lacks both the depth and the subtlety of the original *nouvelle*, nor does it take deep insight to perceive that the restraint and suggestion, playing beneath the realistic surface of the story, proved more successful than James's bald attempt to exploit the plot for the theater.

Several qualities emerge, then, in James's developing fictional methods of the Seventies. The interplay of romantic and realistic elements, of humor and seriousness, of comedy and melodrama, is apparent in varying proportions. Differences of emphasis occur according to the national scene concerned. England brought out the passionate pilgrim in James, but equally provoked him to democratic criticism of the system of social privilege. Italy inspired his aesthetic emotions, his idealism, and interest in the visual arts, but the stories of Florence and Rome likewise carried a strain of scepticism. In *Roderick Hudson,* as we have seen, the roles of passionate pilgrim and disappointed observer are divided between the two main characters, with Roderick's romantic abandon and Rowland's cautiousness weighed about equally in the scale. Disillusion, however, is the note most strongly felt in the French stories. An undercurrent of provocation and moral deviation and a tendency toward melodramatic incidents, intrigue, betrayal, duels, and "arch romance" testifies to James's too ready acceptance of an Anglo-Saxon stereotype of France, on the one hand, and to his personal frustrations and disappointments with French intellectual and cultural circles, on the other. French fiction, especially that of Flaubert and Balzac, was associated in James's mind with the developing "realism" of subject and method. Thus he sought, in his early work, to emulate the French method as an antidote to the localism and provinciality of much American or English fiction. Accordingly, his French stories and novels were an unstable compound of artifice and actuality, yet in such a story as "Madame de Mauves" the resulting synthesis proved highly successful.

It was in the mid-Seventies that James first discovered, with an assist from Howells and the example of Turgenev, the young American *jeune fille* as an international type and explored various combinations of the type in his fiction. This discovery was to become a trademark of all James's work to the latest period and was to become increasingly more complex as his work matured. In the early work his character portrayal showed the influence of the flat, one dimensional characters of Hawthorne or George Eliot, but beginning with Daisy Miller he experimented more and more with the "complex" character. Daisy was "an inscrutable combination of audaciousness and innocence." Bessie Alden in *An International Episode* was a Bluestocking girl whose bookishness and seriousness are mildly satirized and gently treated at the same time. By the end of the 1870's, however, James had begun to see the international predicament with more humor and detachment, and to emphasize its comedy of manners rather than its deeper problems or near-tragedies as in his longer works of the middle years of the decade. *Daisy Miller* is a pivotal story, marking this transition, in its lightness of tone followed by the serious, rather sudden and unprepared for denouement of Daisy's death. More and more in these stories he chose contemporary situations and neutral settings (London, Switzerland, Boston) rather than Roman ateliers or Parisian domestic mysteries.

The direction of his "realism" lay in depicting the effects of social conditions upon his characters. These conditions were not necessarily determining, however, and the drama of these stories lay in watching through the eyes of a neutral observer, the interplay of character *and* circumstance. James sought a kind of realism which would repudiate both the novel of romantic incident and that of domestic local color. Melodrama played a diminishing role, but provided a substructure for James to inject anti-romantic touches and counter-thrusts in the interests of reality. His "vision of the real," during the Seventies, was viewed through a screen of romance, but gradually he worked his way toward a middle zone in which comedy, irony, and gentle satire took the place of seriousness. This newer mood looked ahead to the broad satire of *The Bostonians* or to the skillful vignettes of literary life in the Nineties. Nevertheless, his work in the first decade of his fiction contained a quality of its own which cannot be dismissed as merely experimental, and the best books of that time belong to the permanent body of his work. Despite his own self-deprecation toward it in the later Prefaces, it can be read and re-read alongside the later fiction without apology or condescension.

6.

Victorian Bookmen and the New Novel

In 1879 Henry James, commenting on a review by G. P. Lathrop of his study of Hawthorne, wrote to his friend, T. S. Perry: "The amount of a certain sort of emasculate twaddle produced in the U.S. is not encouraging."[1] To James, already seriously dedicating himself to the art of fiction, there was little aid and comfort to be found in much of the criticism which filled the American periodicals in the Seventies. Only Howells and Perry were among his correspondents in New England when he wanted to discuss his favorite subject, the novel, and the reception of his books. In a letter to Howells, referring to some comments on *The American* and *Daisy Miller* by T. W. Higginson, Emily Dickinson's "mentor," he complained: "My tender (or rather my very tough) flesh is prescient already of the Higginsonian fangs."[2] What James had in mind in such comments was the characteristic mingling of provincial attitudes with conventional moral judgments which passed for criticism in the literary columns and book reviews in the *Atlantic Monthly*, *Scribner's*, and other popular periodicals. Criticism, during the Seventies, was slow to respond to the new fiction and looked backward, for the most part, to older values and the poetic ideals of the mid-century.

Like the hero of James's story "Benvolio" (1875) the Victorian bookmen of the 1870's vacillated between two loves, the wistful and fragile Scholastica, representing the artistic imagination, and the Countess, a fascinating widow and *femme du monde*, representing worldly things. Confronted by an ever-widening gulf between the earlier idealism and the social facts of the Seventies, aspiring poets, critics, and intellectuals found themselves at a crossroads where two paths diverged, one leading toward beauty and "art," the other somewhat menacingly toward actuality and the contemporary scene. The age-old division between the "ancients" and the "moderns" re-asserted itself during this late Victorian *Sturm und Drang* in criticism, a campaign which grew more violent in the late Eighties and Nineties and which often provided more heat than light.

Among the forces for a traditional aesthetics in the 1870's was the formidable figure of James Russell Lowell, dean of American critics, whose essays centered upon the earlier English poets and contributed to the prevailingly neo-romantic temper of literary theory and expression in that decade. Lowell's powerful influence worked against the winds of doctrine which were blowing in the direction of evolutionary science, positivism, and empirical modes of thought, and although he was not altogether a disciple of Coleridge, his work seemed to confirm the inescapable fact that it was nearly impossible to speak of literary matters without returning in some form to the older questions—the romantic elevation of the artist, the organic theory of art, the moral function of literature, the "shaping" imagination. The most advanced critical minds of the period were able to refine upon such concepts, but not to do without them. In 1872 Charles Bristed discussed "American Criticism: Its Difficulties and Prospects" in an article in the *North American Review* which was candid enough about the existing deficiencies, but rather vague about "prospects." The "difficulties" were clear to see—a tone of provinciality, sectional differences, self-consciousness, and timidity. When Bristed came to define the critic of the future, he described him as a man eclectic in taste, widely cultivated and well-read, but definitely not an evolutionary positivist. He would be more like Lowell standing for a critical program rooted in the past and shaped in the academy.

The younger generation of critics, however, hoped to formulate a philosophy of letters which could supersede the older romanticism and somehow express the rising age of science and Spencerian evolution. Conscious of both old and new they searched for a compromise which might encompass the extremes of thought of the period, comprehend the direction of the new fiction, and adjust earlier values to the demands of contemporary life. With a few notable exceptions, however, this collective effort was premature in the Seventies for a variety of reasons. There was, first of all, far too little knowledge of the critical thought and experimental work being done in Europe, especially in France. Furthermore, a tone of evangelical piety entered into some of the commentary on the novel to muddy the waters and carry criticism away from a serious discussion of the new fiction and the principles upon which it could be fruitfully studied. Finally, there was a diffusion of talent into a variety of channels on the part of some of the essayist-critics whose natural gifts, could they have been more directly centered upon literature, might well have produced some lasting critical work.

Thomas Wentworth Higginson, James's *bête noir*, is a case in point. A Unitarian minister, journalist, and follower of such causes as negro rights and women's suffrage Higginson possessed genuine literary gifts, enthusiasm, and large hopes for the future of the national literature. In an article entitled "Americanism in Literature" (1871) he spoke in boldly Emersonian language of the need for native writers to infuse the vigor of the "American spirit" into literature and urged novelists to follow Cooper and Mrs. Stowe in handling "daring" American subjects like the Indian and the Negro. Higginson was honest enough to recognize that this American spirit consisted of more promise than performance. He went on to point out that its strength was balanced by a weakness, a fatal inattention to matters of technique and execution in art.

As yet we Americans have hardly begun to think of the details of execution in any art. We do not aim at perfection of detail even in engineering, much less in literature.

In a passage which accurately forecast the nature of his own future career and characterized at the same time the literary fraternity of the 1870's, he touched on the tendency of writers to diffuse their subjects and spread themselves too thin.

The popular preacher becomes a novelist; the editor turns his paste-pot and scissors to the compilation of a history; the same man must be poet, wit, philanthropist, and genealogist.[3]

That Higginson's taste in art was something less than sound was to be demonstrated in the Nineties when he attempted to "improve" the poetry of Emily Dickinson, nor did he quite see in this essay that it was not only lack of attention to detail and the dissipation of interests which hindered American critics, but likewise insufficient knowledge of the literary theories and experiments in fiction emanating from Europe, lack of wide experience and travel, and an undue infatuation with the national pride.

The critical spirits of the Seventies were men of varied talents and trades. Most, but not all of them, were interested in the novel as the literary type of the future. Individually, their criticism is fragmentary and now almost unread. As a group, however, their work contains historical import and even their failures provide us with case histories which are relevant to the earlier realism. New England produced a group of critics under the guiding influence of Howells. Higginson was one, George Parsons Lathrop another, Thomas S. Perry, a third. The last two did notable work toward understanding and working out guidelines for the new fiction. In New York, Brander Matthews was just beginning a long and distinguished career as a dramatic critic, but his literary efforts in the Seventies, appearing in the *Galaxy*, *Appleton's Journal*, and *Scribner's*, were ephemeral, concerned, as he put it, with the "curiosities of literature."[4] Richard Grant White, the Shakespeare scholar, indirectly abetted the cause of realism (though not in fiction) by his staunch attack upon Coleridgean principles and German eulogistic commentary on Shakespeare.[5] William Crary Brownell, a promising young critic and editor just beginning a long and distinguished career, wrote some of the best native criticism of Henry James in the *Nation* around 1880.[6] All these contributed something to the critical effort of the Seventies.

In the midwest a small band of idealists and ordained ministers like W. C. Wilkinson, George W. Cooke, or the novelist Edward Eggleston interested themselves primarily in George Eliot as the spokesman of the new psychological novel. Their criticism was often diluted, however, with a kind of evangelistic form of ideality which led them to seek in literature a lay form of inspiration. What they mainly saw in Eliot was her "ethical quality" and her "moral spirit" and her novels became too often the material for a sermon of the uplifting sort. George Eliot became a focal figure in the critical debate over "realism" during this period. Her novels satisfied the ethical bias of many American critics and at the same time revealed many of the advances of the newer school in their detailed psychological analysis (as it was called) of her characters.[7] In the South, Sidney Lanier, too, singled out George Eliot as a guiding spirit and symbol of the ideal Victorian woman. Lanier, like his New York counterpart, Edmund Clarence Stedman, was both poet and critic who envisaged a great future when science and literature would be harmonized into a new poetics. Both Lanier and Stedman lectured at The Johns Hopkins University. Both made ambitious efforts to work out an evolutionary system of aesthetics which would preserve the past and include the present. To understand the nature of their thought and critical work is to understand a good deal about the temper of Victorian criticism in the Seventies and early Eighties.

Edmund Clarence Stedman, New York poet and Wall Street broker, lover of beauty and art, summed up in himself, perhaps better than any of his fellow critics, the strains and discords of his time and the divisions which confronted the literary mind in America during the critical period of the shifting of the center of activity from Boston to New York. He was a leading figure in the circle of New York literati including Thomas Bailey Aldrich, R. W. Gilder, editor of the *Century*, Richard Grant White, H. C. Bunner, the poets R. H. Stoddard and Bayard Taylor, and many others. Stedman was a member of the New York stock exchange and the Author's Club, a defender of ideality and an admirer of the Victorian poets. He was also a "Pan in Wall Street," singing songs of tender melancholy strain and Tennysonian sentiment. Like Aldrich, he lamented the passing of the older romance, resented the intrusive demands of realism and prose fiction, and he envisioned a new revival of poetry in which the transitional "lull" would give way to a new millennium of verse and a shimmering harmony of "the lens, the laboratory, and the millennial rocks." For many years the leading critic of *Scribner's* and its successor, the *Century Magazine*, Stedman was a successor to Lowell, a lesser Matthew Arnold, preaching the gospels of beauty and Hellenism in the marts of trade. Like Pan in his poem he piped pastoral ditties on the steps of the Treasury building while the bulls and bears watched curiously and newsboys capered to the melody.

For succeeding generations he became the epitome of the genteel in poetry and criticism.

Stedman's life was a long struggle with ill-health and the necessity of making his living by stock-speculation in order to provide enough hard-won freedom to pursue his literary ambitions. His father died when he was still an infant. A precocious young student of Latin and Greek, he was a romantic dreamer and writer of verses. At fifteen he entered Yale College, the youngest of his class of a hundred freshmen. Left in charge of his uncle and guardian, when the mother he idolized remarried and left for Europe, Stedman struggled against homesickness and loneliness to become a model student. Among the "Rules" he wrote down during his Freshman year were the following: "I will make it a point to come to every recitation with my lessons perfectly prepared. I resolve to abstain *entirely* from profane swearing, gaming, drinking, or disorderly behavior."[8] At the end of his sophomore year, he fell in with a rebellious group of companions, neglected his studies and began "howling around town." During one escapade he was arrested with a group of friends and his activities reported to the college authorities. He was "rusticated" to Northampton where he spent a year tutoring. This terminated his college career, though he had already achieved a reputation for excellence in poetry and English composition, and he was forced to make a living as a journalist. Twenty years later he wrote a long and contrite letter requesting the authorities at Yale for reinstatement, and he was awarded his degree with his class of 1853. Stedman never quite recovered from this experience, and something in the overwrought intensity which marked his dedication to poetry and beauty may have been the result of a guilt-feeling which drove him to succeed in later life where he had failed in his college career.

In his two most important volumes of criticism, *Victorian Poets* (1875) and *Poets of America* (1885) he became the spokesman for many of the neo-romantic ideas in criticism and established himself as one of the representative critics of his time. He applied to poetry the Spencerian principle of progress, proceeding from homogeneity to heterogeneity. He envisaged a harmony of art and science. According to George De Mille, Stedman's career heralded the break, about 1880, from ethical to aesthetic criticism in America in his championing of Poe, Tennyson, and the cult of beauty.[9] He set himself against the rising tide of realism in fiction, but at the same time he was one of the first critics to defend Whitman and to revive Poe's warfare against the heresy of the didactic. Stedman predicted that a new Lucretius would arise to interpret the nature of things, and that the Muse of poetry would once again replace the novel as the true form of expression. He defended the romantic theory of poetic inspiration and the dichotomy between genius and talent which Coleridge had learned from the German transcendentalists.

In his use of Schopenhauer and Eduard von Hartmann's *Philosophy of the Unconscious*, however, he brought psychological methods to the defense of a romantic philosophy of criticism.[10] Although he adopted the historical methods of Taine, he drew back from the implications of determinism in his theory.

Stedman did not concern himself directly with the novel as a form of art, regarding literalism and realism as a hostile tendency and the novelist as a man applying detective methods "to the movements and gabble of doughy nonentities." In his series of lectures on poetry at The Johns Hopkins University he attempted to construct a new system of aesthetics and to stem the tide of realism. The lectures were published in *The Nature and Elements of Poetry* (1892). Here he approached certain of the ideas of functionalism in an effort to work out a compromise with pragmatic ideas, but it was a limited concession which clearly left him a defender of ideality and of the Victorian poetic mode of Landor, Hood, or Matthew Arnold.[11] Nor did he possess the clarity and precision of thought necessary to construct a system of aesthetics such as his master, Poe, had done.

Stedman's prose style suffered from excessive embellishments and overwriting. His tendency was toward a Tennysonian prettiness but without Tennyson's skill. It was his mission to recapture the lyrical impulse in a materialistic age and he insisted that the decline of poetry was merely an "interregnum." Studying the causes for this transitional state of things, he came to the conclusion that, although the advance of science had wrought a profound disturbance of romantic traditions and made necessary a new poetic language, the "years of transition are near an end" and "a creative, poetic literature, adapted to the new order of thought and the new aspirations of beauty, will speedily grow into form."[12] In his struggles against poverty and poor health, his devotion to poetry and beauty, and his heroic effort to revive the romantic canon of aesthetics, he stands as a symbol of the currents of criticism in the postwar decades and almost a reincarnation of his model, Poe. It was in his life and career, as much as in his accomplishment as a critic, that Stedman epitomized the disparities of his age. He became, like Sidney Lanier whom he resembled in many ways, a voice crying in the wilderness, a poet and critic of talents and natural gifts born out of place and out of time.

Sidney Lanier similarly tried to discover in the ideas of evolution and science basic standards of authority for his lectures on literature in the late 1870's at The Johns Hopkins University and the Peabody Institute in Baltimore. Many of the tendencies of literary theory and speculation of that period can be found in his curiously learned lectures and books of criticism which ranged over German aesthetic theories, evolutionary science, and the modern novel. His *Science of English Verse, Shakespeare and his Forerunners,* and *The English Novel* are a strange melange of historical scholarship, moral fervor, and prophetic vision. They glow with a message of harmony and rhythm for a world of conflict and change. The impact of Darwin and Spencer, the conflict between science and literature, the relation of the arts, the function of the novel, the quest for a science of criticism, the reconciliation of opposite poles of thought, the high regard for the individual, a chivalric idealization of Victorian women, an upward law of social progress, an exact science of acoustics for music and poetry, a physics of metrical systems—all these ideas find expression in Lanier's work, eclectic and confusing in its multiplicity of themes, yet held together somehow by a glorious vision of the democratic millennium when men, wafted on the wings of love and beauty, would become self-governing.

Like Stedman, but with even greater poetic passion and a stronger sense of order, Lanier's criticism may be regarded as a summary effort, about 1880, to weave together into a pattern all the singular elements of critical thought which impinged upon the literary mind of the Seventies. For his *Science of English Verse* he went to the German physiological aesthetics of Helmholtz and Heinrich Schmidt, as well as to Tyndall, Alfred Mayer, and Blaserna for their theories of sound and acoustics.[13] Although he seems to have rejected the theory of biological evolution, he found in Darwin, Spencer, and John Fiske an evolutionary foundation for principles of criticism.[14] Likewise, he sought inspiration in German romantic philosophy, especially Novalis, and to Emerson he partly owed his fondness for drawing analogies between science and moral laws. Finally, Poe's *Eureka* helped him to formulate, along with Spencer's system, his view of the universe as a harmony of rhythmic motions.[15] It was Spencer, Lanier said, "who has formulated the proposition that where opposing forces act, rhythm appears, and has traced the rhythmic motions of nature to the antagonistic forces there found."[16]

Lanier understood with the passionate feeling of his nature the deeply conflicting currents of doctrine which confronted the artist and sensitive mind in an age of science and materialism. For this reason he felt the need to establish a broad, philosophical groundwork on which to rest his system of aesthetics—a system which allowed place for his neo-romantic ideals without denying the truths of science or the methods of scientific thought. His work has been regarded as both contradictory and eclectic, but it was in accord with the advanced thinking of his day in its effort at harmonization of extremes of thought. Against the overwhelming odds of physical illness which gave him only a few short years to work out and set down his ideas, he formulated an aesthetic philosophy which was more comprehensive than that of any of his contemporaries.

Harmony among opposing forces of the universe Lanier discovered in "that great principle" of rhythm by which "the whole universe came to present itself to us as a great flutter of motions."[17] The "fret and sting," the "no of death"—all evil in the world were to him the necessary antagonism and the friction of life, like the cross-plucking of the taut bowstring to bring melody and harmony out of conflict. In both the physical and moral world "this beautiful and orderly principle of rhythm thus swings to and fro like the shuttle of a loom and weaves a definite and comprehensible pattern into the otherwise chaotic fabric of things."[18]

In his speculation on social progress Lanier held that society had evolved upward from the primitive to the modern state, and this social progress (here he was close to Herbert Spencer's sociology in *The Man Versus the State*) centered not in the group, but in the individual in his development toward a condition of personal responsibility for his own fate. Arguing from Darwinian premises and citing Fiske's "Sociology and Hero-Worship," Lanier found in the concept of the "spontaneous variation" of species justification for his faith that the social order existed for the highest development of the individual.[19] A new complexity, arising out of the earlier simplicity of man's moral life, called for a new literary form having greater flexibility than the older poetic forms of the epic and the drama.

It is at this point in Lanier's comprehensive theory of aesthetics that *The English Novel* finds a significant place. The novel, in his view, achieving its finest development in the work of George Eliot, contained this freedom of expression together with an ideal balance between the claims of science and those of poetry upon man's understanding. "The enormous growth in the personality of man which our time reveals," Lanier said, can be traced from the Prometheus of Aeschylus, who is devoid of moral responsibility in his dependence on a ruling hierarchy of gods, to Shelley's Prometheus, who only partially approaches ethical freedom and choice, and thence to modern man who possesses a large degree of personal responsibility and "heterogeneity" of mind. The novel, beginning with Richardson, has become a medium through which this higher moral nature and greater subtlety is being gradually revealed. It is not, however, the novel of Zola, based upon a too exacting application of scientific techniques, nor even that of Dickens and Thackeray (whose work tended toward the satiric and partial view of human nature), but the work of George Eliot in which Lanier discovered the reconciliation of science, in the best sense, and art. "The great modern novelist is at once scientific and poetic. And here, it seems to me, in the novel, we have the meeting, the reconciliation, the kiss, of science and poetry."[20]

In his discussion of George Eliot's novels, Lanier touched upon most of the questions vital to the Victorian theory of fiction: the relation of art to morality (he defends her didacticism as beyond priggishness in its intolerance of evil and its loving view of human nature); *l'art pour l'art* (citing Keats and Emerson, he reaffirmed the romantic faith in the inseparability of beauty and truth); the comparison of the drama and the novel (the latter is a finer form evolving out of the earlier drama—"simply another phase of the growth of man from Shakespeare to George Eliot"); and the idealization of Victorian women (he groups the heroines of Eliot's books along with Mrs. Browning, Florence Nightingale, and Charlotte Cushman). Thus the novel, in its superior knowledge of human motivation and greater psychological analysis of character, surpassed the drama and became, for Lanier, "the highest and holiest plane of creative effort." George Eliot he considered the supreme novelist who had laid bare the workings of the human heart with something near god-like omniscience.

Lanier's quest for an all-encompassing theory of aesthetics was nothing less than a vindication of the Victorian mind to God. He possessed a passion amounting to religious zeal for a theory of art which could include both science and poetry. In his upward-spiralling view of man's development he found a high place for the art of the novel. His criticism suffered, of course, from a predilection to system and a commitment to the theory of evolution. At a time when the novel, in James's hands, was to move toward a greater dramatic conciseness, he was less than prophetic in his praise for George Eliot's lengthy, authorial analyses of her characters. Nevertheless, his interest in the novel as a type of the modern, and his sound, historical approach to the subject led him well beyond his fellow poet Stedman in the effort to comprehend the significance of the newer fiction. Possessing little practical experience in fiction (except for his much earlier "novel," *Tiger Lilies*), he was ill equipped to deal with its more technical aspects, and one must therefore turn to the criticism of two New England critics, George Parsons Lathrop and Thomas Sergeant Perry for a closer examination of the principles of the new fiction and an effort to place the American writers in the mainstream of the European novel.

George Parsons Lathrop was one of the young *Atlantic* critics who typified in many ways the transitional state of criticism in America of which Bristed wrote in 1872. He was symptomatic of its enthusiasms, and at the same time of its difficulties and limitations. He contributed in 1874 two long historical essays on the novel to Howells's magazine, essays which set out bravely to overcome the deficiencies which he clearly saw in the reviews and commentaries of the day—a fragmentary and fuzzy vagueness of purpose, a want of systematic principles and sound ideas upon which a serious discussion of the novel could be formed. Lathrop shared and even anticipated certain of the problems of fiction which concerned Howells and Henry James. He possessed ambition and a clear sense of the importance of establishing fresh approaches, but his reach exceeded his grasp. An understanding of Lathrop's relative failure as a critic involves both his own faults of perception and the uncertain state of American criticism in the early Seventies.

Poet, essayist, traveller, critic, and the author of three not very successful novels, Lathrop was born in Hawaii and educated in New York City and in Dresden, Germany, where he met his future wife, Rose Hawthorne. They were married in 1871 and returned to Boston where Lathrop began writing for the *Atlantic*, becoming assistant editor under Howells from 1875 to 1877. In 1876 he published his *A Study of Hawthorne*, the first full-length biographical and critical study of the man and his work. Like so many of the critics of the Seventies, Lathrop was engaged in a variety of activities without achieving significant success in any one. His novel, *An Echo of Passion* (1883) was conventional, and a later novel, *Would You Kill Him?* (1890) elicited only some perfunctory praise of Howells. He continued to review novels for the *Atlantic* during the 1880's but increasingly devoted himself to causes such as international copyright. His strongest claim to attention now, however, aside from his effort to provide a system of principles for the novel, is his biography of Hawthorne and his later editing of Hawthorne's works. His poetry is best forgotten.

His two long essays in the *Atlantic Monthly*, "The Growth of the Novel" and "The Future of the Novel" were notable for several things—the recognition of the "indolence" of criticism on the novel and of the absence of clear principles for its discussion; the application of historical methods to the novel (he traced the form from its beginnings in the Greek romance to his own time); the comparison of dramatic methods in fiction with those of the stage; and the association of the novel with realism. In the early Seventies these were all relatively new approaches. If Lathrop had applied them with more perception and greater critical skill, he might have achieved a permanent place in the history of American criticism. The first of the two essays, for example, anticipated Henry James's "The Art of Fiction" by a decade. It opened with a pioneering note in its plea for serious consideration of the principles by which "the variously modified forms of the novel now extant are to be judged."[21] Like James, Lathrop took issue with the prevailing opinion among readers and would-be novelists that anybody could write a novel without the necessity of learning a difficult discipline. Tracing the origins of the novel from the Greek romances of Heliodorus, he centered his inquiry around the gradual emergence of a dramatic method in fiction, discovering germs of the technique in the Renaissance and after, especially in Cervantes, Le Sage, Richardson, and Fielding.

Such an evolutionary-historical approach to the novel had behind it the weight of system and authority, but Lathrop tended to apply it with a certain mechanical inflexibility. Richardson, Fielding, Goldsmith, Scott, Dickens, Thackeray, and George Eliot are all brought before the bar of judgment, measured by the yardstick of "dramatic" fiction, and each is found wanting, in varying degrees. Fielding, for example, used some of the methods of the stage in his fiction, but he "did not carry the dramatic movement far enough." Lathrop appears to have missed entirely the purpose of the epic structure of *Tom Jones*, seeing in that book only a rambling, discursive tale of adventure without form. After similarly disposing of Fielding's successors in the English novel, he turned to the novels of George Eliot. Her rank is high, indeed. She has, Lathrop says, "almost perfected" the novel, yet at the same time her work fails to realize fully the dramatic method. In her technique of "minute and deliberate analysis" of the characters and in her "wordy" examinations into their mental states, she has left too little to the imagination of the reader, and despite her "brave and noble genius" she has restricted the range and power of the novel by limiting its impartial presentation of life. Thus, despite his rather wooden balancing off of faults and virtues in George Eliot, Lathrop emerges with a concept of dramatic fiction which anticipated by many years Henry James's enunciation of the principle of a "center of consciousness" whereby reality is rendered indirectly through the mind of a "reflector." Lathrop concludes that the portrayal of character in fiction gains from a certain obscurity achieved by the dramatic method in which "the essence of the matter" is finally reserved for the imagination of the reader.

But it is in the work of Turgenev that Lathrop discovers the most complete illustration of this method. At this point in his development of the thesis, Lathrop fails to pursue his line of thought toward technique in the novel and turns to consider content and idea. Turgenev, for all his detachment and objectivity of method, is finally brought to judgment because he is "all too unpoetical." By excluding himself entirely from his scene of action the author of *Dmitri Roudine* and *Smoke* has invoked "despair" and failed to allow "a single note of hope or convincing joy" to redeem the "horror" of his stories.[22] Praising the Russian writer for his dramatic impartiality, Lathrop paradoxically accuses him of excessive "scientific analysis," pessimism, and of "hinting at the agonies of a vivisection." Lacking those qualities of mind which enabled Henry James to hold in balance the opposed implications of a dramatic detachment of method and a neo-transcendental commitment to "higher" things than fidelity to facts, Lathrop failed in his final effort to define realism in the language of romantic critical theory:

> Let us consider the import of realism. It is without doubt an essential to the best dramatic novel-writing. . . . Realism sets itself to work to consider characters and events which are apparently the most ordinary and uninteresting, in order to extract from these their full value and true meaning. It would apprehend in all particulars the connection between the familiar and the extraordinary, and the seen and unseen of human nature. . . . In short, realism reveals. Where we thought nothing worthy of notice, it shows everything to be rife with significance.[23]

Lathrop's weakness here is both that of language and of inconsistency of thought. The language is Coleridgean and Wordsworthian, hardly suitable to a discussion of the fiction of Turgenev. His final standard of judgment is a romantic pantheism, a faith "in some corresponding and essential beauty pervading and including all things."[24] This disparity is only partly concealed beneath a hedge of Emersonian language, and Lathrop is unable to bridge the gap between his theory of dramatic fiction and his inheritance of romantic critical terminology. There was promise in his announced intention of demonstrating the evolution of the novel as "portable drama," but when his philosophy became tenuous, he could only find comfort in his one fixed star in the firmament of fiction, Hawthorne, who combined for him a "fine spirituality" with a realism which was "careful, detailed, perfectly true, and perfectly finished."[25]

While Lathrop's criticism was, therefore, a necessary first step toward a critical position it was seriously wanting in execution. He was aware of the need for a closer examination of the techniques of fiction and his tastes were formed by the work of the best contemporary realists. He was eclectic in his methods, but lacked the flexibility and elasticity to apply them effectively. He spoke against moralizing in fiction, but could not resist the tendency to moralize in criticism, and his analysis, in the end, rested upon words rather than upon examples. His work typified the waverings and divisions of the mind of the Seventies as between "Art" and "reality," and he fell short of his effort to cast upon the novel "a ray thrown out from the strong, central light of systematic mediation."[26] While he recognized the need for clarity and made a large historical gesture toward providing it, his own powers of perception and analysis were insufficient for the task.

A critical mind of greater penetration and broader training than Lathrop's was that of Thomas Sergeant Perry, friend of Henry James from his Newport days and lifelong correspondent of the novelist. Perry helped educate both Howells and James and, in his capacity as editor and teacher, he was an important influence on their thinking and writing about realism. It was Perry who first translated Turgenev and turned Howells's attention to the European writers. As Howells later recalled, Perry "knew not only more of current continental literature than any other American, but more than all other Americans." With his "unrivalled knowledge," he "literally read (Howells testified) every important French and German book which appeared, not only in fiction, but in history, biography, criticism, and metaphysics, as well as those exact sciences which are nearest allied to the humanities."[27] In criticism of the academic and theoretical kind, Perry became the most active crusader in the periodicals for a realism which superseded national boundaries and provincial attitudes. Astute enough to recognize that his own forte was not that of an active novelist, concerned with methods, he was content to translate and to illustrate by European models. His role was that of guide and counselor for the movement, but not of systematizer or lawgiver. As such he performed the true function of a critic, helping establish a fresh current of ideas which advanced the cause of realism and encouraged the creative endeavors of his contemporaries.

Perry's American roots were deep and illustrious. On one side he was in direct descent from Benjamin Franklin, whom he was said to resemble in feature, and on the other he came from a family of distinguished naval heroes, Oliver Hazard and Matthew Perry, the latter the Commodore who opened Japan to the West. Thomas Perry was the first to give to this family of action a literary name. Graduated in 1866 from Harvard, he spent two years studying language and literature with William James at Heidelberg and other European centers. In the Seventies he taught French and German, as well as English literature, at Harvard, became an editor of the *North American Review,* and contributed dozens of articles and translations of European literature to the periodicals. His learning was prodigious, as all his friends acknowledged, and his tastes catholic. In temperament he was inclined toward irony and cynicism and his manner was reserved and self-effacing. He belonged to the most enlightened intellectual circle in Boston and Cambridge during the 1870's, and was a charter member of "The Club" in its early period where he shared stimulating conversations with William and Henry James, Howells, Henry Adams, John Fiske, Oliver Wendell Holmes, Jr., and others. His influence, thus, went beyond his published articles. He made a marked personal impression upon his contemporaries.

As his biographer, Virginia Harlow, has depicted him, Perry embodied in himself much of the New England intellectual mind during its Indian summer. He had the pride of tradition and family, a strong, though concealed, patriotism, learning combined with European travel, and a broad knowledge of European languages and ideas. Despite a large measure of ability and natural gifts, however, he was somehow deficient in confidence and lacked the impulse necessary to enforce his ideas. His scepticism and a certain stiffness of personality prevented him from making full use of his powers so that his books, written during the decade of the 1880's, did not succeed enough to satisfy him, and he gradually lost interest in original work, becoming instead the student and appreciator of others.[28] His three main historical studies, *English Literature of the Eighteenth Century* (1883), *From Opitz to Lessing* (1885), and *A History of Greek Literature* (1890) were notable primarily for his application of evolutionary theories to literature. In this, Perry was among the forward-looking literary spirits of his time, sharing with his friend, John Fiske, the methods and ideas of positivism. Yet, after 1880, he turned increasingly to the literature of the past where the theory of progress and development lost much of its vitality.

It was his championing of the fiction of realism during the Seventies for which he is best remembered, beginning in 1871 with a translation of Turgenev in the *Galaxy* magazine. It was Perry who taught both James and Howells the importance of the Russian writer for American realists and who helped wean them away from the powerful influence of Hawthorne. James had read Turgenev first in his teens, but it was not until Perry called him in 1873 "perhaps the greatest living novelist"[29] and pointed to the lifelike studies of human nature which his books revealed, that James began to see the full possibilities of the Russian writer's fiction as a model for his own. James's essay on Turgenev in the *North American Review* appeared almost simultaneously with Perry's in the *Atlantic Monthly* in 1874. Although James's is superior as a literary portrait there are insights in Perry's essay which strike one as more closely reflective of the deeper currents of Turgenev's work. James was less willing, for instance, to accept the Russian's gloominess for what it was, and he chided him for "the element of error" in his sadness. Perry, on the contrary, held that the pessimism of Turgenev derived simply from his "lifelike pictures" of Russian peasants. "He is a realist in the sense of hiding himself, and in the painstaking accuracy he shows with regard to everything his pen touches."[30] James's reference, in his later essay "The Art of Fiction," to Turgenev's story of the deaf and dumb servant was quite likely recalled from Perry's translation of "Mou-Mou" and his commentary upon it. Perry particularly emphasized Turgenev's exclusion of himself from his fictional portrayals of people. He admired his ability "to draw men and women as they are, with their faults and virtues ever merging into one another," and he urged American writers to emulate him in arousing "our sympathy for some of the most serious matters of human experience."[31]

Perry and James thus held interests in common, and in different ways they each helped define the nature of realistic fiction. Like James, Perry knew the artist John La Farge and he early came to associate in his mind the methods of painting and those of literature. Like both James and Howells, he worked out a compromise between the French novel and his own Victorian sense of decorum, and between the scientific ideas of the time and the traditional values of literature.

Perry has been called a "crusader for realism," a "Back-Bay humanist," a "Boston Brahmin." Edwin Arlington Robinson described him as "one of the great appreciators."[32] Much like his own master Turgenev, as described by Henry James, Perry combined in himself the "impalpable union of an aristocratic temperament with a democratic intellect."[33] His place in the developing conception of Victorian realism in America, especially during the 1870's, was a conspicuous one. A mediator between extremes, and an admirer of continental writers and thinkers as diverse as Gustave Droz, Victor Cherbuliez, Balzac, Flaubert, Auerbach, and Julian Schmidt, he was at the same time a spokesman for the best sort of American fiction.

Taking issue with the narrower nationalists like T. W. Higginson, Perry did not believe that our literary interests were best served by novels which consciously sought an "American spirit" in fiction. "There is an American nature," he wrote, "but then there is human nature underlying it, and to that the novel must be true before anything else."[34] Like James, too, he ranked Balzac at the head of the masters of realism, naming Daudet and Zola his "somewhat degenerate successors."

Perry's strongest attributes as a critic lay in his cosmopolitan interests, his linguistic facility, his wide reading, and broad humanistic mind. His name has become known and his work appreciated partly for his early recognition of the continental realists and partly through his friendship with Henry James. He possessed qualities which in another country might have produced a critic of the stature of Taine, Sainte-Beuve, or Edmond Scherer. Something of a misfit at Harvard, he became disillusioned after his disagreement with President Eliot and his dismissal from his teaching post. His books of literary history were not warmly reviewed and he gradually ceased his writing in later years. His years of teaching at the University of Keiojiku, Japan, in 1898-1900 were a final gesture toward restoring his place in the academic world and an interesting case of a filial return to the nation first opened to the West by his uncle, the Commodore. Perry's biographer has stated concisely his relationship to the movement of realism as follows: "With Howells and James, he stands as a representative of those who apprehended an artistic realism as a remedy for the lush extravagances of romanticism, but who were trying to hold back the oncoming flood of naturalism."[35]

III

THE EIGHTIES:
Social Adjustment and
Literary Fulfillment

'It is time that we ceased to be dominated by the negative aspects of the Brown Decades. To dwell upon their ailments, infirmities, mischances, is to show, as in the invalid's preoccupation with his disease, that the remains of the poison are still operating in our own systems.'

LEWIS MUMFORD

By the end of the 1870's a perceptible change had taken place in the climate of American political and social life, a change which was reflected in literary and intellectual circles as well. The turbulent era of Grantism came to an end in 1876 with the defeat of Blaine for the Republican nomination by Hayes, comparatively unknown and untouched by the corruptions of the second Grant administration and the influence of the railroad tycoons. The strong showing of the Democrats under the reformist candidate Tilden likewise served to indicate that a spirit of purification was in the air. The political appeal of the bloody shirt was no longer an all-powerful instrument, and the nation grew tired of the continued oppression of the South. An time of change, an era of relative peace, was heralded by the repeal of the Reconstruction Act. The depressions of 1873 and 1877 were past, and the violence of labor strikes had subsided. A rising economic index during the early Eighties promised a greater degree of prosperity, at least for the "haves," and for the time being labor organizations bided their time. Conservatism was still the ruling force in American politics, but the policies of Hayes, Garfield, and Arthur were more defensive than aggressive, indicating a willingness to hold to the *status quo*. Reform activities were limited to the Civil Service movement, the bringing to justice of Guiteau, Garfield's assassinator, and the exposure of the Star-Route frauds in the postal department.

Even the election of Cleveland in 1884, marking the close of twenty-five years of Republican rule, failed to mar the outward serenity of the early 1880's. As Allan Nevins described it, most Americans knew that the Democratic party was conservative and that Cleveland was a man of caution. "Men expected Cleveland to display not an excursive boldness, but simply a greater honesty and earnestness than his predecessors, and he understood this perfectly. His campaign speeches, reticent upon policy, had been emphatic in hammering upon the need for a new moral attitude toward the business of government."[1] Civil Service reform, the main issue of his campaign, was recognized as a safe and sane policy of all but the most partisan adherents of the spoils system. Beneath the surface of this interlude of conservatism, prosperity, and labor truce, powerful forces were at work—the aggregation of capital in large corporations, the organization of labor for greater battles in the future, the accumulation of personal fortunes, the agitation for women's suffrage, and Greenback discontent at the resumption of specie payments and the return to the gold standard. Such problems, however, were for the moment distant clouds upon the horizon or, more accurately, they were not recognized at all except by a few forward-looking individuals. Optimism, orthodoxy, and a waking dream of self-contentment ruled the official mind of the early Eighties. "The truth is," wrote Henry Adams in 1884, "our affairs were never in so good a condition; public opinion was never healthier; and barring a few doubtful jobs, no government was ever so economically and sensibly conducted."[2]

Looking back upon the 1880's, historians have been impressed by their complacency and their refusal to sense the coming economic storms. There seemed but little awareness of future disturbances in those secure and prosperous years. The emergence of the nation into the electric splendor of the 1880's seemed to promise the fruits of experience without its penalties. A feeling of growing up prevailed in the new urban centers. The era of electric lights, the telegraph, the typewriter, birth control, and the further emancipation of women temporarily blinded the nation to the deeper maladjustments of society—the dangerous exploitation of natural resources, the Negro problem, the hardships of agricultural life on the frontier, the concentration of population in big cities, the maldistribution of wealth. Newspapers editorialized about the servant problem and forgot the slums. The fashionable aristocracy in New York concerned itself with the problem of the "swells," a new pushing aristocracy of wealth, which threatened the social rule of the "nobs" who held their pedigrees by divine right. There was a sudden jump in the extravagance of parties and balls. Where one million was a fortune in the Seventies, ten, fifty, or a hundred now became essential to social distinction; gold plate replaced silver in the best establishments; six servants greeted the guests at the door. A Napoleonic magnificence dazzled the imagination—Japanese interiors, *Salles de danse*, Gobelin tapestries, servants in pumps and silk stockings with powdered hair—infinite riches in a crowded room.[3]

All such forms of urban "magnificence," showily and awkwardly displayed by an increasing number of wealthy and socially ambitious families, became the source material for episodes in novels such as James's *Roderick Hudson*, Howells's *The Rise of Silas Lapham*, or Twain's *The Gilded Age*. Satire on the newly-rich became a part of realistic fiction. James's account of the millionaire Mr. Leavenworth purchasing treasures in Italy to furnish his "little shanty" at home in the best foreign taste was one of the most barbed of such portraits. Mark Twain's broader burlesque of the bizarre habits of the "Aristocracy of the Parvenus" in Washington ("The Hon. Patrique Oreille was a wealthy Frenchman from Cork") was raucously devastating, and Howells's deftly skillful jabs at the Laphams' efforts to emulate the social manners of the Bromfield Coreys in Boston similarly pilloried the taste of the period. In answer to the desperate needs of many such Laphams or O'Reillys, eager for but inexperienced in the ways of aristocratic behavior, books of etiquette and good manners were in great demand.[4] The aspiring elite were solicited by such titles as *Hints of Etiquette*, *Gems of Deportment*, or *The Art of Dining*. Lapham could have learned from them whether or not to wear his gloves in the house when calling, which fork to use at dinner, or how to decorate his new house in the fashionable Back Bay district near Beacon Street. Young ladies, the prototypes of the Lapham daughters or the Dryfoos girls of *A Hazard of New Fortunes* were cautioned against making "unusual noise" when eating soup, advised against plunging necklines and overdressing in "nice" society, or instructed in the language of love, flowers, sentiment, and the gentle art of pleasing.[5] In its zeal to imitate the high tone of English drawing room life, this new American social class displayed frequent lapses of taste and an uncouthness of manner which became the target of later critics of the manners and mores of Victorian society. The activities of the parvenus were vulnerable to contemporary humorists, as well, in the pages of contemporary humor magazines. *Life*, newly established in the 1880's, found in the antics of the social climbers rich material for cartoons and caricatures. It satirized dudes, Anglomaniacs, fortune-hunters, exhibitionists, and similar "types" of the "Elegant Eighties." C. Gray Parker, one of the most skilled illustrators of *Life*, specialized in the "horsey" set with sketches of the showy carriages and equipages of America's nobs and swells whose "postillions and posteriors," as J. K. Bangs put it, were skillfully and amusingly pinpointed.[6]

The picture has become almost too familiar and the comic aspects disproportionately interpreted in socially significant terms. Much of this display must be explained, if not excused, as the expected behavior of a new and thrusting society, without the guidance of established traditions or socially accepted usages. It expressed the needs of a democratically oriented population for certain stable, or at least socially dignified, manners and habits. Objective commentators like E. L. Godkin were inclined to excuse such lapses of good taste on the ground that over-refinements of manner were better than under-refinements and that good breeding was better learned from books than not learned at all. Some writers, Howells, for one, preferred to take an evolutionary view of the situation and to associate improving manners and social progress. He spoke of decency in the American novel in the pages of *Harper's*, and defended decorum in fiction by maintaining that "the manners of the novel have been improving with those of its readers." Howells admitted that this improvement had been accompanied by a certain squeamishness, but he felt that the change had been, on the whole, for the good.[7] And the "lesson" taken to heart by the more conventional-minded readers of *Daisy Miller* had been that this young Charlotte Temple of "The Age of Innocence" had become a victim to the laws of society and the social verities. Nevertheless, it has not been convincingly demonstrated by the historians that the table manners or the courting habits of a generation are certain marks of its general taste, or that violations of taste are the prerogative of any historical period. When used as historical yardsticks, they must be measured against more important evidence.

In architectural design, for example, the detractors of Victorian taste have gone nearly unchallenged in their opinion that the style of residence and public building construction represented the worst in American over-decoration and non-functional gimcracks. Critics like Charles Beard, who tend to color history excessively with economic implications, condemned the taste of the Victorian generation, applying non-aesthetic standards of judgement. His castigation, for example, of the "masters of urban wealth" for plundering the architectural styles of the European and Oriental past to provide a "Trimalchio's Feast" of showy splendor for "the buildings of men absorbed in making soap, steel rails, whiskey, and cotton bagging" is more of a social criticism than a judgment upon a question of taste in design.[8] Some recent students of art, however, have begun to re-examine the evidence upon which such attitudes rest and to discover certain positive values in Victorian buildings. Lewis Mumford was one of the earliest to interpret the architectural accomplishments of the "Brown Decades" in favorable terms. He was followed by T. B. Hamlin in tracing the beginning of an original American spirit in architecture to the period of the 1880's, acknowledging the contributions of H. H. Richardson, Richard Morris Hunt, Louis Sullivan, and the New York firm of McKim, Mead, and White toward a more functional and indigenous sense of design in public building.[9] Along with the many awkward attempts to adapt Old-World forms to the American scene and to imitate "gingerbread" decor with scroll-worked minarets, cupolas, cornices, and Gothic devices, there were many examples of excellent Victorian construction. Art historians have described the Eighties as the beginning of a renaissance in architecture. The Brooklyn Bridge, built between 1869 and 1883, has been called by a recent critic "the perfect symbol and crowning masterpiece of Victorianism." Eclecticism in architecture did not always result in a riot of confusion, as the majestic Grand Union Hotel at Saratoga Springs, the oriental Temple Emmanuel in New York, or the beautiful Romanesque Trinity Church in Boston, designed by Richardson, testify.

Residential designs, both interior and exterior, have been the most commonly criticized examples of the taste of the Victorians. The Victorian house has become the primary barometer for social historians of the period, to the point where the alleged mingling of styles and excessive ornamentation of buildings have become the symbol of a generation of bad taste, and an historical artifact too sacred to dispute. Criticism of the residential palaces of the railroad kings, however, has seldom been free from the "robber baron" thesis—namely that feudal "castles" along the Hudson River or on Fifth Avenue were anachronisms in a democratic society and an affront to the principle of equality. Yet the fretwork and "gingerbread" which adorned porches, roofs, and cornices on the Victorian house was as frequently in good taste as in bad, and only a few monstrosities such as the often-pictured "Carson Mansion" in Eureka, California, built by a lumber tycoon to display the possibilities of wood construction, have given a disproportionate emphasis to the building standards of an entire generation. The million-dollar dwelling designed by Richard M. Hunt for the Vanderbilts on Fifth Avenue and adapted from the French Chateau de Blois was, whatever the political implications, a magnificent structure inside and out. Many examples of houses of lesser size and scope, scattered across the country, amply justify the recent revaluation of Victorian building and decoration and the reinvestment of the term "American Gothic" with a certain measure of positive meaning and good taste. Of the Victorian house, a recent sympathetic observer whose European training frees him from many of the inherited prejudices of American critics, writes:

> The Greek Revival house was designed to fit behind a traditional façade, it belongs in a formal garden, is best viewed from the fixed standpoint of Renaissance perspective. The Victorian house broke free from this academic scheme. It is planned from the inside out, the free layout of rooms determines the outward look; the broken "picturesque" exterior makes the most of the effects of sunlight, shade, and foliage. . . . Inside they have a happy, hide-and-seek quality of surprise.[10]

The same writer has defended the Victorian house from the charge that it was gloomy and sinister, as portrayed in the cartoons of Charles Addams. This criticism probably derived from the dislocations of urban centers in which the older houses have been left to decay in unfashionable neighborhoods, giving them the aspect of neglect. The fact is that such houses in their prime were neither dark nor forbidding, but full of pleasurable fancy and exuberant color.[11]

Interior decoration was a different matter. Heavy muslin or velvet drapes, layers of shutters, heavy furniture, and fringed cushions tended to discourage the light intended by the architect's design. Houses were cluttered with bric-a-brac—bronze statues, stuffed birds, gilt vitrines, *petit-point* mottoes, draped statuettes, and disguised spittoons. The habit of overdecorating everything may have come from the days when Yankee traders brought back prized possessions from all parts of the world as trophies of travel, but whatever the cause the result was scarcely defensible. Yet the best Victorian houses were not thus overdone. Howells describes the home of the Bromfield Coreys in Boston as "stately" and tall wearing an air of "aristocratic seclusion." Outside were slender, fluted columns, a portico with "delicate mouldings" than which, he writes, "nothing could be simpler, and nothing could be better." Inside, a classic taste was in evidence and an ample staircase climbed in an easy, graceful curve from the tesselated flooring. "A rug lay at the foot of the stairs; but otherwise the simple adequacy of the architectural intention had been respected, and the place looked bare to the eyes of the Laphams." And in Edith Wharton's *The Age of Innocence*, Newland Archer is discouraged by his fiancee's taste for "sham Buhl tables and gilt vitrines full of modern Saxe," and he hoped she would let him arrange his study with "sincere" Eastlake furniture and plain bookcases without glass doors.

The social tone and temper of the early 1880's, especially in the urban centers of the eastern seaboard, showed many of the paradoxes and crosscurrents of the previous decade, yet somehow the atmosphere had become more mellow, more settled, and more stable. No doubt the brilliant displays of the newly rich and the success of the great business organizations created an illusion of progress and general prosperity which obscured underlying social dislocations and class friction. On the other hand, the congestion of populations in the large cities and the complex mixture of creeds and races offered certain compensations for the loss of the more sanative influences of rural life which had prevailed before the war. Ideas were more easily communicated in the busy publishing center of Manhattan. The vigorous, stepped-up tempo of life in the cities spread cultural influences more widely, if not deeply, among the reading public. New ideas were more easily disseminated, controversy stimulated, interest quickened. The turmoil and the ferment of the Seventies had perceptibly sobered. The uncertainties and conflicts of that decade were slowly blending into a new climate of social peace. The nervous apprehension over Darwinism, the self-conscious Americanism which had centered around the international novel, the political tension of the Reconstruction Era, East-West antagonisms over freight rates and currency standards which had given birth to the Society of the Grange and strengthened the Greenback party, the abortive labor riots and the economic depressions— all these tendencies had altered somewhat in degree and in character. A youthful fretting over untried issues gave way to a more practical desire to do something about them. The Knights of Labor, consolidated in 1878 under Terence Powderly and provided with a philosophy and a platform, proceeded to increase its membership from 28,000 in 1880 to four times that number by 1885. While this group had always been highly idealistic and ineffectually humanitarian, the new American Federation of Labor, first organized by Samuel Gompers in 1881, adopted a more utilitarian and workable program. When the Haymarket Riot provoked violent public and newspaper distrust of labor movements, it marked the decline of the more emotional and revolutionary Knights. The Federation of Labor, a trade union modelled upon the conservative English pattern, became increasingly influential.

A greater utility, common sense, and objectivity marked the 1880's. Pragmatic solutions were applied to economic problems as in *Progress and Poverty* (1879) where the emphasis was placed on workable reform through taxation. Collectivism became more articulate in the first years of the Eighties in the work of Henry George, Lawrence Gronlund, Richard T. Ely, Lester Ward, and H. D. Lloyd. Lloyd attacked corruption in the Standard Oil Company and, surprisingly, found an audience. Ward pointed out that laissez-faire and Herbert Spencer's individualistic sociology were behind the times in a social complex which was moving gradually toward government intervention in economic affairs. "There is no necessary harmony between natural law and human advantage," he said.[12] But these were minority voices in the Republican Indian summer of Garfield and Arthur. In 1883, when Ward's *Dynamic Sociology* appeared, the *Nation* responded by saying that it "might please the German Socialists, who love a little more dictation of ends and means by government; but no others would call it practical."[13] The same year saw the appearance of William Graham Sumner's *What the Social Classes Owe to Each Other*, a plea for a laissez-faire economy and an attack on the grounds of natural selection against communistic and socialistic doctrines emanating from Germany. In 1885 Andrew Carnegie's *Triumphant Democracy* trumpeted his conservative gospel of wealth to British audiences—"a paean of the splendid material progress wrought by free capitalistic enterprise."[14]

Philosophers and historians reflected the change from the higher idealisms and roseate speculations of positivism and cosmic evolution to the more stable ground of the functional and the demonstrative. John Fiske, with the encouragement of Huxley and Spencer, began to apply his theories of progress and evolution to the interpretation of American history. Henry Adams, after his two experiments in the fiction of idealogical "romance", *Democracy* and *Esther*, plunged into his monumental *History of the Administrations of Jefferson and Madison* in search of values which seemed lost or fast disappearing from the political scene. Edward Eggleston gave up writing fiction to become a professional historian and president of the American Historical Association. Charles Pierce in an article entitled "How to Make Our Ideas Clear" (1878) first defined the elements of pragmatism, pointing out that the validity of an idea lay in our sensible understanding of its function,[15] and William James in "Are We Automata?" (1879) stated the essentials of his later psychology, his will to believe and pragmatism.[16] The Pragmatic Acquiescence was in its formative stage during these years when utilitarian modes of thought began to be applied to older orthodoxies. As Santayana said of William James, "he was bent on finding new and empirical reasons for clinging to free-will, departed spirits, and tutelary gods."[17] James's philosophy strongly buttressed the earlier individualism and stood opposed to the threats of determinism and collectivism. He urged that emotional and semi-conscious states of mind were active elements of reality and he made an effort to invest the individual (as opposed to the group or the state) with dignity and responsibility by emphasizing the validity of such mental states as desire, feeling, love, aspiration, and habit.

The changing social and intellectual atmosphere after 1880 was accompanied by a notable florescence of literary activity. New York suddenly rose to cultural prominence, partly as a result of the appearance of two new literary periodicals, the *Century* and the *Critic*. In 1881 the *Century*, under the editorship of Richard Watson Gilder, became the successor of *Scribner's* which in the Seventies had been under the editorial control of the schoolmasterish Dr. J. G. Holland. The *Century* dropped much of the domestic preaching of Dr. Holland and published in its early years, serially, some of the best fiction of the realists. Howells's two finest novels, *A Modern Instance* and *The Rise of Silas Lapham* first appeared in its pages. John Hay's greatly successful *The Breadwinners* attacking the power of the labor unions was published anonymously in the *Century* in 1882. In 1884 *Huckleberry Finn* first saw the light of print in the same periodical when several of the early chapters appeared there just prior to the book publication. Henry James's *The Bostonians*, Cable's *Dr. Sevier*, and fiction by many lesser but still important names of the period, such as Eggleston, Marion Crawford, and Mrs. Catherwood—all were in the *Century* during the Eighties. In 1881 Jeanette and Joseph Gilder founded the *Critic*, devoted primarily to book reviews, literary essays, the arts, and the drama. The Gilders printed in their early numbers some of Walt Whitman's verse and prose, many of Joel Chandler Harris's *Nights with Uncle Remus*, and the work of Stedman, Stoddard, Julia Ward Howe, and Emma Lazarus, among others. James H. Morse, along with the two editors, became a spokesman for the rather conservative literary policy of the *Critic*, whose circulation, though only about 5,000, remained steady for over twenty years.[18]

It is not too much to say that the decade of the Eighties witnessed the appearance of more superior fiction than any previous decade of the century. It was, indeed, a period comparable in many ways to that of the early 1850's when the finest novels of Hawthorne and Melville, as well as Thoreau's *Walden* and Whitman's *Leaves of Grass*, all were published within a span of five or six years. The half dozen years after 1880 could justly be called a renaissance of prose fiction during which the realists who had served their apprenticeship to the new techniques in the previous decade were now ready to produce, in their middle years, some of their most mature work. If 1850 marked the high point of creativity for the romantic period of American literature, the year 1880 deserves similarly to be termed a climax of realism. To explain this development as the result of a temporary adjustment of the social or intellectual influences we have been describing would be to oversimplify or to exaggerate unduly the effects of the milieu upon literary minds which were, in many respects, in advance of their time. It is hard to measure, for instance, the significance for literature of the fact that the careers of Mark Twain, Howells, and Henry James all reached their middle, highly productive years in the 1880's. As for the first two, there is little doubt that the Eighties were their most fruitful decade of writing. James, though less affected by American currents of opinion and less sensitive to changes in the national climate, nevertheless continued to seek American readers and responded in his own way to the newer spirit. In broader perspective the 1880-1886 period displayed many of the marks of literary fulfillment and accomplishment. Furthermore, the momentary adjustment of social conflicts and the equilibrium of intellectual forces did coincide with and perhaps help provide a stimulus for the fruitful work of the major writers and for some of the best books of the minor ones. Henry James, for example, was entering upon the second phase of his career in which he discarded the "international situation" for an American locale (in *Washington Square* and *The Bostonians*) and a social theme (in *The Princess Casamassima*). It was a transitional period, but a highly productive one for James in criticism as well as fiction, for during the early Eighties he wrote the essays which were published in *Partial Portraits*, unquestionably the most significant critical volume to be written between 1870 and 1900.

Social satire, a note of critical realism, and a greater attention to environmental factors affecting character lent a deeper quality to James's work of the 1880's in contrast to the slighter *nouvelles* of travelling young ladies which he had written just before *Washington Square*. Howells, too, broadened the range of his imagination and moved gradually toward, without committing himself to, more serious, multi-peopled novels and a moderate form of determinism. Before 1886, he seemed to strike a happy blend of his own temperamental idealism and the newer scientific methods. Mark Twain had not, in the Eighties, yet become embittered by personal disappointments and by a misanthropic view of the human race. Polemics, which were to disturb the balance of realistic fiction after 1887, were a deepening, not yet a darkening, influence. A firmer, more confident tone, a less conscious nationalism, a soberer optimism, a stronger objectivity of characterization and adherence to a middle zone between tragic and happy *dénouements*—in short a successful interfusion of ripe powers and balanced ideas marked the fiction of the major realists during the early Eighties.

In a special sense this was the era of Howells and James. There was both wit and truth to George Moore's remark that James had gone to Europe to study Turgenev while Howells remained at home to study Henry James. Hamlin Garland, when he arrived in Boston, found reviewers speaking of the two men "as if they were some sort of firm, or at least literary twins." They corresponded frequently, were mutually admiring and yet sufficiently critical of each other to become rivals, writing essays upon each other's work and gently but firmly attempting to persuade each other to move in somewhat different directions. But the work of both during this period showed a deeper understanding of the effects of social conditions upon character, and both writers moved further away from the psychological "romance" toward more amply furnished settings and multiple characters while still preferring the milder realism of Balzac or Daudet to the experimental novel of Zola. The old debate over the nature of "The Great American Novel" re-asserted itself in critical circles during the Eighties, and the battle of the periodicals over "realism" flared up anew. Howells in his article "Henry James, Jr." in the *Century* (1882) touched off a controversy which echoed across the Atlantic Ocean. He wrote from a sense of kinship with James and from a changing philosophy of art in an effort to counteract the critical dissatisfaction in American circles toward James's fiction. He spoke of James as the leader of the new school of novelists which was rapidly relegating Dickens, Thackeray, Trollope, and Reade to an outmoded past. The new school derived, Howells said, from Hawthorne, George Eliot, and the moderate realism of Daudet. As for his own preference between realism and romance, he admitted to a certain wavering, but he stoutly maintained that it was Henry James "who is shaping and directing American fiction."[19]

When *A Modern Instance* appeared in book form James promptly responded in a letter from Europe to Howells, encouraging him to move more strongly in the direction of naturalism. "I say this to you," he wrote, "because I regard you as the great American naturalist. I don't think you go far enough, and you are haunted with romantic phantoms and factitious glosses, but you are in the right path."[20] And in "The Art of Fiction" written also in 1884 James had stated his growing impatience with such distinctions as that between romance and realism. Howells, on the other hand, had emphasized in his *apologia pro* H. J. his lingering preference for the romantic qualities of James's writing, admiring especially his softer portraits such as Ralph Touchett, Isabel Archer, and Claire de Cintre. Thus he attempted to leaven the "realism" of James's fiction while James, contrarily, sought to stiffen Howells's and to offer him the example of the French school. At the same time English critics were blustering over Howells's relegation of Dickens and Thackeray to an outworn past. A *Blackwood's* writer was affronted by his Yankee impertinence. The humor magazine, *Life*, was inspired by the debate to satirize the situation in a cartoon in which Howells, standing shakily on two volumes of the *Century*, is struggling to hoist a rotund James up to the level of a heroic statue of Thackeray.[21] American critics continued to harp on the old string by repeating the charge that both Howells and James lacked "the spiritual quality" and overstressed "scientific analysis of character." They were accused of "morbid analysis" in method and of conspiring against heroic qualities of character and the higher sympathies.

These were critical years for the debate over "modernism." In 1883 Charles Dudley Warner led a flank attack upon the modernists in an article for the *Atlantic*. Not mentioning specifics, Warner, whom a contemporary writer promptly called "Charles Deadly Warning," accused "modern fiction" of excessive photographic fidelity, too much "analysis," and indifference to idealism, nobility, virtue, and justice. He disapproved of the preoccupation with sordid details and the sad neglect of happy endings. He resurrected the cause of Sir Walter Scott in defense of his thesis, pleading for a return to chivalry, "romance," truth, virtue, justice, and the eternal verities. The two universal attitudes toward life open to the novelist, according to Warner, were romance and realism, and their two greatest spokesmen, Scott and Cervantes. When the balance between them had been disturbed by the followers of *Don Quixote*, Scott had sought to restore it. Modern fiction would be well advised, Warner concluded, to reassert the healthier tone of the great romancer and give up "morbidity," pessimism, psychological analysis, and despondent moods. The object of the novel was to "entertain," Warner concluded, "and the best entertainment is that which lifts the imagination and quickens the spirit . . . by taking us out of our humdrum and perhaps sordid conditions so that we see familiar life somewhat idealized."[22]

Warner's "perhapses" and "somewhats" were an open invitation for more stalwart minds to enter the fray on the side of modern methods. Henry James was quick to respond in his essay on Daudet in the *Century* (1883) when he begged to differ with Warner in the definition of the novel as entertainment. "I should say," he wrote with restrained irony, "that the main object of the novel is to represent life." He suggested that Warner was defending the rosewater school of fiction which would make a novel "as comfortable as one's stockings or as pretty as a Christmas card."[23] Although he veered rather quickly in his assertion that much of Warner's complaint against modern fiction was "eminently just," he would not agree that the uncompromising endings of Daudet's stories were morbid. He preferred in this essay to leave the question of the purpose of the novel deliberately ambiguous for "after all, may not people differ infinitely as to what constitutes life—what constitutes representation?" Mark Twain was not so judicious when he undertook to counter the romanticism of his friend and former collaborator, Warner, with a vitri-olic blast in *Life on the Mississippi* against the "Sir Walter disease" of the South. Twain attributed the sentimentalism and unreality of that region to the "pernicious work" of Scott—his "jejune romanticism," his fantastic heroes, his grotesque chivalry. And he lamented the decline of Cervantes' prestige: "As far as the South is concerned the good work done by Cervantes is pretty nearly a dead letter, so effectively has Scott's pernicious work undermined it."[24]

Such was the critical melee during the years 1882-1884 when the realists were producing some of their most finished novels. Later observers like Bernard Smith who described the literary criticism of the "genteel decades" as belonging to "Academy and Drawing Room," or Sinclair Lewis, who called it a "chill and insignificant activity pursued by jealous spinsters, ex-baseball reporters, and acid professors"[25] have established an orthodoxy of denigration which scarcely accounts for such periods of heated and anxious debate. But, as in the Seventies, it was the fiction rather than the criticism of the Eighties which distinguished that decade and which justifies the description of the period as that in which the novel of the earlier realism achieved its fullest expression.

1.

Howells: Maturity in Fiction

In March, 1882, when his first long novel, *A Modern Instance*, was in the midst of its serial run in the *Century*, Howells commented upon its progress to an editor: "I can assure you," he wrote, "that I wish the story had not grown to such length on my hands; it has cost me nearly twice the labor of anything I've written before; I will compress it all I can."[1] His preoccupation with what he considered the unusual length of the novel suggests that he had instinctively written a story which contained larger implications, multiple characters, and certain social ideas which went beyond the proportions of his previous *repertoire*. In short, Howells had achieved an important advance in his methods and in his conception of realism, without first having articulated a rationale to support it. In theory he was still committed to the smaller canvas, with a few characters reacting upon each other—variations upon the perversity of love and courtship which he had learned in the Seventies from Turgenev and Henry James. In 1880, he was still wavering between the newer literary atmosphere and his earlier conception of "romance." He wrote to W. H. Bishop that he was beginning to alter his fictional method, and urged Bishop not to imitate Thackeray "in those pitiful winks to the reader" by which that "bad artist" had undermined our novelists. "For heaven's sake don't be sprightly. I am now striking all the witty things out of my work."[2] By 1882 he had further clarified his thinking about the novel and realism. First, all moving incidents and dire catastrophes were to be rejected. Second, characters were to be dramatically presented without authorial intrusions and their individuality expressed through "their own qualities," not by "downright petting," as frequently in Thackeray and Dickens. And finally, with James as his model for the new realism, Howells began to conceive of the novel less as a "story" and more as an analytic study with the interest centered upon "what the novelist thinks about his material."[3]

His recognition of James's originality was not made without some sacrifice to his own lingering romantic nature, however, and he owned that "I like a finished story." In critical theory, at any rate, he was, in the early Eighties, still hesitant to make an unqualified commitment to the literary atmosphere of the new decade. He admitted in 1884 that realism was "almost the only literary movement of our time that has vitality in it," but hoped that even in the fiction of realism there would be a place for poetry and romance. The highest realism would "show us both of these where the feeble-thoughted and the feeble-hearted imagine that they cannot exist."[4] In his novels of the period there began to appear certain shadowings and a social seriousness which marked a change of temper. In 1884, two years before the Haymarket Affair in Chicago, which has often been cited as the turning point in his interests toward social reform, Howells wrote a review of John Hay's controversial, anti-labor novel, *The Breadwinners*—the first definite indication of the preoccupation with social and economic conditions which was to dominate his thinking in the late Eighties and Nineties. He was careful, however, to conceal his authorship of the review by signing it simply "W." It was an earnest defense of his close friend, Hay, against the charges of his lack of sympathy with the working classes. Howells took the occasion to express cautiously and with reservations some of his own growing convictions. The novelist must realize, he said, that he will be held to account as a public teacher, and that he must "do his work with the fear of the community before his eyes which will be jealous of his ethical soundness." The author of *The Breadwinners*, he went on, did not attack workingmen as a class and showed them no antipathy until they began to burn and kill. Speaking for himself, Howells defended the right of workmen to strike. He would have been content to see the recent telegraph strike succeed, but he agreed with the author that "if the telegraphers, like the railroad men, had begun to threaten life and destroy property, we should have wanted the troops called out against them." We are all workingmen or the sons of workingmen in America, he said, but the real mischievous elements are the idle poor, as well as the idle rich. "It is quite time," he concluded, "that we were invited to consider some of them [i.e. the workingmen] in fiction as we saw some of them in fact during the great railroad strike."[5] The review was a long step forward for Howells. It conflicted, in its acceptance of the legitimacy of literal social fact in fiction, with many of his deepest convictions regarding the "ideal" basis of literature and went beyond his later pronouncements on the smiling aspects.

For the immediate future Howells's work was to shift somewhat uncertainly between the novel of manners and an increased concern for social problems. There was evidence, beginning about 1880, of a greater depth in his fiction, and of effort to record truly, if not photographically, both the temper and outward tone of contemporary life. At the same time he was anxious to avoid the pitfalls of romantic adventure, bold action, and strong effects. Readers and critics expressed their disappointment at Howells's thus hewing to the line of average people and ordinary affairs of life. E. C. Stedman voiced the reaction of romantic criticism toward this sort of realism when he lamented the loss to fiction of what he considered the pathos and passion of an older tradition. "Today we have a more consummate, realistic art," he said, "but where, now, the creative ardor, the power to touch the stops, if need be, of tragedy and superstition and remorse?"[6] Stedman looked for the vogue of science and realism to spend itself first before a revival of the older poetic voices or a renewal of the earlier heroism would appear. Of the realists he sighed: "The novel is their drama, but chiefly the photographic novel of conventional life. They subject their tears to analysis, but do not care for tragic rage."[7] Henry Adams similarly regretted the reduced stature of the novel. In a mood of self-criticism he wrote to Hay that his novel *Democracy* had failed because it spoiled a tragic subject such as Aeschylus might have written. "The tragic element," he said, "if accepted as real, is bigger than ever before. I hate to see it mangled *à la* Daudet in a tame-cat way. Men don't know tragedy when they see it."[8]

Henry James, who had admired and been influenced by Howells's portraits of women in the Seventies, spoke more critically in 1886 when he considered them as uniformly "of the best—except, indeed, of being the best to live with." His heroines, James noted with some irony, were paragons of purity, "fineness of conscience, benevolence of motive, decency of speech, good nature, kindness, charity, tolerance." He failed to point out, however, that one of the marked signs of change and development in Howells's fiction after 1880 lay in the altered character of his American *jeunes filles*. No longer were they like Kitty Ellison or Florida Vervain, triple-armed in innocence, independence, and right-mindedness. As he enlarged his themes to include social and philosophical questions such as spiritualism, medicine, divorce, business, and class consciousness, he subordinated the roles of his "fibrous virgins," as Ambrose Bierce called them, and placed them in less commanding positions. The love theme was still present and usually related with larger problems, but it was increasingly darkened by disappointments, frustrations, or misguided illusions. Both Grace Breen and Helen Harkness, heroines of *Dr. Breen's Practice* (1881) and *A Woman's Reason* (1883), for instance, are partial victims of the conscience-ridden New England tendency to identify happiness with suffering. In his slighter productions of the early 1880's, Howells failed to find social themes of enduring significance, but he gained a firmer realism by the almost hostile way in which he portrayed his heroines. Grace Breen is so neurotically self-conscious of herself as a woman doctor as to become a "case study" in the history of the battle of the sexes. She urges a woman patient to go sailing and, when the boat is upset and Mrs. Maynard catches pneumonia, Grace's self-accusations are masochistically intense. Howells pointedly suggests that her self-torture is a case of the earlier Puritan conscience still working, but turned somehow upon itself in a culture which lacks the religious certainty of the past.

Marcia Gaylord in *A Modern Instance* marks a turning point in Howells's new severity of treatment of his heroines. Unlike her predecessors in the novels of the Seventies, Marcia's innocence cannot prevail over the obstacles placed in the way of her happiness. Howells presents her case in tragic terms, the wronged woman, a modern Medea, but far different from her Greek prototype in strength of mind and determination. Although there is some indication that her home town of Equity, Maine, where religion had become a matter of Sunday picnics and popular entertainments, left her without spiritual foundations, Howells leaves little doubt that her eventual downfall was both her own fault and that of Bartley's vanity and selfishness. She grows jealous, but unlike Medea she is quick to forgive. Olive Halleck's analysis of Marcia, after Bartley has deserted her, comes near to Howells's interpretation when she says to her brother:

> She's grown commoner and narrower, but it's hardly her fault, poor thing, and it seems terribly unjust that she should be made so by what she has suffered.

The real clue to Howells's opinion follows when Olive (the only truly candid and objective observer in the book) places the responsibility for Marcia's defeat upon both her lack of moral discipline *and* her misfortune. "She's so undisciplined, that she couldn't get any good out of her misfortunes; she's only got harm: they've made her selfish, and there seems to be nothing left of what she was two years ago but her devotion to that miserable wretch." Marcia, in Howells's view has become, not an avenging Medea, but a small-town heroine of a domestic tragedy.

> She had a rich nature; but how it's been wasted, and turned back upon itself! Poor untrained, impulsive, innocent creature. . . .

In short, she was vulnerable, inadequately trained and emotionally flighty, and these traits, despite her "rich nature" and the free-thinking infidelity of her lawyer father, were sufficient to invite the misfortune which is then visited upon her by Bartley's pettiness and the harsh blows of chance.

As one might expect, critics were disapproving of this change of purpose in Howells's treatment of his young women heroines. When *The Rise of Silas Lapham* was published, in 1886, he was taken to task by defenders of the national and regional vanity for his disparaging portraits of Boston girls. The *Nation* reported to its readers that the women in the novel were "deplorably unattractive" and that Boston girls were not all as bad as Penelope Lapham, who "mocks her parents and snubs her relations," or as Irene whom Howells described as so ignorant that she wondered vaguely whether Sir Walter Scott was an American.[9] The reviewer no doubt referred to an episode in which Penelope, with a pained sense of the social inferiority of her family to their aristocratic friends the Coreys, answers several of Mrs. Corey's questions with an abruptness which conceals her sensitivities. After Mrs. Corey's departure from her visit, Penelope gives her sister a mocking account of the proceedings before fleeing in tears to her room. Not only did the *Nation* writer miss the significance of this episode, but he was singularly obtuse regarding the central situation of the love-plot in which the Laphams mistakenly interpret Tom Corey's affections as directed toward Irene, because of her beauty, rather than to Penelope. Howells's satire is directed at the single-minded devotion of sentimental fiction to the importance of the master passion. Recent scholarship on Howells has pretty thoroughly exposed the absurdity of such criticism. Edwin Cady, in his excellent biography of Howells, has recounted an anecdote in which a reporter confronted him with the standard charge that he had failed to create noble women. "This criticism," Howells replied, "always seems to me extremely comical. I once said to a lady who asked me, 'Why don't you give us a grand, noble, perfect woman?' that I was waiting for the Almighty to begin." Cady has well summarized Howells's attitude as follows: "A feminist in the best of all senses, he wished to help women become freer psychologically and intellectually, more honest, more mature, more realistic, healthier. What seems to have worried Howells most about women was their susceptibility to quixotism . . . especially the quixotism of self-sacrifice."[10]

Where in his earlier stories, Howells had elevated innocence and placed the spotlight on the romantic situation, he now was assiduous to expose the errors of adolescence and immaturity of mind in the marriage relation. His two novels of the mid-Eighties devoted largely to this theme were *Indian Summer* (1886) and *April Hopes* (1888), both looking back to his Turgenev-like studies of the 1870's in theme and structure. *Indian Summer*, an exception to Howells's work of this period, was a psychological romance suggested initially by the experience of his visit with his family to Florence in 1883. Written in a mood of geniality and reminiscence, it handles the love relationship with amused irony and light satire, but its theme was one which Howells took seriously—the importance of acting one's age. It was twenty years after Howells had courted Elinor Mead in Venice and his mood was nostalgic. In the forty-year-old Colville's flirtation with young Imogene Graham, Howells sought to expose the absurdities of a September-and-May courtship, and in good Victorian style the situation is brought back to reality and propriety by the recognition of his true feelings toward Mrs. Bowen, Imogene's guardian and Colville's contemporary in age.

April Hopes, on the other hand, was a more serious and critical analysis of the dangers of irresponsible dreams of happiness through conventionally romantic ideas of marriage. It was a solemn warning on the futility of expecting a utopian solution to conflicts without the necessity of "perpetual pardon, concession, surrender." Alice Pasmer and Dan Mavering are symbols of typically female and typically male forms of adolescent, self-centered vanity. Each expects a miracle to emerge from the marriage contract and both are doomed to disappointment and unhappiness. Howells finally brings about their union, but he has built up to it with so many qualifications and hedged it around with such scruples and conditions that their marital prospects are viewed in near-tragic terms. The lovers are destined for the fate of Marcia Gaylord and Bartley Hubbard. Howells closes the book with the harshly ironic comment: "If he had been different she would not have asked him to be frank and open; if she had been different he might have been frank and open. This was the beginning of their married life." In his consistent exposure of romantic love conventions and his stubborn opposition to the kind of narcissistic emotionalism which he abhorred in popular fiction, Howells was a good deal more than a Victorian marriage counselor to the lovelorn. His variations on this theme were soundly supported by his realistic doctrine of moderation and his distrust of the spurious.

But anti-romanticism was only the negative aspect of his literary purpose. To understand the reasons for Howells's reputation as a major realist of his time and one of America's important men of letters requires an examination of the larger ideas upon which his best novels of the 1880's were based. Much of the earlier criticism upon them was weakened by short-sightedness, irrelevance, and misplaced patriotic motives. Without quite knowing why, traditional-minded critics felt their security assailed and their world shaken by realism. To measure the revolution of taste which took place in America between 1880 and 1920 one has only to compare a typical neo-romantic comment on Howells in 1886 with a vastly different one given by H. L. Mencken in 1917. Hamilton Wright Mabie, reviewing *The Rise of Silas Lapham* under the title "A Typical Novel" attacked realism and Howells as "cold," "analytical," "skeptical," and his methods as "practical atheism applied to art."[11] Mencken, three decades later, found "The Dean" shallow, uninspired, full of *Ladies Home Journal* morality and amateur psychology—"an Agnes Repellier in pantaloons" with a "college-town Weltanschauung."[12] It has required a half-century of time since Howells's death in 1920 to reach a dispassionate evaluation somewhere between these extremes of opinion and a sensible perspective upon the manners and *ethos* of the period in which he wrote.

Before further analyzing this phase of American literary taste, it will be well to return to 1881 when *A Modern Instance* was running its course in the *Century*. Howells conceived the story of Marcia Gaylord and Bartley Hubbard initially as a classical revenge tragedy of sexual jealousy based upon a performance in 1876 of Euripides' *Medea*. This was exotic material from which to construct a commonplace tale of a contemporary marriage between two immature, but well-intentioned young people in the unromantic setting of New England in the late 1870's. What emerged from it was a realistic account of the gradual failure of the marriage through a long series of ordinary domestic episodes and its ultimate breakup in the divorce court. Read simply as a story, *A Modern Instance* is convincing in the authenticity with which Howells has narrated the trivial matters of incompatibility and exposed the vanities of human nature upon which such a marriage rests. The fault is distributed almost evenly between the two principals—Marcia, whose "fatal flaw (as one recent writer describes it) is an inability to accept the conditions of real life and real marriage" and who "tries to perpetuate the conditions of courtship and ideal love even when she no longer believes in them,"[13] and Bartley, a handsome, egocentric, worldly newspaperman with a clever wit, but a certain shallow trickiness of character which leads him repeatedly into compromising situations.[14] Bartley's sins are venial ones, and he seems hardly deserving of the shower of ill-fate which is visited upon him in the course of the action. His moral laxity, cynicism, and flirtatious tendency get him into hot water with his wife, and his financial borrowings irritate his friends. Accidents multiply his troubles until at the end he finds himself alone in the world, little the wiser for his experience, wondering vaguely how it all happened. His death, at the hands of an enraged subscriber to his gossipy newspaper in "Whited Sepulchre, Arizona," is briefly described by Howells in the closing pages of the novel—a summary dismissal which leaves the central problem unsatisfyingly concluded, while Marcia's exile to her home in Equity, Maine, for an indefinite period of withdrawal and anguish seems an excessive punishment for a fault only partly her own.

The denouement presented Howells with the problem of how to invest a commonplace story with tragic, or near-tragic significance. Murder and revenge were in his source material, but the possibility of his plain New England heroine murdering her husband for divorcing her was too absurdly melodramatic a "modern instance," and the story, already too drawn out, had to be ended in a dying fall. A disproportionate amount of tragic emotion is engendered by what is a commonplace affair. This weakness, combined perhaps with the fact that Howells was seriously ill in the midst of writing the novel, disturbed somewhat the emotional balance which he might otherwise have maintained.

The conclusion, however, was essentially a technical matter. More relevant to an understanding of Howells's blend of realism with the Victorian attitude toward the problem of divorce is the thematic interpretation behind the story. The time was not yet for a wholly naturalistic account of a broken marriage. Divorce was a subject fraught with social taboos and strong prejudices in 1880, as Robert Louis Stevenson's letter to Howells cancelling a proposed visit to him in England testifies. Stevenson, who had married a divorced woman, could not accept the friendship of the author of *A Modern Instance*, a man "who considers himself holier than my wife." This was a mistaken view of Howells's novel, but such

thinking made it necessary to include certain agencies to speak the voice
of Victorian propriety. This role is filled by the "Proper Bostonians," the
Hallecks and Atherton, who provide a running "Greek chorus" of
judgment upon the fortunes of the Hubbards. There is something factitious about the over-serious discussions of ideal love between Halleck and
Atherton. Howells was too much the realist, however, to imply that their
high-minded and rather patronizing views on the Hubbards' marriage
were his own. Halleck and Atherton function as spokesmen of propriety
for a doctrine which becomes the thesis of the book—that is, the doctrine
of "complicity" as applied to the ethics of marriage. Divorce is a crime
against society because it has broad social consequences, encouraging the
general opinion that marriage is to be taken lightly. Ben Halleck, in love
with Marcia and self-sacrificingly dedicated to what he conceives is his
Christian duty of self-denial, speaks the burden of this categorical impera-
tive when he tells her:

> You have a double duty in this matter. You must keep him bound
> to you, for fear some other woman, whose husband doesn't care for
> her, should let him go too, and society be broken up, and civilization
> be destroyed. In a matter like this, which seems to concern yourself
> alone, you are only to regard others.

Howells has been careful to qualify the authority of Halleck, the over-
scrupulous and consciously self-denying lover, and of Atherton, the
lawyer, whose wealth and position of social superiority is pointedly
satirized. In a scene in which Atherton and his humanitarian-minded wife,
the former Clara Kingsbury, are discussing the domestic troubles of
Marcia, he develops the thematic center of the novel into a philosophy
which seems to express Howells's own sense of the inadequacy of undisciplined human nature:

> The natural man [he says] is a wild beast basking in the sun when
> his stomach is full. The Hubbards were full of natural goodness, I
> dare say, when they didn't happen to cross each other's wishes. No,
> it's the implanted goodness that saves,—the seed of righteousness
> treasured from generation to generation, and carefully watched and
> tended by disciplined fathers and mothers in the hearts where they
> have dropped it. The flower of this implanted goodness is what
> we call civilization. . . .

Howells follows this speech immediately by a description of Atherton
reclining comfortably in his Back Bay dining room, with its view of the
river, and lifting "with his delicate slim hand the cup of translucent
china," drinking his Souchong tea "sweetened and tempered with Jersey
cream to perfection." Even Clara with her debutantish conceptions of

charity cannot resist an ironic outburst at the picture of her husband's complacent attitude: "Ah," she says, "it is easy enough for us to condemn. *We* have everything we want!"

Howells's realism suffers somewhat from employing the Atherton and Halleck episodes both as objects of satire and as qualified vehicles for the expression of his own ideas. A recent critic lays much emphasis upon Howells's indictment of these "proper Bostonians" as products of a decaying aristocracy "crippled by uncertainty and fast fading into the obsolescence of a genteel tradition."[15] Reviewers of the novel in 1883, on the other hand, considered their presence in the book as representing saving social standards and "settled social tendencies" by which the falterings of the principal characters could be condemned. As between the two roles Howells preferred to leave the decision to his readers, however, and his refusal to commit himself in the matter is one measure of his stature as a realist. At the same time it was a test of his critics, who too often wanted an unclouded and hopeful solution to fictional conflicts. Bartley and Marcia were frail, not evil. The high-minded idealism of upper-class Boston, itself weakened with hypocrisy, was too far beyond their training to give them assistance. Chance and determining circumstance contributed to the failure of their marriage. Like Queequeg's sword-mat in *Moby Dick* "chance, free will, and necessity—no wise incompatible—all interweavingly working together" combined to bring about the result.

Conventional-minded reviewers were unhappy. Richard Watson Gilder, the cynosure of genteel eyes and editor of the *Century* expressed familiar, neo-romantic objections to the novel by denying that Howells went below the surface in his portrait of New England life. Gilder quarreled with all realists, as he said, because they restricted their angle of vision only to "what they can see and test,—what yields material results, and they end there. They give too little credit to what the mind, by its idealizing processes, adds to character." Such wordplay simply led to the real objection which he phrased as a rhetorical question: "Will it reform the bad or comfort the good?"[16] This criticism, like so much of the commentary in the magazines, ignored both sides of Howells's work—his realistic account of the marriage and his qualified ethical judgment of the characters. Repeatedly, contemporary critics charged Howells with the exhibition of "depressing" episodes and "disagreeable" characters. So preoccupied were they with the social dangers of realistic fiction that they tended to confuse the describer with the thing described. This sermonic purpose vitiated much criticism and postponed serious literary evaluation of Howells's work for generations from the time the books first appeared.

Horace E. Scudder's review in the *Atlantic Monthly* was a notable exception. He found *A Modern Instance* to be a parable "as all great works of art are parables" and considered it "the weightiest novel of the day." He called the main characters "unpleasant" and Bartley's motives "ugly," but he recognized with candidness that Marcia and Bartley were products of "a crude and partly brutal civilization." Marcia was the result of "a life where religion has run to seed, and men and women are living by a copy-book morality," and in a summary remark Scudder acknowledged the two sides of Howells's novel by noting that Bartley's dream of escape from marital bondage was the action of both a corrupt mind *and* a rotten social condition.[17] Howells had prepared for such an interpretation in a final sentence which disposes of Bartley, after his murder. His finish, Howells said, was "the penalty or consequence, as we choose to consider it, of all that had gone before."

The conclusion failed to reform the bad or reward the good because Howells's sense of reality was too subtle for such distinctions. Marcia returns with her father to her home in Equity, Maine, to feed her anguish in a life of withdrawal. Ben Halleck enters the ministry, still longing for Marcia and still agonizing with his conscience. Even Atherton seems in a state of uncertainty. Years later Howells rationalized his conclusion when he explained to an interviewer the attitude of a realist toward tragic endings:

> The culmination of a tragedy, its climax, does not reveal character to the full. It rather stuns all the faculties. . . . Life, on the other hand, is not afraid of anti-climaxes; it produces them daily. No tragedy in real existence but has its tomorrow, unheroic perhaps, artistically, but unavoidable, inexorable. Art may stop where it pleases, life must go on. Realism endeavors to take note of the continuity which nothing can arrest for long, and considers it more important to the individual and humanity at large than the violent interruption.[18]

The Rise of Silas Lapham, first printed in *Harper's* in 1885, is still considered Howells's most balanced work of fiction, and in many ways it is the most complete realization of the Victorian novel of realism, American style. It represents a technical advance upon *A Modern Instance* in its construction. The story of Lapham is carefully plotted, and the wave-like fluctuation of his fortunes, plus the interrelations of the main plot with the love-triangle, all brought to focus in the new house he is building on Beacon Street, make it Howells's most shapely novel. In still another way *Silas Lapham* was an advanced step in the technique of realism. The agency for the resolution of the central conflict, that which brings about Silas's financial loss and moral "rise" at the end, comes from within his own character and not, as in the story of Marcia and Bartley, from many chance episodes beyond their control. Lapham's decision is his own, he judges himself, and the artifice of a genteel commentary upon the action by Proper Bostonians is avoided. Howells has carefully prepared for his denouement by little strokes of portraiture, beginning with the opening chapter where Lapham is interviewed for the Solid Men of Boston Series and the final resolution escapes the criticism that a man of his "coarse grain" should possess moral scruples and a delicate conscience.

Without retracing well-marked paths of comment upon *Silas Lapham*, it will be more rewarding to consider it in the light of later patterns of historical commentary on the tradition of the businessman in America and its relation to "the protestant ethic." *Silas Lapham*, along with its immediate successor, *The Minister's Charge, or the Apprenticeship of Lemuel Barker*, has a significant position in the fiction of the businessman, a tradition which is as old as Franklin's *Poor Richard's Almanack* and as new as the man in the gray flannel suit. Howells's two novels furthermore reflect clearly the influence upon this long tradition of the Horatio Alger theme. *Silas Lapham*, while it ultimately reverses the emphasis of the Alger story by "rising" in a quite different way, nevertheless reveals the essential spirit of the nineteenth-century, middle-class, protestant definition of success through hard work and virtuous conduct. It is not accurate to regard it as a parody of the Alger story. Actually it is a more serious and mature examination of the tradition. *The Minister's Charge*, on the other hand, with its Algeresque subtitle, belongs more clearly to the familiar pattern. It contains many of the classic features. A country boy adrift in the city and confronted by the duplicities of city life, ultimately triumphs over obstacles by innocence, patience, and a stubborn insistence upon the old verities.

It remained for a later generation of economic historians to denigrate the protestant ethic and create the image of "The Gilded Age," and it is necessary to understand the historical reasons for this change before applying all of its assumptions to a judgment of the period in which Howells wrote. During the 1930's when American social critics sought historical causes for the economic dislocation of the depression years, they began to define the meaning of such terms as "Social Darwinism," "the gospel of wealth," and "the protestant ethic." With the assistance of European scholars like Max Weber they identified the spirit of capitalism with the period of the 1870's and 1880's which they regarded as the golden age of American business and the "apotheosis of the protestant ethic." Weber had traced the beginnings of this process back to John Calvin and found a latter-day illustration of it in Benjamin Franklin's success philosophy, especially in *The Way to Wealth*. American critics applied the thesis to the dream of success, the rags-to-riches pattern as seen in Franklin's *Autobiography* and *Poor Richard*. In 1934 Nathanael West wrote a scathing parody-novel entitled *A Cool Million; or the Dismantling of Lemuel Pitkin* which was a great deal more than a clever caricature of the Horatio Alger idea of "rising in the ranks," as parodied in the subtitle. West extended his satire to include the whole concept of American innocence and free enterprise. For him the protestant virtues of middle-class business and virtue, the combination portrayed by Howells in Silas Lapham, were merely an invitation to disaster in the America of the 1930's. Lem and his friend Shagpoke Whipple, former president of the United States, became in West's novel the unconscious dupes of communist and fascist demagogues.

A comparison of Howells's character with West's suggests the way in which Howells remained close to the spirit of the Alger tradition. West's Lemuel Pitkin is gradually "dismantled" of his arms, legs, his sight, his teeth, and his scalp. He has come to the city to make his fortune "in the honorable tradition of his country," but his virtuous efforts to win success bring him the rewards of jail, poverty, violence and death. West's purpose, hilariously and cruelly revealed, turns the original Alger tradition inside out. Howells, on the other hand, preserved the tradition in all its essentials, altering only the surface heroics and popular gilding by which Alger sentimentalized it for his juvenile readers. Lemuel Barker comes to Boston from "Willoughby Pastures" seeking literary success. When he realizes that his verses are not publishable, Lem undergoes the classic Alger experience in the city. He is the victim of confidence tricksters and loses his money. Too proud to ask assistance, he is arrested while chasing the swindlers and is falsely accused of purse-snatching. Jailed for a night, he is judged innocent but is forced to spend a second night in a charity flophouse where Sewell finally rescues him and starts him on the path to success with a job as janitor for a wealthy friend, Miss Vane. Lem gradually learns the ways of the city and the injustices of the social system, but like the Alger hero he educates himself and "rises" to a position of respectability. His rural-bred innocence has played him false in various ways, but it serves him well in the end, and he returns to the farm determined to assist his family in their poverty.

There is no direct evidence that Howells was consciously following the Alger plot, or even that he knew the *Ragged Dick* and *Tattered Tom* stories,[19] but in a letter to James R. Osgood, while writing the novel, he seemed uncomfortably aware that his purpose was misunderstood by H. M. Alden, the editor to whom he had submitted the manuscript. Alden had suggested to Howells that he "make more of the hero and heroine." Howells explained:

> I never meant to make what he seemed to think I would—that is, something farcical or comical. In the first place, I don't believe in heroes and heroines, and willingly avoid the heroic; but I meant to make a simple, earnest, and often very pathetic figure of my country boy, whose adventures and qualities should win him the reader's entire sympathy and respect.[20]

Alger had written in *Ragged Dick:* "I hope my young readers will like him as I do without being blind to his faults. Perhaps, although he was only a bootblack, they may find something in him to emulate." If we subtract the obtrusive sermonizing, the money *mystique*, and the banalities of style of the typical Alger "juvenile" there remains much in *The Minister's Charge* that parallels the Alger stories. Thrift, hard work, respect for elders, self-education, pride are among the virtues Lemuel Barker owns in common with Alger's heroes. Howells insisted that his hero was "anything but a trivial or a farcical figure" (as Alden had apparently interpreted the story) and told Osgood that his tendency was toward tragic, rather than comic, effects. Before publication of the novel, two years after this letter, Howells superimposed upon the account of Lemuel Barker the character of Reverend Sewell and his circle together with the final sermon on "Complicity" which states the central thesis in Tolstoyan terms. *The Minister's Charge*, which began as a modified Alger success story ended as a plea for universal brotherhood and Christian charity.

Howells's social philosophy, first cautiously indicated in his review of *The Breadwinners*, and made explicit in *The Minister's Charge*, was kept beneath the surface in *The Rise of Silas Lapham*. Class distinctions in this novel remain largely matters of taste and etiquette. Only in the brief glimpses into Zerilla Dewey's life, her drunken husband and poor living conditions in a tenement apartment, does Howells desert the generally middle-class setting of the story. If one were to summarize Howells's social views from evidence in *Silas Lapham* alone, they would well represent the Victorian concept of class responsibility, somewhat as follows:

> Poverty and inequality of the laboring classes are increasing problems of American society, but they can best be solved within the existing class divisions, provided enough ethical leadership and responsibility is demonstrated by the two classes which hold places of influence— that is, the traditionally educated Back Bay families like the Coreys and the newer, energetic businessmen like Lapham. The Coreys and the Bellinghams represent the older, established order and the settled social authority of Boston, but they had become, like Bromfield Corey, cynical and withdrawn. Lapham, despite his humble origins, had hold of the driving force of American society. If he could achieve a measure of ethical responsibility, he might compensate for his social deficiencies. But what was needed was the right combination of the two types.

Howells seems to suggest in the marriage of Tom Corey and Penelope Lapham that a hope for the future lay in joining these two classes of citizens. Tom Corey is the mediating force. He possesses his family's superior taste and education, but is equally sympathetic with Lapham's useful and productive ideas of business. And he tactfully brings the two men together and helps break down their reserves of suspicion toward each other.

Thus Howells was concerned to exhibit with the greatest impartiality the faults and virtues of both these families. Bromfield Corey, despite his idleness and caustic sense of superiority, is engaging in his manner, likeable, and self-critical. He sees clearly and states conditions frankly and articulately. It is Corey, not Lapham, who expresses one of the central concerns of the novel: "Money," he says, "is the romance, the poetry of our age. It's the thing that chiefly strikes the imagination. The Englishmen who come here are more curious about the great new millionaires than about anyone else, and they respect them more." Lapham has the money, and he likewise has an acute feeling of his responsibility to less fortunate people, like Zerilla Dewey, his secretary, whose father had saved him in the Civil War at the cost of his own life. Lapham's one act of injustice toward his former partner, Rogers, seems fully compensated in his other acts of charity and fair-mindedness even before the final temptation scene. Howells, too, is careful to limit the satire to matters of taste—his table manners, his ignorance of social amenities, his bragging about his possessions and his money, his crude pleasure in painted signboards advertising the Lapham paint. It is clear from the opening chapter that Howells sees Lapham as a hopeful element for the future of American society, and in the broad picture he has presented of a representative, nineteenth-century individualistic entrepreneur of business, he struck a vein of social analysis which has been a focal point for fiction and social analysis ever since.

The novel echoes the Alger theme mainly in the opening chapter when Lapham describes his boyhood to Bartley Hubbard, a boyhood not unlike that of Howells himself who also had risen from a rural environment to become a Solid Man of Boston and had built a large and comfortable home on the water side of Beacon Street. Howells directs his sympathy toward Lapham in the exchange with Bartley Hubbard when the latter satirically questions him about his boyhood. "Worked in the fields summers and went to school winters," Bartley notes, "regulation thing? Any barefoot business? Early deprivations of any kind that would encourage the reader to go and do likewise?" Lapham replies to Hubbard's professional flippancy "with quiet self-respect;" "I guess," he says, "if you see these things as a joke my life won't interest you." After the opening chapter the novel becomes a more serious examination of a recognizable type of the American business tycoon, a theme which touched a basic chord in the American experience.

Lapham's character does not, however, demonstrate later doctrinaire definitions of the protestant ethic. Nor does it exemplify the "gospel of wealth" or the cluster of ideas suggested by the term "Social Darwinism." As the story developed Howells placed less emphasis upon Silas's acquisitive qualities and his low motives. When Persis, his wife, charges him with making his paint business a religion and with forcing out his partner to gain larger profits for himself, he defends his action on the grounds of sentiment, as a dedication to the memory of his father who discovered the mine on the family property. Though he boasts about his money and the power it gives him, he nowhere suggests that it was a providential sign of God's favor, nor does he imply that his good fortune was the result of an evolutionary process of struggle and competition. Lapham remains a human being, never becoming a symbol or the illustration of a thesis. As such Howells's portrait remains one of the most satisfying in the history of the fiction of the businessman. With his mixture of good and bad traits, he is more convincing than either Dreiser's Frank Cowperwood or Lewis's Babbitt. Without either Dreiser's powerful statement of the robber-baron thesis or Lewis's sharp-edged satire upon small-minded rotarianism, he nonetheless managed to describe a businessman who was neither a monster nor a damn fool. By the oblique use of a popular tradition, he managed to find a large reading public for his realistic examination of a type which had already become central in American life.

Critical opinion of the novel has only recently done it justice. Contemporary criticism and reviews ranged from blind imperception to outright hostility and rage. Scattered amidst perfunctory praise for Howells's accuracy in describing the class differences and social foibles of the new versus the old aristocracy of Boston were the customary scoldings for his "realism" and his omissions of the "inspiring" and the "beautiful" in life. In a comment seldom equalled for obtuseness, the *Nation* remarked that "there is no inspiration for anyone in the character of Silas Lapham" and that his story "suggests no ideal of conduct."[21] But even this was exceeded by an intemperate review in the *Catholic World* which accused both Howells and his subject of a "hopeless depravity" in which was reversed the evolutionary theory of man so as to send him reeling back to apes, worms, and bacteria![22]

The intensity of such native attacks upon Howells in 1886-87 signalled the resurgence of the battles of the bookmen, begun in the 1870's and resumed with increased tempo in the Nineties. From certain European-oriented voices of opinion, however, there came a more penetrating and, at the same time, more sympathetic estimate of Howells's work. Henry James was the first to put his finger on the essence of both the strength and the weakness of his friend's writing in an essay in *Harper's Weekly* in 1886. He pointed to "the unerring sentiment of the American character" in his work. "Mr. Howells knows more about it than anyone else," he said. He admired especially Howells's picture, in *The Rise of Silas Lapham*, of the daughters and their problems of engagement. Lapham himself, James thought, "is magnificent, understood down to the ground, inside and out—a creation which does Mr. Howells the highest honor." As a realist, James considered Howells too complacent, too dedicated to "the colloquial, the moderate, the optimistic, the domestic, and the democratic," and unwilling to introduce unusual, exceptional, or incongruous material into his fiction. In a criticism which has not yet been wholly resolved by Howells's critics, James spoke of the limitations of his "perception of evil" whereby Lapham's immoralities are only "aberrations of thought" and Bartley Hubbard's mere "excesses of beer."[23] While James was perhaps unprepared to estimate the broader significance, for American social conditions, of Howells's portrait of a business millionaire, his general comment remains central to those who would defend Howells from the charge of favoring largely the smiling aspects of life, as the "more American." Hippolyte Taine was more willing to see *Silas Lapham* as a serious social study when he compared Howells's novels to some of Balzac,[24] and H. H. Boyesen, the Norwegian writer who had adopted America, acknowledged the indebtedness of American fiction to Howells for "the ultimate triumph of realism." Boyesen was to write a novel of a businessman who breaks with the ethical code in *The Mammon of Unrighteousness* (1891). He spoke of the need for "the serious chronicling of our social conditions" and gave one of the best definitions of realism written before 1900.

> Broadly speaking, a realist is a writer who adheres strictly to the logic of reality, as he sees it; who, aiming to portray the manners of his time, deals by preference with the normal rather than the exceptional phases of life, and, to use Henry James's felicitous phrase, arouses not the pleasure of surprise, but that of recognition.[25]

Boyesen, furthermore, feared the intrusion of "romance" into the field of realism, especially the effect of the young girl reader on the American novel. Whereas Howells had defended her presence by denying that she had sealed the lips of fiction to "some of the most vital interests of life," Boyesen described her as "the Iron Madonna who strangles in her fond embrace the American novelist; the Moloch upon whose altar he sacrifices, willingly or unwillingly, his chances of greatness."[26] The feminine coloring of Howells's fiction led Mencken to call him spinsterish, and the many echoes of this criticism are still heard today in serious treatments of the cultural standards of the Victorian novel in America. Like James's comment upon his "moderation" it has become one of the sensitive points of controversy among Howells's defenders.

"We are not easy with quiet men," Lionel Trilling pointed out in his essay on Howells in 1951. This observation, as Trilling said, could cut in two directions. It could be a comment upon Howells and his doctrine of moderation, or it could illuminate the present fascination for extremes, not only in literature, but in public affairs. Trilling makes an important distinction between the relation of evil to the creator of a work of literature and that of the reader. "There is something suspect," he says, "in making evil the object, as it were, of aesthetic contemplation." The modern fascination for the literature of power, violence and sexuality has its counterpart in the tendency, politically and socially, to run to extremes, extremes of the right or the left, for the solution of threatening problems. Since Trilling wrote this more than a decade ago,[27] there is evidence in the body social that Americans have less faith in extreme solutions to political questions than they had in the afterglow of military confidence which followed World War II. Threats of nuclear devastation may bring people once more to the simpler experience of man's daily and domestic relations with his fellow man. If so, literary taste, too, will alter so that readers will be more conditioned to the quiet men and to the moderate aspects of life, not only because such experience is more "real," but because it may provide the only recourse of people against mass action and bureaucratic slavery. Something of this sort has already changed the critical attitude toward the Victorians and toward writers like Howells and has helped to qualify in part, at least, Henry James's opinion that his "perception of evil" is small. Although Trilling, following James's lead, was doubtful about the possibility, it may be that James's later prediction, written on the occasion of Howells's 75th birthday anniversary, that "your really beautiful time will come" may prove as much an accurate prognostication as it was a generous compliment to a lifelong friend and literary admirer.

2.

James: The Middle Years

Henry James's two visits to America in the early 1880's were occasioned by the deaths of his parents. The slightly more than a year he spent visiting Boston, Cambridge, New York and Washington were scarcely enough to repatriate him, but he did renew old associations and revive old memories. Also, he provided himself with new "impressions" to work into his international stories. His oblique relationship to his native country became, temporarily at least, somewhat less oblique. As a source of readers, of reputation, and income, if nothing else, James had never lost sight of his native land, and at this period especially he was hoping to be able to repeat the success of *Daisy Miller*. He needed the American audience. "It is a great loss to have one's person in one country and one's glory in another," he wrote William. But Europe remained his home, and after his brief trips to his native country in 1881-83, he again returned, this time for twenty years, to keep his residence in England and to submit himself again to the "Londonizing process." He lived at first in rooms just off Picadilly, later moving to De Vere Gardens, Kensington, and once again adapted himself to the vast "murky Babylon." No longer a passionate and slightly rebellious pilgrim, his attitude now changed to that of an established colonist in his middle years. His friends were a group of expatriate, cosmopolitan artists and writers. The American painters, John S. Sargent, Frank Millet, and Edwin Abbey were among his circle in these years, as were Edmund Gosse, the critic, and George Du Maurier, illustrator for *Punch*. Also, James's warm literary friendship with Robert Louis Stevenson began at this time and lasted until the latter's death in 1894. America was rapidly receding from his personal horizon during the 1880's, although it was to remain essential to his fiction and one of the established poles of his intellectual life.[1]

The Eighties were "middle years" for James not only in his literary development but in age, manner, and outward appearance. No longer the poetic, idealistic youth of 1870, he was now an international novelist, a figure of importance and reputation. He kept himself somewhat aloof and withdrawn, the full, silky beard he wore at this period suggesting the artist-hermit. He did not look "American" nor did he seem English, either. Although only slightly past forty in 1886, he appeared older than his years. At this time Sargent sketched James for the *Yellow Book*, with his beard trimmed, Van Dyck fashion, his dark-complected face in a profile, a somewhat stiffly erect head, rapidly balding on top, and one eye prominently revealed in an intense, penetrating gaze. Women who knew him at this time spoke of the strange power of his glance, more noticeable against his olive skin and dark-bearded face. Tall and erect of bearing (his early back injury exaggerated this posture) and gravely sedate of manner, he had the semitic look of a Renaissance trader or Anglicized merchant of Venice.[2] Edmund Gosse recalled James in 1886 as showing a rather formidable reserve of mien, but a compensating fund of friendliness and indulgence toward others. His talk was "enchanting" and his attitude "mildly avuncular." Gosse remembered a boating party with a group of ladies when James sat stiffly at the prow, like a "bearded Buddha," half afraid the boat would tip, but enjoying himself nonetheless.[3]

Recent scholarship has sought to discover some center for the variable and conflicting elements of his mind during these years, partly in response to Matthiessen's thesis that the novels written after 1900 constituted his "major phase." Philip Rahv, M. D. Zabel, F. R. Leavis and others have considered the Eighties as evidencing the principle of growth in his work and as showing advancing techniques and ideas, an increased mastery of the methods of his apprentice years. Zabel speaks of this mastery in the books of the middle period, especially *The Portrait of a Lady*, as "perhaps the touchstone of his entire achievement."[4] Leavis, seeking to place James in the "great tradition" of Victorian novelists along with Jane Austen, George Eliot, and Joseph Conrad, makes a virtue of the earlier deracinated-artist theme of Van Wyck Brooks and Rebecca West. He regards the middle years as representing a "vital poise" in James's consciousness, a balance of English and American qualities of mind which comes to focus in *The Portrait of a Lady* and more particularly in the character of Ralph Touchett who "represents the ideal civilization which James found in no country." Leavis included *The Bostonians* and *The Princess Casamassima* with other tales of the Eighties as "a cluster of achieved masterpieces."[5] In the general revaluation of the middle years even the once-disparaged *Washington Square* has been grouped with its immediate successors as a minor classic of the second period of James's development.

Such terms as "Victorian" and "realist" should be defined carefully in James's case, but they apply with greater relevance after 1880 when he began to talk of doing a "big novel, rich in paraphernalia" in the manner of Balzac or Thackeray. In his relation to the English novel, as well as in certain of his tastes and habits of mind, his reticences and his guarded freedoms, he was one of the Victorians. His literary realism of this time is best seen in reference to the continental novel of Turgenev, Daudet, or de Maupassant and to his revived interest in the American scene as a social milieu and a background landscape for his fiction. A central conflict in his mind was to reconcile his portrait technique with a desire to write long novels of realism and social conditions. "My artistic conscience," he explained in a letter in 1879, "is so greatly attached to *form* that it shrinks from believing that it can supply it properly for *big* subjects, and yet is constantly studying the way to do so; so that at last I am sure it will arrive. I am determined that the novel I write this next year shall be 'big'."[6] *The Portrait of a Lady* became this "big" novel, but its superiority, as we now see, was in its full realization on a larger scale of the earlier methods of the "portrait" and the international theme, rather than a new departure toward the novel of social reality. It was amply "furnished" with people and places, and it was written with measured pace and gradually revealed undertones of moral ambiguity, but it did not quite achieve the harmony he now sought between "the fictive picture" and the naturalistic treatment of a significant phase of human history in the manner of Balzac. In his letters and criticism of this period, he was searching for a resolution of this conflict, contenting himself in his best statements of the problem with the rejection of doctrinaire theories, embracing the concept of perfect freedom for the artist, and continuing his quest for a form to encompass the different kinds of experience which demanded expression.

His renewed interest in the American scene as a background for his work and a possible way out of the convention of the international marriage-plot began with *Washington Square*, his first attempt to emulate Balzac with a novel about an American *ville de province*. His own later disparagement of the book and omission of it from his collected edition indicated the distance his interests were ultimately to take him away from the novel of local color. He later felt that *Washington Square* was insufficiently artistic, a linear narrative, without artistic design or perspective or the device of a center of consciousness to secure dramatic point. He told Howells that in writing it he felt acutely the "want of paraphernalia," which he defined as density of civilization—the established habits, customs, and usages which European society so amply offered the novelist.[7] He called it a "poorish" story and wrote to William that "the only good thing in the story is the girl."[8] The portrait of Catherine Sloper, brought up in the older New York of James's boyhood, was an American Eugénie Grandet. She represented an advance upon James's earlier heroines, Gertrude Wentworth or Daisy Miller, in a significant respect. She displayed signs of change and development as the story progressed. Daisy Miller had become a type partly because she remained static throughout her story, the various incidents simply reinforcing the essentials of her character. Catherine, on the other hand, was shown as changing from a weak and obedient daughter, afraid of her father's strength of mind and ironic condescension, into a mature and independent woman, holding firmly to her own opinions. At first a plain, dull, and unattractive girl, she gradually develops in appearance and self-respect until, after her return from a trip to Europe, her Aunt Penniman, never a strong believer in Catherine's powers, considered her as "rather handsome."

In this parallel between Catherine's outward appearance and her inward strength of mind, James followed the Emersonian belief in a harmony of natural and moral growth, and at the same time solved the problem of the anti-romantic handling of his heroine without sacrificing an idealistic reading of human nature. After the revelation that Morris Townsend is more interested in her fortune than in her, Catherine withdraws into herself and lives out her life in retired, but dignified spinsterhood. A clue to James's understanding of her character lies in the fact that she maintains her independence of the two pressures upon her—the harsh disparagement of her father and the romantic sentimentalism of her aunt. She neither lapses into a weak surrender to Dr. Sloper's will, nor will she accept the lachrymose sympathy of Aunt Penniman. Instead, calling upon reserves of her own, she holds stubbornly, if not defiantly, to her role as jilted lover.

Washington Square showed few structural or technical advancements over its predecessors, but it did succeed in refining upon methods he had used heretofore. Like both *The American* and *Daisy Miller*, it was an anti-melodrama. That is to say, the essentials of the story were those of romantic intrigue—an heiress, a fortune-hunting villain, a disappointed *amour*, a stern father, a sentimental aunt—but its success lay in James's blurring with a realistic surface all these elements and permitting none of the characters to descend into mere type. Morris Townsend, though treated mainly from the outside view, is never quite the designing Victorian villain. Catherine holds the reader's sympathy, but not to the degree of becoming a conventionally jilted romantic heroine, nor is Dr. Sloper allowed to revert to the role of indignant and protective father only. He retains a measure of sympathy and a considerable respect by virtue of the clarity and reasoned sharpness of his judgment of the true nature of Morris's intentions. Aunt Penniman remains the nearest to a type, but here James has penned a deliciously satiric portrait and a clever parody of the romantic novel, as in the following description of her mental meanderings:

> Mrs. Penniman's real hope was that the girl would make a secret marriage, at which she should officiate as a brideswoman or duenna. She had a vision of this ceremony being performed in some subterranean chapel; subterranean chapels in New York were not frequent, but Mrs. Penniman's imagination was not chilled by trifles; and of the guilty couple—she liked to think of poor Catherine and her suitor as the guilty couple—being shuffled away in a fast-whirling vehicle to some obscure lodging in the suburbs, where she would pay them (in a thick veil) clandestine visits; where they would endure a period of romantic privation; and when ultimately . . . they would be reconciled to her brother in an artistic tableau, in which she herself should be somehow the central figure.[9]

Thus, while the characters in the novel are *of* the type, they remain individuals. James's flexibility and his control, his veering from convention, was one element of his maturing technique and the cause of the bewilderment of critics whose standards were worn smooth in the grooves of conventionally romantic fiction.

The response of contemporary reviewers of *Washington Square* was one of dissatisfaction, especially with the indecisive ending. It was praised with non-faint damns. It was called witty and clever, but a piece of dilettantism, earnest trifling, and a waste of talent on "the elaborate nonentities" who occupy its pages. Scudder in the *Atlantic* said that James had "set himself the task of portraying the mental features of a dull woman capable of a species of dumb devotion to a man who easily assumes the place of an ideal being in the somewhat arid waste of her life."[10] A *Scribner's* critic complained of a want of force in the denouement.

> Like most, and perhaps all, of his novels *Washington Square* seems
> to have been worked up with extraordinary care and skill—and come
> to nothing. We do not care two straws for the fate of the actors.

The same writer could remark that it was one of the cleverest tales James had written, Dr. Sloper was "an admirable study," and Catherine "a true triumph for Mr. James"—one of the "best outcomes of his generalizing realism."[11] One reviewer felt that its great fault was in handling tragedy by the dispassionate-realistic method, another was disappointed that James let the "villain" (Morris) escape and deprived the reader of "joining in the hue and cry after him." Such critical inanities may have helped bring about the long period during which *Washington Square* was underrated even by James himself until its revival recently on the stage and screen.

The Portrait of a Lady (1882) was James's most ambitious psychological portrait thus far and one of the best of his long novels. The young woman, Isabel Archer, was painted in the center of a canvas, surrounded by figures ("satellites," James called the other characters) in varying attitudes of adoration, love, friendly counsel, or hostile intent. The conception was derived from Turgenev, "the beautiful" genius, who along with George Eliot, contended for mastery of James's artistic conscience in this novel. Like *Washington Square* the machinery of the story was that of nineteenth-century melodrama—a betrayed heiress, schemed against by enemies pretending to be friends, and maneuvered into a hypocritical marriage contract with a villain of *Wuthering Heights* proportions. From such stuff James formed a subtle and analytical study of an American girl modelled upon George Eliot's Gwendolyn Harleth. The American expatriate Osmond was even more closely fashioned upon Charles Grandcourt. All this melodrama is deeply embedded in and concealed by a dense atmosphere of psychological interplay and polite manners which were to become James's trademark in his later fiction. The intellectual and literary roots of the novel, as James scholars have elaborately shown in various accounts of its sources, are extremely complex, but at the heart of the story was probably his memories of his cousin Minny Temple who died in 1871 and for whom he was writing a belated memorial.

The Portrait of a Lady disguised melodrama, but it is also a great deal more. It is a study of character and destiny in which freedom and fate are deftly woven into the character of his heroine. It has been interpreted as a romantic story of triumph and self-sacrifice, but recent criticism has pointed more properly to the naturalistic emphasis in the book. As James later viewed the novel from the perspective of his Preface, he must have felt that the deterministic forces had been too firmly written into the character of Isabel Archer. He had meant her personal psyche to be all-important, he said, like the heroines of George Eliot or Shakespeare. She was to be an idealized type, like Cleopatra or Juliet or Portia or Gwendolyn Harleth or Maggie Tulliver—"Frail vessels," as he called them, bearing through the ages the treasure of human affection.[12] This is the initial conception of Isabel in the opening chapters. She is "intelligent and presumptuous," high-spirited and sensitive, yet "liable to the sin of self-esteem." She is romantic about love and marriage and possessed of a certain "nobleness of imagination." In short, she was a combination of "the delicate, desultory, flame-like spirit and the eager and personal creature of conditions."[13]

As the novel progresses, however, toward its subdued climax the force of circumstances is felt increasingly. She early rejects the suit of Lord Warburton because, as she says, "I can't escape my fate." And, at the end, when she has finally cut herself off from the dull but solid American virtues of Caspar Goodwood, she knows that her only course is to return to Rome and Osmond. Her choice of action in this main crisis of her life, paralleling as it does the renunciation theme of "Madame de Mauves" and *The American*, has been interpreted as indicating James's "puritan" attitude toward divorce and his sympathy with the Christian doctrine of the discipline of suffering. More likely, however, it reflected his need to shade off his endings from the climactic and romantic. And one should note that James deliberately blurred the ethical implications of Isabel's return to Osmond. She briefly promises Pansy that she will return, but her frame of mind in this scene is one of resignation rather than moral justification. She follows a course of ever-deepening shadow from her beginnings as a delicate flame-like spirit to a woman of defeated purposes.

Toward the end of the novel, after Isabel has broken with Madame Merle and rejected Osmond's demand that she stay in Rome rather than go to London to visit the dying Ralph Touchett, there is a chapter describing her state of mind when the evil and treachery of life have been revealed to her. Here James deliberately avoids high-principled reasons for her decision to return to Rome and ethical implications in her choice of conduct. Instead he lays stress on the disconnected welter of impressions which pass through her consciousness. Her mind, during the long journey back to Gardencourt,

> . . . had been given up to vagueness; she was unable to question the future. . . . She had plenty to think about, but it was neither reflexion nor conscious purpose that filled her mind. Disconnected visions passed through it, and sudden gleams of memory, of expectation. . . . All purpose, all intention was suspended. . . . To cease utterly, to give it all up and not know anything more—this idea was as sweet as the vision of a cool bath in a marble tank, in a darkened chamber, in a hot land.[14]

The moral ambiguity involved in this passage is significant of the direction his realism was to take in the Eighties. No doubt the reviews of his previous books which had disapproved of his tentative conclusions led James to predict in his Notebook, when the novel was still in serial form, his expectation of unfavorable criticism of its denouement: "The obvious criticism of course will be that it is not finished—that it has not seen the heroine to the end of her situation—that I have left her *en l'air*."[15]

Criticism of the novel was generally favorable. Reviewers began to realize that James was now an influential force in literary circles; the usual strictures against his "disagreeable" people and disappointing endings were played down, and critics concentrated instead upon the technical advancements which his work showed. They discussed his analytical method, his lack of action, and his device of carrying on the story without the usual plot element. Orthodox-minded critics continued to berate James for his cynicism, his decadence, his literary Pyrrhonism, and his artificial and "repulsive" characters, but the *Atlantic Monthly, Scribner's,* and the *Nation* praised his skill in characterization and Scudder extended himself to describe Isabel as "representative of womanly life today." Scudder, in his analysis of Isabel's character, seemed to understand what James was attempting to do in his handling of an idealized type within determining conditions.

> The fine purpose of her freedom, the resolution with which she seeks to be the maker of her destiny, the subtle weakness into which all this betrays her, the apparent helplessness of her ultimate position, and the conjectured escape only through patient forbearance,—what are all these, if not attributes of womanly life expended under current conditions?[16]

The most discriminating of the contemporary reviews, however, was that of W. C. Brownell in the *Nation*, who described the change in

James's fictional method from "the field of imaginative romance," as in *Roderick Hudson*, to a new kind of novel which he called "romantic sociology." He discovered signs of this new technique in *The American*, but considered *The Portrait* to be James's masterpiece and the culmination of his new style. He mentioned Turgenev and George Eliot as the strongest influences and pointed out that James was striving for "the imaginative treatment of reality." Brownell's comments suggested that there were two sides to James's artistic nature and that the novel had succeeded in combining "a scientific value with romantic interest and artistic merit."[17]

Though more discerning than most of the contemporary criticism of the novel, Brownell's remarks were insufficient to clarify the complex technique of *The Portrait*. It is not surprising that he failed to divine the method of the psychological portrait of Isabel Archer, when James himself came only slowly to recognize what he was trying to accomplish. There is nothing in the Notebooks of the time to suggest the device as he described it much later in his Preface to the novel. "Place the centre of the subject in the young woman's consciousness," he wrote, "and you get as interesting and beautiful a difficulty as you wish. Stick to that—for the centre."[18] The other characters, as he later realized, were to remain contributory to the central figure. Sociological elements played a relatively minor role in Isabel's fate—only insofar as her American innocence, given free rein by Mr. Touchett's bequest, placed her in the equivocal situation where she became a victim of intrigue. The ultimate resolution of her fate was determined by the qualities of mind she had from the start, and the "realism" the novel displayed lay in its dramatic revelation of the heroine's gradual awareness of evil.

Isabel Archer was a generic portrait, evolved from James's moral conscience as much as from the literary sources he used. Like Christopher Newman, she began in abstraction and only gradually acquired roundness and living habiliments in the course of her story. The theory of her origin in Minny Temple has been questioned and is a tenuous connection at best, but it is likewise true that James was aware of his tendency to abstraction and he sought to base his people upon live originals, whenever he could. He discussed this question in his *Hawthorne* where he noted the close resemblance of Zenobia in *The Blithedale Romance* to certain events in the life of Margaret Fuller—her reformist ideas, her flamboyant nature, her known connection with Hawthorne at Brook Farm, even her eventual death by drowning. This autobiographical source, James felt, made Zenobia more concrete as a person than any of Hawthorne's creations. On the other hand, he shifted his ground on the matter, arguing that the writer can take "hints" from living models, but he "does what he likes with them, and imports new elements into the picture."[19] He began in the early Eighties, however, to consider more seriously the use of actual people in his own work. He admired Daudet's method of transposing historical persons into his fiction, noting that Daudet "proposed to himself to represent not only the people but the persons of his time" and that this temptation was not only "legitimate" but "inevitable" for a writer.[20] In his own case, he found it difficult to emulate Daudet or Balzac in this because of his lack of intimacy with such public figures, but he continually sought a more solid reality in his characters. There have been many recent discoveries of live sources for James's fictional people, but the most famous instance was his basing Miss Birdseye of *The Bostonians* upon Elizabeth Peabody, Hawthorne's sister-in-law. When the similarity was noticed to the horror of Bostonian readers, James defended himself on the ground that his character had evolved entirely from "my moral consciousness" and only after he had "got going" did he become aware of the resemblance to Miss Peabody. The well-known defense was a prime instance in which theory and practice were at odds and James worked out a rationale in defiance of consistency to bridge the gap.[21]

A different and less restraining form of portraiture, however, was the literary portrait in criticism. Here the writer was free to work directly with living persons or those recently dead, and the essays James wrote about literary persons he knew were among his most vivid recreations. The chapters in the volume, *Partial Portraits* (1888), were mostly narrative portraits of literary personalities. They were "lives," reminiscences, memorials, retrospective estimates, or impressionistic portrayals. The method, already used effectively in *French Poets and Novelists* and in *Hawthorne*, was a mixture of critical appraisal and what James called "the pleasant fashion of the literary portrait," which he recognized as a little old-fashioned. *Partial Portraits* has been described as the first of his critical books in which James achieved a real mastery. Morris Roberts gave it "a central place in his criticism, like that of *The Portrait of a Lady* among his novels."[22] This may be unjust to the earlier criticism, especially to the admirable study of Hawthorne, but it points to a maturing and mellowing of James's critical method in the Eighties, a development parallel to the advancement of his techniques of fiction. A more intimate, more tactful and warmer tone characterizes the studies of literary figures in *Partial Portraits*. A deeper sense of the technical problems confronting the artist can be felt in his essays on such writers as George Eliot, Daudet, de Maupassant, and Trollope, while a strong personal feeling entered into the portraits of Emerson, Stevenson, and Turgenev.

In all there were eleven separate essays included rather haphazardly in the volume. The range of subjects and the editorial organization suggests no clear pattern. All but one of the chapters were first published in the magazines between 1883 and 1888. The opening chapter on Emerson, one of the latest in date, established the rationale for the method. In this essay James objected to J. E. Cabot's *Memoir* of Emerson for its lack of pictorial quality and sense of personality. Cabot, James felt, had short-suited the background, the New England of the transcendental time, the people who surrounded his subject—in short, much-needed local color. "We know a man imperfectly," he wrote, "until we know his society, and we but half know a society until we know its manners."[23] Similarly, in the chapter on Turgenev, James wanted to give his readers, not just another critical estimate, but a sense of the living person—his face, his talk, his temper—a vivifying impression of the Russian writer whom James had known for almost a decade. Robert Louis Stevenson, whose relationship with James was a warmly personal literary friendship, is portrayed as an ideal model for the painter. James considered him "essentially a model," one of the people with character and pictorial quality. The chapter on Du Maurier, another personal friend, was the only non-literary essay in the book, dealing with the artist's illustrations for *Punch*. Here James was primarily interested in the "London Society" which emerged from Du Maurier's drawings.

The now famous essay, "The Art of Fiction," placed last in the book, almost as if by afterthought, was the only chapter exclusively devoted to general principles of the craft of fiction. It was, as he confided in a letter to Stevenson, "simply a plea for liberty," for James had grown impatient with rules and doctrinaire abstractions which hampered the freedom of the novelist to pursue his own way. Artificial distinctions, such as that between "realism" and "romance," which had occupied much of his speculation in the earlier period, he now called "clumsy separations" which readers and critics liked to employ "for their convenience and to help them out of their occasional predicaments."[24] He defined his ideal of the critic as "the very genius of observation, art, discretion, and taste," and he resented the intrusions upon it of those who simply played narrow law-givers or rigid censors. The aim of criticism, he now felt, should be justness of characterization and among its important requisites James listed study, inquiry, observation, and finally, interpretation. One of the key passages in *Partial Portraits* set forth, in the language of satire, the damage done to criticism when it deserts the older, more genial and pleasant role of sympathetic portraiture. In its place there had arrived, he lamented, a gross form of literary prosecution, a court trial with the author placed in the witness chair and the critic taking "sides" and keeping "score" and rendering a final verdict, usually guilty. In place of the modern criminal trial, James said, the role of the critic should revert to something nearer to that of the familiar, personal essay—the portrait in which he attempts to "fix a face and figure, to seize a literary character, and transfer it to his canvas." In *Partial Portraits* there is everywhere evident the application of "the amiable, uninvidious" tone and the desire to "catch a talent in the fact, follow its line, and put a finger on its essence."[25]

Two of the chapters in the volume bear special mention, giving the book its distinctive quality. The essay on de Maupassant is, by general consent, James at his best in literary appraisal, and "The Art of Fiction" represents his finest summary in short compass of the delicate and serious art of the novel. "Guy de Maupassant" carried to the farthest limits of paradox James's Victorian compromise between French and Anglo-Saxon literary ideals. de Maupassant he terms "a case" and adds that "the critic is intelligent in proportion as he apprehends and enters into that case." To the Anglo-Saxon imagination in its conventional blinking of the mean, the sordid, the erotic, and the cynical, de Maupassant has become a "lion in the path," and James makes it the burden of his criticism to find a way around the "embarrassment" of the French writer for his English readers. By the end he has found it, in a remarkable embracing of opposites whereby the French writer, prodigious in the gifts of genius, sharp visual perceptions, and keen sensibilities, is a figure "at once so licentious and so impeccable," a tribute to the perfect freedom of the artist and "this magnificent art of the novelist."[26] The essay was for James a triumph in his effort to resolve the conflict between the artist and the Victorian gentleman in himself, and though it was the artist who prevailed the victory was not lop-sided, for the result is to reveal the astonishing lengths to which he could go in allowing perfect license for the writer without quite abandoning the Anglo-Saxon moral preferences of his own temperament.

In the same way, paradox rests at the heart of "The Art of Fiction." Only the verbal skill and flexibility of language which James displayed could have succeeded in weaving something like a harmony out of the contrarieties of this essay, such antitheses as freedom for the artist against moral responsibility, literalism versus selection in "the interests of the typical," character vis-a-vis incident and plot, "romance" as opposed to the "novel." On the one hand, the novel aims primarily to represent "life" which embraces nothing less than "all feeling, all observation, all vision." On the other, "art is selection, but it is a selection whose main care is to be typical, to be inclusive." While a moral conscience and a sense of responsibility to society are integral to the highest art, the artist must not be deprived of his freedom of subject or restricted in his way of handling it. James insisted upon a finely shaded conscience, as much a matter of good taste as anything else, whereby the moral tone of a work of art is finally determined by the refinement and the intelligence of the artist. In an Emersonian sentence he summed up: "In proportion as that intelligence is fine will the novel, the picture, the statue, partake of the substance of beauty and truth."

Only such of his contemporary readers and critics (and they were few) who were capable of resting within a series of contrarieties and who were content with a "negative capability" of suspended meaning, could fully appreciate James's conception of art in this essay. Most reviewers expressed impatience with the elusiveness of his dialectic and the rapid turns of his thought. George Woodberry expressed this feeling toward *Partial Portraits* as a whole when he lamented James's refusal to make clear and direct judgments. He ascribed this fault to a lack of convictions. "He does not favor what is known as final criticism," Woodberry wrote, and his essays are in the main "an expression of the personal preferences of his own temperament, which may or may not be valid in the case of others."[27] Today, it is generally felt that James reached in two or three of the essays in the volume his own highest achievement in critical writing and literary portraiture. On de Maupassant, Turgenev, and Stevenson he raised the level of American criticism from its habit of didacticism and moral judgment to a fine art of discriminating taste and rounded, three-dimensional portrayal. "The Art of Fiction" in its attention to theoretical matters was something of an exception in the volume, but it has come to be considered a milestone in the history of American criticism and a minor miracle of the art of shaping existing doctrines of critical theory to the artist's personal predilection for latitude and license. Along with a few of the famous Prefaces, it remains his most widely quoted and best-known piece of criticism. And in James's intellectual development it stands at the point where he could go no further toward preserving a framework of ideas in his strong drift toward a subjective and impressionistic position. The art of fiction encompassed for him every province of life. It had no limitations. "It is," he wrote in one of his most impressive statements, "an immense sensibility, a kind of huge spider web of the finest silken threads suspended in the chamber of consciousness and catching every air-borne particle in its tissue."

A somewhat stronger American accent is noticeable in his fiction of the early Eighties. James wrote a series of homecoming stories in which a long-absent countryman returns to America to refresh his memories and gain new impressions. The narrator and point-of-view character is either an artist carrying his sketch pad or a writer with his notebook in hand with which to record his impressions and gather material. The American cities and landscape provide the imaginative starting point in this group of tales, such stories as "The Point of View," "The Impressions of a Cousin," "A New England Winter," "Pandora," or "Lady Barberina." They were not among his more successful, only the last two being ultimately selected for the New York edition. The American scene, as seen through the eyes of a European American, is far from lovingly painted. Mostly, it is shown as harsh, cold, angular, vulgar in its taste, and wanting in dignity and cultural depth. A young painter, in "A New England Winter," with the fantastic name of Florimond, returns to visit his mother in Boston where the white glare of the snowy streets and the icy wind strike him in the face like an insult and become symbols of the wintry

New England moral climate. In "The Impressions of a Cousin" a young woman artist returns to New York hoping to sketch the streets and vistas of Fifth Avenue, but the narrow, impersonal houses with their "dry, hard tone" of brownstone prove fatal to her imagination. In "Pandora" James sought the authentic by transcribing scenes of local color drawn from his two visits to Washington and his impressions of its social life. The capitol and Mount Vernon were worked in for "realism," but he likewise drew the Bonneycastles directly from Henry Adams and his wife. Alfred Bonneycastle "was not in politics, but politics were much in him." They gave the best parties for the best people and they regarded it as a great joke to "be vulgar" and invite the president!

James was not content to be merely a painter of surfaces, and in Pandora Day he brought a new and bolder Daisy Miller back to her American environment and asked himself what would become of her at home. "The 'self-made' girl," he wrote in his Notebook, "a good subject for a short story. Very modern, very local; much might be done."[28] Pandora is a step forward in the evolution of the type which would eventuate in the still more worldly Julia Bride. She is the daughter of "vulgar" parents who combines beauty with social success. She was possible, James wrote, only in America. "She hadn't been born with the silver spoon of social opportunity; she had grasped it by honest exertion." Looking back on the story twenty-five years later James felt that Pandora had become a dated figure and the rapid passage of history had rendered her a much less novel type than her multiple sisters of the 1900's. "The evolution of varieties moves fast; the Pandora Days can no longer pass for quaint or fresh or for exclusively native to any one tract of Anglo-Saxon soil."[29]

James's limitations as a realist and social historian stemmed in part from his growing quarrel with his homeland as a source of materials for fiction. Yet he was not prepared in the Eighties to admit that Howells had surpassed him in this vein, and he looked with some envy upon the success his rival and friend was winning among American readers. In this frame of mind he continued his own search for authenticity—"Actuality must be my line at present."[30] In a review in the *Atlantic* for 1882 of Howells's *Dr. Breen's Practice*, Horace Scudder had compared the author's warm and natural treatment of New England life with "the somewhat thick, heavy air" of *The Portrait of a Lady*. Howells, Scudder felt, was more successful than James in describing "people whom we meet in actual life."[31] James's letters to Howells during the Eighties contained an undercurrent of challenge and a note of irritation. He had debated sharply with his friend for the opinions expressed in the review of his *Hawthorne*. He praised the "naturalism" of *Dr. Breen's Practice*, but qualified his remarks by suggesting that Howells had not yet done for America what Balzac and Thackeray had done for their countries. Howells was, James told him, a naturalist with certain romantic elements and his perception of evil was small. Behind his remarks was an unexpressed ambition to "do" the American scene himself à la Balzac or Daudet and to compete with Howells for readers and critical acclaim in his own country.

In his Notebooks of the period he steadily sought to be "very national and typical." In April, 1883, two years before he finally completed *The Bostonians* he outlined with remarkable completeness his plan for the characters, the subject, and the interpretation of a long novel of the "so-called woman's movement." The novel was to be his bid "to show that I *can* write an American story" and that it should be "as American as possible and full of Boston."[32] The underscoring of "can" suggests both a strong determination on James's part to write a realistic novel about America, and some doubts about his ability to succeed. He wished, he said, to write "a very *American* tale, a tale very characteristic of our social conditions" and he asked himself what the most salient point of our social life was. In choosing the subject of "the situation of women, the decline of the sentiment of sex, the agitation on their behalf,"[33] James felt that he had a better subject than he had ever had before. He expected the novel would become "much the best thing I have done yet."[34]

To call *The Bostonians*, and its companion novel about the English anarchist movement, *The Princess Casamassima*, social novels scarcely describes their special character, except to indicate that they belonged to a distinct category of his fiction—different from almost all of James's other long novels. They are different, writes Lionel Trilling, "by having in common a quick responsiveness to the details of the outer world, an explicit awareness of history, of the grosser movement of society and civilization."[35] Of the two, *The Bostonians* is the less typically "Jamesian" perhaps by virtue of its tone of high comedy, satire and burlesque. On the surface a comedy of manners and a study of strange contrasts of character, it becomes not only an examination of the "situation of women," but a subtle probing of a highly vulnerable aspect of the nineteenth-century American mind. It is both socially and psychologically realistic, but at the same time touches chords of tragedy and melodrama. Basil Ransom, the Southern gentleman-chevalier and champion of old-fashioned standards of romantic love, contends against a New England enchantress (Olive Chancellor) for possession of the beautiful Verena Tarrant who has been symbolically confined to the Back Bay home (dungeon) of Miss Chancellor. As Charles Anderson has happily phrased the plot, "it reaches a climax in the romance of rescue: he snatches her from the enchanted castle of Boston's Music Hall just as she is about to be sacrificed on the lecture platform, and escapes with her into the night (a horse car presumably serving as his fiery charger)."[36] James's skill in burlesquing and at the same time gaining dramatic force from such romantic equipment is equalled only by the realism and symbolism by which he makes of the latter-day feminist-visionaries an analogue of the national psyche and a study of regional contrasts. Despite James's own devaluation of the novel, its poor press, and his ultimate rejection of it from the collected edition, there are many reasons for restoring it to a position among his best long novels.

The history of its reputation is greatly revealing both of James's mind and that of the American literary world in the middle Eighties. Before it had been well started serially in the *Century* magazine, outraged cries of protest were heard from local patriots. The opening chapters provoked a series of letters between William James and Henry over his drawing a portrait of Elizabeth Peabody, the aging Bluestocking who was still seen on the streets of Boston. William called his brother's character, Miss Birdseye, a piece of "bad business" and Henry, "appalled" at this blow from within the family circle, struck back with acrimony and heat in a clash which came close to causing a rift between the two.[37] Behind this filial quarrel lay William's envy of his younger brother's success as a novelist. Henry replied by accusing "the public mind" of "ignoble levity and puerility" in its refusal to allow a novelist to base his characters upon a solidly real foundation. At the same time, he admitted to having "overdone it" and blamed this on his not having had a chance to see the proofs before printing.[38]

His attitude, as revealed in this letter and in later comments he made upon *The Bostonians*, was clearly ambivalent. The total effect upon him was a psychological defeat equalled only by his experience a decade later when he was hooted and jeered by an audience gathered to watch his play, *Guy Domville*. While writing the novel, James told his brother that he expected to be abused for the title he had selected, but when the abuse materialized he was hurt and angry, disclaiming any "invidious intent" in the title and insisting that he had not meant to generalize, but only to designate as Bostonians Olive Chancellor and Verena "as they appeared to the mind of Ransom, the Southerner and outsider looking at them from New York."[39] Of Miss Birdseye, who is the object of some of the sharpest satire, he wrote that she was meant to embody "the purest philanthropy" and that she had been handled with sympathy and respect. Although he had said in 1885 that he thought *The Bostonians* his best fiction thus far, he wrote of it the following year calling the "whole thing too long and dawdling," and spoke of knowing "terribly little" about the life he had sought to describe.[40] And he criticized the method of going behind his characters with authorial explanations and editorial intrusions. His final opinion, twenty years later, on the book was the decision not to revise it for the New York edition or to write a preface for it, though he still would not admit, as he wrote Howells, that the book had received "any sort of justice." It was not reprinted after its original publication until 1945, sixty years later, an incredible neglect of a major American novel. Today, however, with the James revival at full tide, the novel has at last vindicated James's own prediction, made at the lowest point of his

American reputation in 1888, that his "buried prose" would someday "kick off its various tombstones" and be given a just hearing.[41] Several new editions and much commentary have been devoted to it. It has been termed a "masterpiece" and a brilliantly satiric account of a vulnerable aspect of the American social experience.

The conspiracy of silence which greeted his novel in New England circles, after the first outraged cries of dissent, wrought what James considered an "inexplicable injury" to his reputation and reduced the demand for his work to "zero." From that time to the present, the revolution of taste in America has been so complete and the recognition of James's stature so altered that one can only wonder at the degree of critical blindness which missed entirely the satiric thrust of *The Bostonians* upon its first appearance. The *Atlantic Monthly* politely praised a few of James's character-portraits as skillful and called Miss Birdseye "the one redeeming feature of the book," but described the others as "repellant" and scolded him for pushing them "too near the brink of nature."[42] The *Nation* admitted the accuracy of the social analysis, but without really seeing its larger implications, while the *Critic* touched new levels of condescension in saying that James said nothing in 449 pages, but that he said it with an art that is constant and charming.[43] Today the novel is mentioned in the same breath with the plays of Strindberg or the novels of D. H. Lawrence for its penetration into forbidden areas of sexual behavior, and it has been ranked along with such acute diagnosticians of the national psyche as Henry Adams, de Tocqueville, and George Santayana for its exposé of American idealism gone awry. Its literary sources have been fully scrutinized from Daudet's *Evangeliste* (James's one admitted "source") to Hawthorne's *The Blithedale Romance*, Howells's *Dr. Breen's Practice*, and even the *Antigone* and the *Lysistrata* of Greek tragic and comic drama. And, despite James's admission that he knew "terribly little" about the life he sought to depict, scholars have admired the way in which he drew analogies between the transcendental abolitionists of New England's golden time and the visionary reformers who comprised the lunatic fringe of the later period—the short-haired women and effeminate men of the "so-called woman's movement."

James himself seemed somewhat naive about the devastating possibilities of his own satiric powers when they were directed at so vulnerable an aspect of American life as the feminist agitation in the post-Civil War era. Some years earlier, commenting upon Hawthorne's handling of New England reformers in *The Blithedale Romance*, he had noted as a weakness of that novel its "absence of satire" and its tendency to run to fantasy and unreality. His own portrait of Olive Chancellor was compounded from mingled echoes of Zenobia (Hawthorne's Margaret Fuller), Madame Autheman, the fanatical Calvinist in Daudet's novel, Howells's Grace Breen, and his own imaginative reconstruction of a morbid, spinsterish, Back Bay aristocrat who enjoys slumming among the Bohemians of the "movement," but who disdains their grubby parlors and bare meeting houses. Olive possesses a neurotic fear of the male animal and channels her womanly instincts toward Verena in a sublimation of the natural impulses which become actively Lesbian. In his choice of a southerner from Mississippi as her rival for the gifted young girl, James discovered a ready-made stereotype of the romantic conservative and a champion of the Old South. His portrait has been subjected to close examination for its authenticity and found partly wanting,[44] but there is little adverse criticism of the skill with which he substituted the stereotype for the real thing and worked it into the texture of his drama. Ransom is a good deal more than a point-of-view character. For one thing, he is one of James's most successful masculine heroes, a far cry from the poor sensitive gentlemen and priggish consorts of the heroines of his international stories. He has a well-developed social philosophy and is opposed to all forms of agitation and freedom causes. He reads Comte and de Tocqueville, writes for the "Rational Review" and stands foursquare for the old-fashioned values. Dramatically, he stands for a vindication of the sentiment of sex against Olive who is the enemy of the sentiment. In the larger meaning of the book Ransom becomes a representative of the male principle and the double standard in a world of superannuated females, spiritualists, eccentrics, canting reformers, and long-haired agitators. In a key passage he is described as saying:

> The whole generation is womanized, the masculine tone is passing out of the world; it's a feminine, nervous, hysterical chattering, canting age, an age of hollow phrases and false delicacy and exaggerated solicitudes and coddling sensibilities, which if we don't soon look out, will usher in a reign of mediocrity, of the feeblest and flattest and the most pretentious that has ever been.

James's enlargement of the theme from a satiric account of certain types of spiritualists and reformers of Boston into a penetrating comment upon the whole problem of sexual maladjustment of American life after the Civil War has been the burden of some of the best modern criticism of *The Bostonians*. Lionel Trilling, Irving Howe and others have in various ways pointed out the advanced nature of James's searching examination into the disarrangement of American social and sexual life.[45] They have seen in the book a depiction of a "cultural crisis" and a tracing of a fundamental "sexual disorientation." Furthermore, they have noted the way in which James deepened its implications by viewing the question of feminism as the aftermath of the struggle between North and South over slavery. Irving Howe sees the novel as "infected with ideology" and as showing "the vast uprooting of American life which begins after the

Civil War and has not yet come to an end." Ransom, its hero, has been carefully analyzed as the advocate of an ante-bellum *status quo* and even as the representative of a conservative imagination which was to find expression in the twentieth century by the Southern agrarians or by such literary spokesmen of conservatism as T. S. Eliot and Yeats.

"I should have liked to write that Preface to the Bostonians," James wrote to Edmund Gosse in 1915.[46] He had always intended to include the novel in his collected edition, but the prospect of extensive revision, which he felt necessary, prevented him from doing so. What would he have written in the Preface? The question is an intriguing one, and one can only speculate on the basis of his later scattered opinions and observations about the novel. It was "too diffuse," he told Howells, and would take a good deal of artful "retouching." If he had written a Preface, he would no doubt have dwelt upon this weakness. It is certain, too, that he would have touched on the fact, as he told William, that the life he had attempted to describe was too remote from his experience to be made convincing. He would have devoted several paragraphs to the matter of technique. *The Bostonians* belonged to those of his novels which went "behind" the characters—that is, he talked to his reader about his characters' thoughts and feelings rather than revealing them dramatically through the center-of-consciousness of a narrator. In a letter to Mrs. Humphrey Ward, he had discussed this question, defending the looser method of delineation as occasionally necessary even to the best writers, though admittedly at the cost of authenticity and dramatic consistency. But above all, if James had written a Preface to *The Bostonians*, he would have defended it against the critical disparagement it had received. He spoke in later letters of its having never received "any sort of justice," that it was "a tolerably good and full novel," and he considered it "a remarkable feat of objectivity" which might have been a notable contribution to the collected edition.

It is less likely that James would have hinted at the symbolic and prophetic import of the book which has been seen by modern critics. A half century of social history has intervened to make possible such readings as those of Trilling, Howe, and other recent critics. But *The Bostonians* has come to be regarded as a culmination of the fiction of James's middle years, and his most successful long novel of social commentary. Conceived within the framework of the Victorian novel of realism, it is seen as a brilliant example of a melodramatic plot raised to the level of social analysis. Furthermore, written as it was at the time of the fruition of the earlier realism in America, it may be seen as a capstone of achievement in the fictional manner begun fifteen years earlier by John De Forest in another novel of North and South, sectional rivalry, and large social meaning. De Forest's *Miss Ravenel's Conversion* and James's *The Bostonians* were in certain ways antipodal expressions of Victorian realism. Their methods are divergent, the special talents and experience of the two authors widely different, their literary purposes unlike. Yet, a comparison of the two books as representative expressions of the earlier realism can be highly significant to the present study.

Both novels were an affront to the delicate taste of the time and to the effeminate reader, of either sex. Both authors had read widely in the continental novel and had brought the experience of European standards and literary methods to enrich American fiction. A family resemblance is apparent between some of the more devious characters of De Forest and those of Henry James. The former had invented and developed the type of aging and scheming coquette in both Mrs. Larue and Mrs. Chester, the latter in his *Kate Beaumont.* James's version of the type in Mrs. Penniman (*Washington Square*) and Adeline Luna (*The Bostonians*) clearly recalls De Forest's characters. Nothing the equal of Olive Chancellor's morbid neuroticism and sexual deviation can be found in *Miss Ravenel,* but female ambition and waywardness were carried as far as they would be in Mrs. Larue before James portrayed Christina Light, Madame Merle, and Miss Chancellor.

A still more striking comparison between the two novels, however, lies in their interpretations of the social effects upon American life of the oppositions growing out of the conflict between North and South. Both De Forest and James exploited fully the melodramatic implications of this central experience without sacrificing a uniformly realistic surface and treatment. Lily Ravenel and Verena Tarrant are both Victorian heroines, placed in the middle between competing forces representative of the two sections, and each becomes a prize of love and war. De Forest's Colonel Carter and James's Basil Ransom represent, in different ways, the chivalrous ideal mingled realistically with human failings. Both symbolize masculinity, set over against the feminized culture of New England, and each serves the author as a point of reference for satiric treatment of Bostonian life. In short, from quite different directions and techniques, *Miss Ravenel* and *The Bostonians* approached a center and achieved similar ends. De Forest's sociological panorama of the American experience and James's psychological analysis of certain eccentric types of the feminist movement both arrived at a significant reading of a highly vulnerable aspect of the national life. Considered together the two books framed and drew together a cycle of fiction during the postwar decades.

IV

POSTSCRIPT:

Mark Twain and the Earlier Realism

> To know Mark Twain is to know the strange
> and puzzling contradictions of the Gilded Age.
>
> V. L. PARRINGTON

V. L. PARRINGTON, in the first comprehensive discussion of Victorian realism in America, used the language of evolution to describe the period after the Civil War as arising out of "the ashes of romantic faith." He dismissed the work of Howells and Henry James as genteel and ineffectual, out of harmony with the steady march of the realistic emphasis. Now, however, his basic assumption of an evolutionary "rise" of literary aspirations from "gaudy romantic altars" and decadent social patterns to new and vitally "real" ones has ceased to carry the conviction it once had. It is no longer possible to accept his premise of an upward-curving spiral toward "reality," or to share his condescension toward nineteenth-century America. The decades here designated as "Victorian Realism" constituted more than a "transitional" phase of literary history. Both in its social and its literary manifestations the period deserves to be considered not as a side current in the stream of letters, but as an independent unit of cultural history. It had a development of its own marked by distinct chronological and historical limits—from the end of the war to the outbreak, about 1885, of a new form of turbulence and social strife—and it accomplished a life cycle of its own. It coincided with the formative and maturing years of three of America's leading novelists. During that period the novel was a potent social force and an accurate barometer of taste and manners. Literature was both an art and a social record, but it was not yet an instrument of reform. As a cultural unit, the period is one of great interest to the student of the American mind. And in its purely literary manifestations—the critical issues raised, the flourishing "monthlies" read and supported, the excited discussions of "art" and "reality," the lively exchanges of letters among its major writers—the age of Victorian realism had all the signs of a "movement."

The heated critical battles in the journals marked the literary phase of the larger struggle of intellectual conflict and swift social change. Great issues hovered in the background. The ideals of the Enlightenment and the political experiment of 1776 seemed to hang in the balance. As a moment of intellectual history, the twenty years between 1865 and 1885 were the stage-setting for a drama of survival in which the promise of democratic idealism and the threat of a deterministic and mechanistic philosophy seemed in fatal opposition. A re-orientation of American thought took place in which social Darwinism and the Victorian orthodoxy represented the polar extremities. Between these two extremes thoughtful Americans sought some new basis and a new stabilization of opposing pressures.

The rapid movement after the war of social and economic forces toward an industrial economy, the aggregation of capital, and the consequent rise of the leaders of finance found philosophic sanction both in the traditional American faith in the individual and in the evolutionary argument of natural selection. This powerful swing of the pendulum toward integration, however, created the momentum for a reverse movement—labor and agrarian protest, group psychology, and a class-conscious society. Collectivism gradually drew support in opposition to rugged individualism and business enterprise. The intellectual expression of this conflict was a gradual re-orientation of the prewar attitudes of individualism and equalitarianism. Psychological and analytical study of the springs of conduct supplanted the older exaltation of individual worth; similarly, economic and sociological disciplines, based upon science, took the place of the earlier philosophic abolitionism with its ethical concept of human rights. Both the new psychology and the new sociology contained seeds of determinism. Regional oppositions grew more complex. The rapid expansion westward into the unsettled frontier established a third section with its own claims to recognition to complicate the existing tensions between North and South. New rights of man needed to be integrated with the old—the rights of women, the rights of sections, the rights of labor. Increasingly diversified religious and racial types sought a place alongside the predominantly Anglo-Protestant strain. The impact of such forces upon the earlier idealistic-individualistic heritage produced a climate of intellectual and social disparity.

Against this background of controversy intellectuals and literary-minded men and women envisioned some sort of synthesis of opposing points of view. Sensitive to both the old and the new, they sought a temporary equilibrium of conflicting forces. It is this quest, as it took shape in the two decades following the truce of 1865, that one must regard as the essence of the problem of realism in fiction and criticism. For the most part, it was a conservative quest. American critics, for instance, did not turn at once to espouse a critical realism of protest against political corruption and economic graft. Instead, they grounded their hopes upon a return to the earlier democratic faith that the individual consciousness contained the will and strength to bring about necessary reforms in society. In short, the Victorian orthodoxy was conservative in temper, Christian in spirit, and humanitarian in outlook. It turned away from militant and outward means to reform, and, sustained by the strong infusion of mid-century idealism, it looked to the natural endowments of the democratic man to bring about the American dream. It is inaccurate to regard this effort as a genteel escape or a priestly withdrawal into the academy and drawing room. More sympathetically seen, it was a belief that the frictions of society might be assuaged by a literature which, without sacrificing the authenticity of the newer analytical methods and contemporary themes, could still maintain inherited standards of ethical and aesthetic idealism. During the twenty years we have been considering, the literary pendulum swung back and forth between the ideals of "romance" and those of "realism," and the values which emerged from this controversy may be discovered in the antithetical and reinforcing counterpoint between the two.

There were various literary "realisms." In one meaning, the word was associated with the novel as opposed to the "romance." In another, it signified realism of the commonplace and "poor real life" which Howells found so precious. The realism of contemporary life found expression in the work of De Forest, Howells, and James. Anti-romanticism was still another form of realism, and Henry James became the master of transposed melodrama. Victorian realism, when broadly defined, contained something of all these attitudes and points of view. There remains to be accounted for in the literary climate of the Seventies and Eighties another form of realism—the realism of native humor and local color. The frontier thesis as applied to literary history, puts this tradition in a conspicuous place in the growth of a realistic literature. Its roots lie far back in the nineteenth century, but in the early work of Mark Twain it became something more than dialect humor and newspaper eccentricity. It achieved the status of a genuine American style.

Although Mark Twain's best books have achieved the rank of greatness in American and world literature, it is difficult to define his precise relationship to the pattern of realism as we have attempted to portray it. In his own way Mark Twain was both a realist and a Victorian, yet his literary method and his highly original personality place him somehow outside of the tradition of Victorian literary realism. His best books depicted an earlier, rural America. His angle of vision was reminiscent, nostalgic, retrospective. His genius was unique and his method autobiographical. He was uninterested in aesthetic ideas or the art of fiction. Analysis and psychological character delineation were not in his repertoire. He did not carry over, as did James and Howells, a strong heritage of transcendental idealism. Criticism, metaphysics, philosophy, and social criticism were outside the circle of his interests which he once described as "history, biography, travels, curious facts, strange happenings, and science."[1] He once told Howells that he could not stand George Eliot, Hawthorne "and all those people." He detested Jane Austen and preferred to be damned to John Bunyan's heaven than be forced to read *The Bostonians*. Scott and Cooper were not literary models to be followed, but convenient targets for burlesque. In contemporary fiction he read only the novels of

Howells for enjoyment, more out of his strong friendship and attachment than from any special interest in realistic fiction. His own books he wrote, he once said, with one eye on the lecture platform and the other on sales.[2]

Still, Mark Twain's contribution to a realistic literary attitude was important and lasting. In the 1870's it took the form of burlesquing the excesses of what he felt was an outworn romanticism. Building upon the dialect and tall-tale tradition of western humor, he wrote in *Innocents Abroad* and *Roughing It* books which were implicitly and explicitly broadsides against the serious tradition of letters. He poked fun at Benjamin Franklin's moral earnestness, parodied Scott and Coleridge, rebuked the noble savage, and slashed away at European culture and American tourists who became cathedral-hounds and culture-seekers. Together with his predecessors and contemporaries in this humor tradition, he attacked by means of colloquialism, slang, parody, buffoonery, and plain ridicule all forms of "goody-goody-ism," "flim-flam charlatanism," and "sappy inanities." By deflating the polite tradition of the East and the culture of Europe, he contributed to an amorphous but effective campaign of deflation and demonstrated in riotous terms the *un*importance of being earnest. Along with John Phoenix, Artemus Ward, G. W. Harris, Bill Nye, John Hay, and others, Mark Twain sought to expose artifice, sentiment, and pretentiousness and thus helped clear the ground for others to articulate a more positive program for realism.

But in more constructive ways Mark Twain contributed to the literary climate of realism during the Seventies and Eighties. His humor was in itself a protest against what he once called "a sad false delicacy" which had emasculated literature and feminized culture. If his humor more often ran to travesty, burlesque, or ribaldry, he could also employ satire as a weapon of the realist, and he once drew a distinction between travesty, which left the reader a "joked and defrauded victim," and satire which had as its aim the advancement of knowledge or wisdom. In his special province of western life, Mark Twain sought for veracious coloring and authentic tones. He was offended, for instance, when Bret Harte referred in one of his early stories to "twilight" along the Pacific slope, remarking that there was no such phenomenon. Commenting upon a painting by Bierstadt, he pronounced the peaks and valleys correct, but objected that the "atmosphere" in the picture was "imported." Nothing like it, he noted, "was ever seen in California." Making a comment on E. W. Howe's *The Story of a Country Town*, he said it was "vivid and true. I know for I have seen and lived it all." He distrusted the meretricious wherever he found it. Summing up his literary creed late in life, he felt that he had experienced much that had equipped him for the building of novels. "I surely have the equipment," he said, "and a wide culture and all of it real, none of it artificial, for I don't know anything about books."

The association of realism with local color and especially with the western story was Twain's one positive contribution to theoretical criticism of the novel. Looking at his own career in retrospect he concluded that it was only through years of "unconscious absorption" that a writer can report the soul of a nation—its very life and speech and thought. But even this is too broad a scope for a single novelist. He must not try to generalize a nation.

> No, he lays before you the ways and speech and life of a few people grouped in a certain place—his own place—and that is one book. In time he and his brethren will report to you the life and the people of the whole nation.[3]

Every section and racial type can provide subject matter for the writer and not until "a thousand able novels have been written," can you have "the soul of the people, the life of the people, the speech of the people; and not anywhere else can these be had."[4] Thus Mark Twain defined the place and function of local color. In his cooperative approach to the American novel he was characteristically western. He agreed with a fellow westerner, Eggleston, who said in 1892 discussing the regional movement and its achievement in Americanizing our literature:

> The taking up of life in this regional way has made our literature really national by the only process possible. . . . 'The great American novel' for which prophetic critics yearned so fondly twenty years ago, is appearing in sections.[5]

Hamlin Garland likewise found localism to be the key to the realistic trend and saw the work of Cable, Joel Chandler Harris, Eggleston, Jewett, Wilkins, and Harte as "varying phases of the same movement which is to give us at last a really vital and original literature."[6] The local color movement seemed to Garland a signal for "the advance of the democratization of literature."[7]

In a different perspective, however, Mark Twain's relation to realism in the 1880's paralleled that of Howells and brought him closer to the pattern of Victorian realism as we have indicated it. Like Howells, he reached his artistic peak in the early and middle Eighties when *Life on the Mississippi* and *Huckleberry Finn* were published. In 1883 he wrote to Howells that he was piling up manuscript rapidly for the new book: "I'm booming these days—got health and spirits to waste—got an overplus."[8] The humor of *Innocents Abroad* and *Roughing It* was the rollicking gayety and coarse laughter of the romantic West. Although the satire of *The Gilded Age* was sharp at times it was without rancor; but in the Nineties his humor had turned to bitterness and misanthropic scorn in *The Mysterious Stranger* and *What Is Man?* Somewhere between *Tom*

Sawyer (1876) and *A Connecticut Yankee* (1889) Clemens achieved a period of adjustment and equilibrium among the variable and quixotic elements of his literary personality. It was not the middle zone of romance and realism which Howells sought, nor the "ideal real" of Henry James, but rather the coming to terms in middle life with the psychic conflict between his youthful enthusiasm and the cynicism of age. Passages of reminiscence in *Life on the Mississippi* contained this note of ripeness. But in *Huckleberry Finn* the mood was sustained throughout in a stronger handling of plot structure, social history, symbolism and skillful characterization. The nice adjustment of point of view, for instance, between the realist Huck and the romantic Tom show the two sides of Twain's nature in happy combination. This greater depth and harmony of mood indicates his work at its best. *Life on the Mississippi* and *Huckleberry Finn* are fundamentally great regional portraits. In them the romancer and the poet, the humorist and the cynic, the realist and the satirist, and the rich narrator of the American past were all suffused by the imaginative strength of his style. It was in the early Eighties that he found the most successful expression for his theories of localism, his keen ear for dialect, his nostalgia, and his autobiographical understanding of people and scenes along the Mississippi. In these ways he made significant contributions to the development of literary realism.

Much importance has been attached to the incident by which *Huckleberry Finn* was banned as an indecent book by the Concord Library Association. *The Springfield Republican* called it "trashy and vicious," its moral level low, and Clemens's sense of propriety unreliable, as in the notorious speech at the *Atlantic* dinner.[9] But the few authentic voices of criticism which were heard in review of the book recognized at once its superior artistry. T. S. Perry in the *Century* praised the humor, descriptive power, and characterization. He called Huck "its immortal hero," and a young scapegrace whose "undying fertility of invention, his courage, his manliness in every trial, are an incarnation of the better side of the ruffianism that is one result of the independence of Americans." He likewise admired its "autobiographical form" which gave the book a unity of narration superior to the more fragmentary *Tom Sawyer.* In the Grangerford-Shepherdson feud, Perry saw the method of Twain at its best. Here was "objectivity" and truth, one of the marks of realism in its mature form. The account is told as it appears to "a semi-civilized boy of fourteen, without the slightest condemnation or surprise."

> That is the way a story is best told, by telling it, and letting it go to the reader unaccompanied by signposts or directions how he shall understand it and profit by it. Life teaches its lessons by implication, not by didactic preaching; and literature is at its best when it is an imitation of life and not an excuse for instruction.[10]

Brander Matthews, one of the so-called "genteel" critics, likewise recognized that *Huckleberry Finn* was more than the work of a funny man. In an article entitled "Mark Twain's Best Story" he wrote: "that Mark Twain is a literary artist of a very high order all who have considered his later writings critically cannot but confess." Matthews acknowledged the "marvelous" skill of characterization and, like Perry, complimented him upon his objectivity and refusal to moralize. He thought the scene between Colonel Sherburn and the mob "one of the most vigorous bits of writing Mark Twain has done." On the subject of the portrayal of Huck, Matthews anticipated and refuted the expected genteel criticism of the novel: "Old maids of either sex will wholly fail to understand him, or to like him, or to see his significance and his value." Huck and Jim were both true to life, he thought, and concluded:

> That Mr. Clemens draws from life, and yet lifts his work from the domain of the photograph to the region of art, is evident to anyone who will give his writing the attention it deserves.[11]

There is, indeed, ample evidence that the vituperation and abuse of Mark Twain's vulgarity and buffoonery which greeted many of his books is hardly a fair representation of the criticism which the "Age of Decorum" rendered him. Setting aside comments by European critics such as those of Andrew Lang and Kipling, who ranked him with Cervantes, one recalls Howells's high opinion of his work and Joel Chandler Harris's defense of the wholesomeness of *Huckleberry Finn*.[12] J. G. Huneker followed Perry and Matthews in the serious view of his work. He wrote in 1899:

> Mr. Clemens is one of the most original writers America has produced and more of an artist than is generally believed. Being a humorous soul the public was slow to recognize his power in other fields. I pin my faith to 'Huckleberry Finn.' For me it is the great American novel, even if it is written for boys.[13]

Mark Twain was in many respects typical of the age whose name he coined. He was typical of its puzzling contradictions and disharmonies. He shared with Colonel Sellers dreams of great wealth. Money was his theme, but unlike Horatio Alger his endings were often bitter and disillusioning. He was defensive about art, Europe, age, tradition, culture, and bookishness. Yet he was one of the most widely travelled of his contemporaries. Full of ribaldry and profanity, he was a sensitive writer and one of the most "exquisite" of men. Travel made him the more conscious of his own limitations and threw him back upon the main affirmation of his life—a democratic faith in the value and dignity of the individual. His realism was a special blend, born of experience and frontier skepticism, schooled by such hard disciplines as the printing office of a newspaper or the pilot house of a Mississippi steamboat. But in his best books of the middle 1880's he found a successful harmony in his strain of idealism and his love of authentic reporting and local color. In his own way he portrayed a passing America with accuracy and with skill. If it was not the contemporary world of the eastern seaboard or the international set, it was a significant phase of the American experience which has remained in myth and imagination and belonged as much to the period as did the more serious fiction of James and Howells and De Forest.

After 1885 it became increasingly difficult for writers and thoughtful Americans to maintain a moderate attitude toward social problems. A change began to manifest itself in many areas of the national life which marked the decline of the earlier form of realism and transformed the ideas and tastes which we have called "Victorian." The intensification of conflicts between labor and capital, the alarming increase in strikes, the emotional response to the Haymarket "anarchists," and the tendency once more to take sides in social disputes brought about a period during the late 1880's and early 1890's which can be called "The Years of Protest." Utopian and socialistic solutions like Edward Bellamy's *Looking Backward* caught the popular fancy and liberals like Lawrence Gronlund, Richard T. Ely, and Jacob Riis proposed remedies and pointed out the seriousness of the disparities between "haves" and "have-nots." In fiction the change in Howells's novels was symptomatic of the socio-economic trend of the late Eighties. In his vigorous championing of liberal causes, he became the guide and inspiration for a group of younger writers whose interests had been formed by the Populist movement and the mood of protest. But the moderate realism of Howells's best books of the mid-Eighties was not equalled in his reform novels. The plots moved more slowly, interrupted by long sermonic passages, and the characters became symbols of class distinctions. Only *A Hazard of New Fortunes* among his books of this period achieved something of the balance between a social thesis and a psychological study of character. More and more he allowed his sympathy for social betterment to color his reading of human nature.

By 1890 Henry James had lost touch with the American scene as a subject for fiction and turned to London theater for new worlds to conquer. Mark Twain, beset by personal trials and financial reverses, had grown embittered by "the damned human race" and, despite desperate efforts to recover the mood of *Huckleberry Finn*, he was not able to achieve anything like its harmony of tone and style. The critical battles in the journals between the adherents of "realism" and those of "romance" continued, but the debates grew shrill and acrimonious and produced little of the blending that had marked the earlier period. A younger generation of novelists and critics began to explore different areas of the national experience in an atmosphere which could less and less be termed "Victorian." The essential tone and quality of the earlier realism had changed and the literary world had begun to search for another and greatly altered concept of reality.

NOTES

I. GILT AND INNOCENCE: IDOLS OF THE TRIBE

1. In his *Novum Organum*, Part II, Bacon discussed "True Directions Concerning the Interpretation of Nature" in a series of "Aphorisms" which described the "idols and false notions which are now in possession of the human understanding, and have taken deep root therein."

2. Thomas Beer, *The Mauve Decade* (New York, 1926), ch. 1.

3. Lewis Mumford, *The Brown Decades, A Study of the Arts in America, 1865-1885* (New York, 1931) portrayed the social character of the period in these terms, applying the color "brown" to the industrial and materialistic tone of the time. Mumford recognized, however, more clearly than most critics of the 1920's and 1930's, the positive accomplishments of the age. "It is time," he wrote, "that we ceased to be dominated by the negative aspects of the Brown Decades." Furthermore, he realized that the earlier age had become a mirror for his own time and saw points of resemblance between the Brown Decades and "our own post-war difficulties" so that "one has the sense of following our own history, told in a slightly foreign language." Cf. ch. 1 *passim*.

4. Godkin's essays defining "chromo-civilization" appeared in the *Nation*, volumes XIX and XXII for September 24, 1874, and June 29, 1876.

5. Ch. III entitled "The Gilded Age," pp. 51-72, contains Brooks's interpretation of both the period and the novel. He described the latter as "artistically, almost an unqualified failure," and the period as one of effeminacy and general cultural sterility in its creative life.

6. Beard's reading of the period is found in *The Rise of American Civilization* (1930), volume II, ch. XXV. His colorful style brought convincingly together many of the representative views of the Twenties toward the Victorian decades, but it should be balanced by more judicious and objective studies such as Merle Curti's *The Growth of American Thought*, pp. 505 ff.

7. Hicks's language seems excessive in its description of the conditions reflected in Mark Twain's novel as a "debauch," and the "demoralization of a nation," *The Great Tradition* (1935), pp. 69 ff. A valuable antidote to the interpretations of Van Wyck Brooks and Granville Hicks on the meaning of the novel, *The Gilded Age*, is in W. F. Taylor, *The Economic Novel in America* (1942), p. 126. Taylor sees the principal force for evil in the book as a "Spirit of Speculation" of which the main characters are victims, not instigators. For an opinion that Colonel Sellers was not intended as a caricature-portrait of the Jay Cooke or Jay Gould type of industrial baron see F. W. Chapman, "The Germ of a Book," *Atlantic Monthly*, volume CL (December, 1932), p. 720.

8. Parrington's familiar and much-quoted description of the post-Civil

War decade is included in his third volume *The Beginnings of Critical Realism* (New York, 1930). Parts I and II of Book One are entitled "The Gilded Age" and "The Culture of the Seventies." See esp. pp. 10-17 and 48-69.

9. Weber's term "The Protestant Ethic" has been used by recent sociologists to describe the period of social Darwinism and Horatio Alger as one of business enterprise in the older, individualistic meaning of the term. David Riesman, *The Lonely Crowd* (1953), pp. 32 ff. equates the term "inner direction" with that of the "protestant ethic." Similarly, in *The Organization Man*, ch. II, W. H. Whyte, Jr. discusses the "Decline of the Protestant Ethic" and compares it with the "organization ethic" of the 1950's.

10. *Winds of Doctrine* (New York, 1913), pp. 187-88.

11. See esp. ch. 1, pp. 10-11, 13 ff., and 27 ff. Brooks's succeeding studies of the two major writers of the period, *The Ordeal of Mark Twain* (1920) and *The Pilgrimage of Henry James* (1925), though still regarded as brilliantly written, now seem dated by their "theses" and by the over-emphasis upon the analogy between "The Gilded Age" and the postwar Twenties. Their tone is one of tragic drama in which the major figures, Twain and James, were defeated by the corroding forces of an acquisitive society and forced either to surrender to its principles (Twain) or flee the country (James). Both books underrated the stature of the two authors and overstressed the corruptive effects of the period.

12. "The Beginnings of Critical Realism in America, 1860-1920" (New York, 1930), p. 237. Parrington does not make clear his chronology, apparently directing his comment to the 1890's almost more than the 1870's. For example, he cites the reaction to Crane's *Maggie* (1894) and Hardy's *Jude the Obscure* (1895) as illustrating the prudery and persistent romanticism of the Seventies and Eighties.

13. *The Liberation of American Literature* (New York, 1932), p. 87. Calverton's attack on reticence in literature, like that of all the anti-genteel critics, failed to take account of the fact that there are strong literary uses of gentility. Such qualities as restraint, indirection, and ambiguity brought, for example, much subdued power to the writing of Henry James.

14. *Forces in American Criticism, A Study in the History of American Literary Thought* (New York, 1939), pp. 20-21, 242-3, and *passim.*

15. Erik Axel Karlfeldt, *Why Sinclair Lewis Got the Nobel Prize* (Stockholm, 1930), pp. 16-23. For a discussion of Lewis's address see M. Cowley, *After the Genteel Tradition* (New York, 1936), pp. 9-16.

16. A good expression of this principle was in the essay, "The Critic and American Life" (*Forum*, 1928) where Babbitt, provoked by what he regarded as the irresponsibility of "Menckenism" wrote: "It may be that the only way to escape from the unduly complacent cynicism of Mr. Mencken and his school is to affirm once more the truths of the inner life. In that case it would seem desireable to disengage, so far as possible, the principle of control on which the inner life finally depends from mere creeds and traditions and assert it as a psychological fact."

17. T. S. Eliot, *Selected Essays, 1917-1932* (New York, 1932), p. 388. The essay was a reply to Babbitt's and originally appeared in the *Forum* for July, 1928. Eliot, seeking some larger authoritarianism, objected to the individualistic doctrine of Babbitt's inner check, as "pretty precarious."

18. Pp. 22-23.

19. See esp. pp. 43, 84-85, and 238 ff.

20. *After the Genteel Tradition* (New York, 1936), pp. 17-23.

21. Ch. XII, "The Industrial Mind," pp. 255 ff. Parkes drew a connection

between the industrial mind and the "genteel tradition" and regarded the intellectual movements of the Eighties and Nineties, such as pragmatism, instrumentalism, and functionalism in art, as serving only to expose illusions, not as setting forth new affirmations.

22. In an address in 1922 at St. Andrews, Scotland.

23. From a letter in the Paris *Temps* cited by Henry James. See *Henry James, Parisian Sketches,* ed. by Edel and Lind (New York, 1957), p. 182. Renan's reference was made at the time of the death of George Sand, whose life and career he considered as typical of the 19th century.

24. P. 295. Unfortunately Brooks did not develop this idea. It was stated as an opinion of the pseudonymous critic, Oliver Allston.

II. THE SEVENTIES: A DECADE OF HESITATION AND LITERARY EXPERIMENT

1. The Writings of Mark Twain, Author's National Edition, X, "The Gilded Age," volume 1, p. 176.

2. *New England: Indian Summer* (New York, 1940), pp. 189, 200.

3. *Walt Whitman, An American* (New York, 1943), p. 210.

4. *Miss Ravenel's Conversion from Secession to Loyalty* (New York, 1939), p. 56.

5. *Trumpets of Jubilee* (New York, 1927), p. 197.

6. *Ibid.,* p. 141.

7. *What the Social Classes Owe Each Other* (New York, 1883), p. 101.

8. *Notes of a Son and Brother* (New York, 1914), p. 305.

9. *From Opitz to Lessing* (Boston, 1885), pp. 8-9.

10. *Life in Letters of William Dean Howells,* ed. Mildred Howells (New York, 1928), I, p. 172.

11. *Victorian Poets* (New York, 1877), p. 13.

12. *The Education of Henry Adams* (New York, 1931), Modern Library Edition, p. 225.

13. *Ibid.*

14. *The Emergence of Modern America, 1865-1878* (New York, 1927), p. 247.

15. *Atlantic Monthly,* XXV (Jan., 1870), p. 63.

16. *North American Review,* CXV (Oct., 1872), p. 368.

17. F. O. Matthiessen, *Henry James: The Major Phase* (New York, 1944), p. 185.

18. *Life in Letters,* I, p. 233.

19. *North American Review,* CII (April, 1866), p. 591.

20. *Atlantic Monthly,* XXV (Feb., 1875), p. 238.

21. *Atlantic Monthly,* XLI (Jan., 1878), p. 132.

22. *Scribner's Monthly,* IX (Nov., 1874), p. 33.

23. *North American Review,* CXV (Oct., 1872), p. 366.

1. JOHN W. DE FOREST: THE PANORAMIC NOVEL OF REALISM

1. *Atlantic Monthly,* XXXIV (Aug., 1874), p. 230.

2. *Harper's New Monthly Magazine,* XXXV (Aug., 1867), p. 401.

3. *Atlantic Monthly,* XXIX (March, 1872), p. 365.

4. *A Volunteer's Adventures,* ed. J. H. Croushore (New Haven, 1946) and *A Union Officer in the Reconstruction,* ed. J. H. Croushore and D. M. Potter (New Haven, 1948).

5. "A Checklist of the Writings of John William De Forest (1826-1906)" by E. R. Hagemann, *Papers of the Bibliographical Society of the University of Virginia* (1956).

6. See Clara F. McIntyre, "J. W. De Forest, Pioneer Realist," *University of Wyoming Publications*, IX (1942), pp. 1-13, and Thomas F. O'Donnell, "De Forest, Van Petten, and Stephen Crane," *American Literature*, XXVII (Jan., 1956), pp. 578-80. The latter establishes Crane's indebtedness to De Forest's battle scenes through his history teacher who was one of De Forest's comrades-in-arms during several of the campaigns.

7. *Atlantic Monthly*, XX (July, 1867), p. 120.

8. *Literary History of the United States*, II (New York, 1948), p. 882.

9. *Atlantic Monthly*, XXIX (March, 1872), p. 364.

10. In his Introduction to a 1955 edition of *Miss Ravenel's Conversion*, Gordon Haight, writing of Lillie's marriage to Carter, made the suggestion that Howells borrowed De Forest's theme "of a fine young girl who against her father's advice married a man of weak character and lived to regret it." He added that Howells "refined it to the taste of genteel readers." There is a certain parallel between the two, but the Armitage-Beaumont marriage contains similar elements and Howells may well have had both couples in mind. It was also a conventionally Victorian situation which need not have required a specific source.

11. *Heroines of Fiction* (New York, 1901), II, pp. 153, 162.

12. *Atlantic Monthly*, XXIX (March, 1872), pp. 364-5. Howells added that both Randolph Armitage and Mrs. Chester were characters "more entertaining to middle life"—a mark of his excessive sensitiveness toward the young reader.

13. *Heroines of Fiction*, II, p. 153.

14. Clarence Gordon, "Mr. De Forest's Novels," *Atlantic Monthly*, XXXII (Nov., 1873), p. 614.

15. See *A Volunteer's Adventures, A Union Captain's Record of the Civil War*, ed. J. H. Croushore (New Haven, 1946), p. 13.

16. *Atlantic Monthly*, XXX (Dec., 1872), pp. 676-684.

17. Drawn from accounts of the *Credit Mobilier* affair in Don C. Seitz, *The Dreadful Decade, 1869-1879* (Indianapolis, 1926), ch. III; Allan Nevins, *The Emergence of Modern America* (New York, 1927), ch. VII; and Claude Bowers, *The Tragic Era* (New York, 1929), ch. XIX.

18. *Atlantic Monthly*, XXXV (Feb., 1875), p. 238.

19. *Nation*, XIX (Dec. 13, 1874), p. 442.

20. *New England: Indian Summer, 1865-1915* (New York, 1940), pp. 242-3.

21. In parallel passages Gordon Haight compares De Forest's "true realism" with Crane's "somewhat decadent impressionism." The former describes things "as they are," while everything that Crane describes "looks like something else." Haight prefers De Forest's simplicity and directness to the melodramatic effects of Crane. He also states: "There is no doubt that Crane knew De Forest's battle scenes." See Introd., *Miss Ravenel's Conversion from Secession to Loyalty* (New York, 1955), pp. xiv-xvii.

22. Ms. letter to Howells, *ibid.*, p. xviii.

23. Ms. letter, *ibid.*, p. vii.

24. Letter to Howells partially reprinted in "The Editor's Study," *Harper's New Monthly Magazine*, LXXIV (May, 1887), p. 987.

2. WILLIAM DEAN HOWELLS: THE ROMANCE OF REAL LIFE

1. *Their Wedding Journey* (Boston, 1872), pp. 86-87, 106.
2. *Atlantic Monthly*, XL (Nov., 1877), pp. 601-3. Howells later called Goldoni "the first of the realists" who at the same time observed "the proprieties" in the "almost English, almost American" sense (*My Literary Passions*, pp. 208-11).
3. *The Writings of George Eliot* (New York, 1907), III, ch. XVII, 257-8. The role of George Eliot in the early growth of realism in American fiction can scarcely be overemphasized. She became a champion of the newer psychological school of characterization without espousing French license and naturalistic methods. Henry James, almost alone among the many American writers who discussed her work, demurred at her didactic tone. James's essay in *French Poets and Novelists* (1878) was one of the best on her work. But many other American critics discussed it in detail. See below ch. 6, n. 7.
4. *Atlantic Monthly*, XXVIII (Apr., 1870).
5. See Howells's review of *Liza*, *Atlantic Monthly*, XXXI (Feb., 1873), p. 239. American realists learned dramatic objectivity from Turgenev and were encouraged in their preference for character representation of a few people by his example. Howells's scholarly friend, T. S. Perry, had written on the Russian novelist in the *Atlantic Monthly* (May, 1874), pp. 572-4, pointing out that the power of Turgenev's work lay in a deep insight into his fellow men and in his skill at placing them before the reader with detachment and objectivity. In the mid-Seventies Turgenev's influence began to be widely recognized. G. P. Lathrop praised his work highly in the *Atlantic Monthly* (Sept., 1874). Henry James wrote two essays on him in the same decade, the best one in *French Poets and Novelists*. See Royal A. Gettmann, *Turgenev in England and America* (Urbana, Ill., 1941), which discusses the reception of his work by American critics.
6. *Life in Letters of William Dean Howells*, ed. by Mildred Howells (New York, 1928), I, p. 233.
7. *Atlantic Monthly*, XXXIV (Nov., 1874), p. 624.
8. *Ibid.*, XXXV (Apr., 1875), p. 492.
9. *Life in Letters of William Dean Howells*, I, p. 175.
10. *Atlantic Monthly*, XLIV (Aug., 1879), p. 265.
11. *Ibid.*, XLV (Feb., 1880), p. 283.
12. *Century Magazine*, XXV (Nov., 1882), p. 27.
13. *Century Magazine*, XXVIII (Aug., 1884), p. 633.
14. *Nation*, XXXI (July 15, 1880), p. 50.
15. *Letters of Emily Dickinson*, ed. by Mabel L. Todd (Boston, 1894), pp. 11, 329.
16. *Nation*, XXVIII (March 20, 1879), p. 205.
17. *Mark Twain's Letters*, ed. by A. B. Paine (New York, 1917), pp. 11, 455.
18. *Nation*, XX (Jan. 7, 1875), pp. 12-13.
19. "William Dean Howells," *Century Magazine*, XXIII (March, 1882), p. 683.
20. Everett Carter, "The Palpitating Divan," *College English*, XI (May, 1950), p. lxxx n.
21. *Nation*, XVI (June 12, 1873), p. 405.
22. *Century Magazine*, XXXIII (March, 1882), p. 682.
23. *North American Review*, CXX (Jan., 1875), p. 212.
24. *Ibid.*, p. 211.

25. See his letter to Charles Eliot Norton: "If I had been perfectly my own master . . . the story would have ended with Don Ippolito's rejection." Yet he prolonged the story to the conventional ending with the marriage of Ferris and Florida Vervain—in deference to "others." *Life in Letters of William Dean Howells*, I, p. 198. See also C. M. and R. Kirk, *William Dean Howells* (New York, 1950), p. lxxx.

26. *Atlantic Monthly*, XXXIV (Nov., 1874), p. 624.

27. *My Literary Passions* (New York, 1895), p. 77.

28. *Life in Letters of William Dean Howells*, I, p. 175.

29. *Atlantic Monthly*, XLIV (Aug., 1879), p. 265.

30. *Ibid.*, XLV (Feb., 1880), p. 283.

31. *Nation*, XXXI (July 15, 1880), p. 50.

32. *Prejudices, First Series* (New York, 1919), pp. 53, 56.

3. HENRY JAMES: AESTHETIC THEORIES AND CRITICAL METHODS

1. Studies of James's early critical writing include Morris Roberts, *Henry James's Criticism* (Cambridge, Mass., 1929), a detailed and balanced account of the subject; Cornelia Pulsifer Kelley, "The Early Development of Henry James," *University of Illinois Studies in Language and Literature*, XV (Urbana, 1930), a study of the criticism and its influence upon the growth of James as a novelist; Laurence Barrett, "Young Henry James, Critic," *American Literature* (Jan., 1949); René Wellek, "Henry James's Literary Theory and Criticism," *American Literature* (Nov., 1958). There are many books and articles on James which touch aspects of the subject including my essay on the literary theory of the 1870's and 1880's in *The Development of American Literary Criticism*, ed. F. Stovall (Chapel Hill, N.C., 1955).

2. *The Selected Letters of Henry James*, ed. Leon Edel (New York, 1960), pp. 19-20.

3. "A French Critic," *Nation* (Oct. 12, 1865). Reprinted in *Notes and Reviews by Henry James*, ed. P. de Chaignon La Rose (Cambridge, Mass., 1921), p. 105.

4. *Henry James's Criticism*, Preface.

5. *Library Table*, IV (March 30, 1878), p. 197.

6. "Recent Literature," *Atlantic Monthly*, XLII (July, 1878), pp. 118-9.

7. *Ibid.* Characteristic of Howells's tendency to protect the interests of propriety and decorum is his comment on James's "not altogether pleasant jocularity in the treatment of those dubious relations between men and women which the themes selected naturally involve."

8. *Little Review* (Aug., 1918). Reprinted in *The Question of Henry James*, ed. F. W. Dupee (New York, 1945), pp. 108-119. See esp. pp. 109-110.

9. "Henry James's Literary Theory and Criticism," *American Literature* (Nov., 1958), p. 320.

10. *Literary Reviews and Essays by Henry James*, ed. A. Mordell (New York, 1957), p. 15.

11. "The Novels of George Eliot," *Atlantic Monthly* (1866). Reprinted in *Views and Reviews by Henry James*, ed. L. Phillips (Boston, 1908), pp. 1-37.

12. *Notes and Reviews by Henry James*, p. 104.

13. *Henry James's Criticism*, pp. 45-46.

14. *The North American Review*, C (Jan., 1865), p. 272. See also *Notes and Reviews*, ed. La Rose, p. 23. Balzac was for James at this period the model of realism in fiction. He was, James wrote, "literally real." Furthermore, his

work was distinguished from popular American fiction because he conceived his characters fully before writing. "His story exists before it is told; it stands complete before his mind's eye."

15. *Ibid.*

16. The quotations are from James's reviews of Harriet Prescott's *Azarian* (*North American Review*, Jan., 1865), Trollope's *Miss Mackenzie* (*Nation*, July 13, 1865), and De Forest's *Honest John Vane* (*Nation*, Dec. 31, 1874). Reprinted in La Rose and Mordell (*supra*).

17. *Atlantic Monthly*, XVIII (Oct., 1866), p. 48. Reprinted in *Views and Reviews by Henry James*, ed. Leroy Phillips (Boston, 1908), pp. 4-5.

18. *Notes and Reviews by Henry James*, p. 102. Originally in the *Nation* (Oct. 12, 1865).

19. *French Poets and Novelists* (New York, 1878), p. 113. Originally in the *Galaxy* (Dec., 1875), pp. 814-36.

20. *Ibid.*, p. 318.

21. See note 3, *supra*.

22. "Robert Louis Stevenson," *Partial Portraits* (London and New York, 1888), p. 138. James described the method of critical portraiture again in this essay as "the effort to seize a literary character and transfer it to the canvas of the critic."

23. *The Notebooks of Henry James*, ed. F. O. Matthiessen and K. Murdock (New York, 1947), pp. 24-25. He had come back to New York after an extended trip to Europe, mostly in Italy, to "try" his native country once more "thinking it my duty to attempt to live at home . . . and not take for granted too much that Europe alone was possible."

24. "Ivan Turgenieff," *French Poets and Novelists*, p. 317.

25. *Partial Portraits* (New York, 1888), p. 296. Originally in the *Atlantic Monthly* (Jan., 1884).

26. "Gustave Flaubert," *French Poets and Novelists* (London and New York, 1893), p. 201. Originally in the *Galaxy* (Feb., 1876).

27. *The James Family*, ed. F. O. Matthiessen (New York, 1948), p. 552.

28. "James's Hawthorne," *Atlantic Monthly*, XLV (Feb., 1880), pp. 282-5.

29. *The Letters of Henry James*, ed. P. Lubbock (New York, 1920), I, pp. 72-73.

30. *Nation*, XXX (Jan. 29, 1880), pp. 80-81.

31. *Hawthorne* (New York, 1879), p. 126.

32. *French Poets and Novelists* (New York and London, 1893), p. 210.

33. "The Next Time," *Embarrassements* (New York and London, 1896), p. 197.

34. *The Crack-Up*, ed. Edmund Wilson (New York, 1956), p. 69.

35. The phrase is used in a letter of Keats on December 21, 1817. See the discussion in Lionel Trilling, "Introduction" to *The Selected Letters of John Keats* (New York, 1951).

4. JAMES'S STUDIO STORIES: THE DISINHERITED OF ART

1. Preface, *The Novels and Tales of Henry James* (New York, 1908), XIII, p. xx.

2. *The Destructive Element* (Philadelphia, 1953), p. 29.

3. Preface, New York edition, XIII, p. xviii.

4. *Ibid.*

5. *The James Family*, ed. F. O. Matthiessen (New York, 1948), p. 289. In his Notebook for November, 1881, he wrote that his experience in Italy, in

the early 1870's, had given him "some very discouraged hours" and "lovely and desireable though it was" it did not "seem as a permanent residence, to lead to anything." *Notebooks of Henry James* (New York, 1947), p. 24.

6. *The James Family*, p. 289.

7. Cornelia P. Kelley, "The Early Development of Henry James," *University of Illinois Studies in Language and Literature* (Urbana, 1930), pp. 150-1.

8. *The Letters of Henry James*, ed. P. Lubbock (New York, 1920), I, p. 21.

9. *The James Family*, p. 122.

10. *A Small Boy and Others* (New York, 1913), p. 263.

11. *Notes of a Son and Brother* (New York, 1914), p. 97. See the discussion of James's experience of the arts in Edwin T. Bowden's *The Themes of Henry James* (New Haven, 1956), pp. 1-22.

12. "Miss Prescott's *Azarian*," *North American Review*, C (Jan., 1865), p. 275. Almost twenty years later James echoed this statement in "The Art of Fiction" where he said: "The analogy between the art of the painter and the art of the novelist is, so far as I am able to see, complete."

13. "The Art of Fiction," *Partial Portraits* (New York, 1888), p. 392.

14. *The Method of Henry James* (Philadelphia, 1954), p. 26.

15. "Introduction," *Roderick Hudson*, ed. Leon Edel (New York, 1960), p. xiii.

16. *Scribner's Magazine*, XI (Feb., 1876), pp. 588-9.

17. G. P. Lathrop, *Atlantic Monthly*, XXXVII (Feb., 1876), pp. 237-8.

18. *The James Family*, p. 561 n.

19. *The Method of Henry James*, p. 196. Beach explained the source of this weakness in "the unhappy choice" of Rowland Mallet as narrator and the resulting division of interest between his "judicial" point of view and the "more vivid and naughty" Roderick.

20. "The Hawthorne Aspect," in *The Question of Henry James*, ed. F. W. Dupee (New York, 1945), p. 117. Eliot holds that James "too much identifies himself with Rowland, does not see through the solemnity he has created in that character."

21. *Henry James* (New York, 1951), p. 87.

22. Oscar Cargill, *The Novels of Henry James* (New York, 1961), pp. 27-28 has discussed the origins of the split-personality theory of the novel and modifies the interpretations of its principal exponents. James, he says, "kept himself wholly outside" of his two male characters.

23. Richard Poirier, *The Comic Sense of Henry James* (New York, 1960), pp. 11 ff.

24. Dupee, *Henry James*, p. 87.

25. *Ibid.*

26. *Ibid.*

27. *The Letters of Henry James*, ed. P. Lubbock, I, p. 13.

5. JAMES AS PASSIONATE PILGRIM AND DISAPPOINTED OBSERVER

1. Howells's review appeared in the *Atlantic Monthly* (Apr., 1875), pp. 490-5. Lowell's was in the *Nation*, XX (June 24, 1875), pp. 425-7. Other notices, mostly favorable, but less discriminating, were those in *Scribner's*, IX (Apr., 1875), pp. 766-7, the *Literary World*, V (March 1, 1875), p. 157, and *Appleton's*, XIV (Feb. 13, 1875), pp. 214-5.

2. The only story separately mentioned by Lowell was "Madame de

Mauves" which he used to illustrate James's delicacy of method and the use of gradually accumulating effects, each of itself "unemphatic."

3. This was the only reference in the review to his bowdlerizing of two episodes in the story, referred to in the previous chapter in my discussion of "The Madonna of the Future."

4. See his Preface to *The Reverberator*, Volume XIII (New York edition). James remembered having taken "the adventure" of his twenty-sixth year "hard" as "A Passionate Pilgrim" sufficiently attests.

5. See *The Letters of Henry James*, ed. Percy Lubbock, I, p. 28.

6. *The James Family*, ed. F. O. Matthiessen (New York, 1948), pp. 253-4.

7. Christof Wegelin, *The Image of Europe in Henry James* (Dallas, Texas, 1958), p. 35.

8. Lubbock, *op. cit.*, I, pp. 33-35.

9. This phrase was used by a *Scribner's* reviewer speaking of the character of Longmore in "Madame de Mauves."

10. Preface to *The Reverberator, Novels and Tales of Henry James*, XIII (New York, 1907-1909).

11. *Century Magazine*, XXV (Nov., 1882), p. 27.

12. William James's advice in this instance was apropos of Henry's early story, "A Most Extraordinary Case," dealing with the psychology of a Civil War veteran, his physical breakdown and nervous illness.

13. *North American Review*, CXXVIII (Jan., 1879), p. 106.

14. The article was published in the *Literary World*, X (Nov. 22, 1879), p. 384. Reprinted in *The Question of Henry James*, ed. F. W. Dupee (New York, 1945), pp. 1-5.

15. See *The James Family*, p. 500. James's commentary here is somewhat at variance with his remarks much later in the Preface to the novel. Here he sought to justify the tragic tone of the story, and also gave his first expression to his doctrine of sacrifice. He denied being a pessimist, but added that "the interest of the subject [of *The American*] was, for me ... its exemplification of one of those insuperable difficulties which present themselves in people's lives and from which the only issue is by forfeiture—by losing something."

16. *Atlantic Monthly*, XL (July, 1877), pp. 96-97.

17. See *The Complete Plays of Henry James*, ed. Leon Edel (New York, 1949). Also, for amplification, R. A. Gettman, "Henry James's Revision of *The American*," *American Literature*, XVI (Jan., 1945), p. 292, and R. P. Falk, "Henry James and the 'Age of Innocence,'" *Nineteenth-Century Fiction* (Dec., 1952), pp. 182-6.

18. *The Complete Plays of Henry James*, p. 241.

19. *The Letters of Henry James*, ed. Lubbock, I, p. 180.

20. Preface to *The American* (New York edition), Volume II.

21. *The Image of Europe in Henry James*, p. 61.

22. See the summary of reviews of *Daisy Miller* in R. N. Foley, *Criticism in American Periodicals of the Works of Henry James, 1866-1916* (Washington, D.C., 1944), p. 19.

23. Preface to Volume XVIII (New York edition). The views expressed here may safely be taken as James's own, despite his putting them dramatically in the mouth of a woman friend with whom he is discussing the story while waiting on the water steps of a hotel on the Grand Canal in Venice.

24. *Ibid.*

25. *The Letters of Henry James*, ed. Lubbock, I, p. 66.

NOTES

6. VICTORIAN BOOKMEN AND THE NEW NOVEL

1. James's letter, dated September 14, 1879, was printed in Virginia Harlow, *Thomas Sergeant Perry: A Biography* (Durham, N.C., 1950), p. 303. Lathrop's reviews of *Roderick Hudson* and *The American* had appeared in the *Atlantic Monthly* pointing out certain defects, along with praise, for the two novels. James's irritation may have been given added pique by his sense of debt to Lathrop's earlier book on Hawthorne. "G. P. Lathrop will hate me for writing it; though I couldn't have done so without the aid (for dates and facts) of his own singularly pretentious little volume."

2. *The Letters of Henry James*, ed. P. Lubbock, I, p. 73. The reference is to Higginson's reviews of James's *The American* and other stories in the *Literary World*. Higginson's remarks were largely admiring, though he found the ending of *The American* "disappointing."

3. *Atlantic Essays* (Boston, 1871), p. 55.

4. See *These Many Years, Recollections of a New Yorker* (New York, 1917), ch. VIII, pp. 166-8. Unlike some of the American critics, Matthews had travelled abroad, and in the 1880's and 1890's he concentrated his attention on the European and American stage, writing and editing many volumes of dramatic criticism.

5. White evolved a "business man" theory to explain Shakespeare's genius. He found reason, sanity, and conscious art, rather than mysterious powers of creation, to be the sources of his superiority. His independent position in this field modified some of the more extreme Coleridgean attitudes and contributed to the growth of a more realistic approach to Shakespeare. He also wrote some rather conventional commentary on *Daisy Miller* and some of Howells's early fiction.

6. Brownell's best work was done after 1890 when he became literary advisor to *Scribner's*. In such books as *French Traits* (1889), *American Prose Masters* (1909), and *Standards* (1917) he raised the level of Victorian criticism to an art and he has been compared with Matthew Arnold as a precursor of the New Critics of the 1920's and 1930's.

7. See besides the essays of Henry James and the opinions of Howells on George Eliot (previously cited) W. C. Wilkinson, "The Literary and Ethical Quality of George Eliot's Novels," *Scribner's Monthly*, VIII (Oct., 1874), pp. 685-703; G. P. Lathrop, "The Growth of the Novel," *Atlantic Monthly*, XXXIII (June, 1874), pp. 684-97; Edward Eggleston, "George Eliot and the Novel," *Critic*, I (Jan. 29, 1881), p. 9; and G. W. Cooke, *George Eliot* (New York, 1883). Also, Lanier, *The English Novel* (New York, 1881), discussed below.

8. *Life and Letters of Edmund Clarence Stedman*, ed. by Laura Stedman and George M. Gould, 2 vols. (New York, 1910), I, p. 55.

9. *Literary Criticism in America, A Preliminary Survey* (New York, 1931), pp. 136-7.

10. *Genius and Other Essays* (New York, 1911), p. 23. Originally published in the *Princeton Review* (1886).

11. See the discussion by Willard Thorp in *The Literary History of the United States* (New York, 1948), II, pp. 817-8.

12. *Victorian Poets* (New York, 1887), p. 31.

13. *Complete Writings of Sidney Lanier*, Centennial Edition (Baltimore, 1945), II, pp. 25 n. and xxix. The manuscript in the Lanier Room at Johns Hopkins contains seven pages of notes on Blaserna's *Theory of Sound* (Lanier's *Works*, II, p. xxvi).

14. Edwin Mims, *Sidney Lanier* (Boston, 1905), p. 317.
15. Aubrey H. Starke, *Sidney Lanier: A Biographical and Critical Study* (Chapel Hill, 1933), p. 372.
16. *Complete Writings of Sidney Lanier*, II, 193-5; III, pp. 301, 317.
17. *Complete Writings*, III, p. 317.
18. *Complete Writings*, II, p. 250.
19. Compare Whitman's glorification of "great persons" in *Democratic Vistas* and elsewhere. Lanier, however, differs from the earlier individualism of Whitman and Emerson by applying the principle of evolution to justify the concept of individual differences. Like William James, he explained his belief in the value of the individual on the Darwinian grounds of spontaneous variation of species. See R. B. Perry, *The Thought and Character of William James* (Boston, 1935), I, p. 470.
20. *The English Novel and the Principle of Its Development* (New York, 1883), p. 70.
21. *Atlantic Monthly*, XXXIII (June, 1874), p. 684.
22. *Atlantic Monthly*, XXXIV (Sept., 1874), p. 323.
23. *Ibid.*, p. 321.
24. *Ibid.*, p. 323.
25. *Ibid.*, p. 321.
26. *Atlantic Monthly*, XXXIII (June, 1874), p. 684.
27. "Recollections of an Atlantic Editorship," *Atlantic Monthly*, C (Nov., 1907), pp. 596-7.
28. For biographical facts and certain interpretations, such as this one, I am indebted to Miss Harlow's biography of Perry.
29. *Atlantic Monthly*, XXXI (Jan., 1873), p. 111.
30. *Atlantic Monthly*, XXXIII (May, 1874), p. 569.
31. *Ibid.*
32. The phrases are quoted from the *New Republic* (Jan. 1, 1930), pp. 174-5 and the *New York Times* (Feb. 16, 1930) in Virginia Harlow, *Thomas Sergeant Perry*, p. 230. For Robinson's phrase, see E. A. Robinson, *Selections from the Letters of Thomas Sergeant Perry* (New York, 1929).
33. "Ivan Turgenieff," *French Poets and Novelists* (London and New York, 1893), p. 243.
34. "American Novels," *North American Review*, CXV (Oct., 1872), p. 366.
35. Harlow, *Thomas Sergeant Perry*, p. 93.

III. THE EIGHTIES: SOCIAL ADJUSTMENT AND LITERARY FULFILLMENT

1. *Grover Cleveland* (New York, 1933), p. 340.
2. *Letters of Henry Adams*, ed. by W. C. Ford (New York, 1930), I, p. 357.
3. See Ward McAllister, *Society as I Have Found It* (New York, 1890), pp. 245 ff., 350, 369, 376 and *passim*.
4. A. M. Schlesinger, *Learning How to Behave, A Historical Study of American Etiquette Books* (New York, 1947), p. 35.
5. C. J. Furness, ed., *The Genteel Female* (New York, 1931), pp. 138-51.
6. J. H. Bangs, *John Kendrick Bangs* (New York, 1941), pp. 67-68.
7. "Editor's Study," *Harper's Magazine*, LXXIX (June, 1889), p. 154.
8. *The Rise of American Civilization*, II (New York, 1930), p. 437.
9. *The American Spirit in Architecture* (New Haven, 1926), p. 166. Included as Volume XIII of *The Pageant of America*, ed. R. H. Gabriel and others.

NOTES

10. John Maass, *The Gingerbread Age, A View of Victorian America* (New York, 1957), p. 64.

11. *Ibid.*, pp. 36-37.

12. Lester Ward, *Glimpses of the Cosmos*, II, pp. 336-7. Cited in R. Hofstadter, *Social Darwinism in American Thought, 1860-1915* (Philadelphia, 1945), p. 56.

13. *Nation*, XXXVII (Oct. 11, 1883), p. 318.

14. W. F. Taylor, *The Economic Novel in America* (New York, 1936), p. 39.

15. See H. W. Schneider, *A History of American Philosophy* (New York, 1946), pp. 522-33. Also M. Curti, *The Growth of American Thought* (New York, 1943), pp. 560-1.

16. Schneider, *op. cit.*, p. 524.

17. *Character and Opinion in the United States* (New York, 1921), p. 7.

18. F. L. Mott, *A History of American Magazines, 1865-1885* (Cambridge, Mass., 1938), pp. 457 ff., 548-51.

19. *Century Magazine*, XXV (Nov., 1882), p. 29.

20. *Letters of Henry James*, ed. P. Lubbock (New York, 1920), I, p. 104.

21. William Linneman in an article "Satires of American Realism, 1880-1900," *American Literature* (March, 1962), pp. 80-93, has described this cartoon with its accompanying dialogue. Howells asks James if he is now higher than Thackeray. James replies: "Be so uncommonly kind, H-w-lls, as to let me down easy; it may be we have both got to grow." Linneman also points out that the cartoon was probably inspired by the acid comments of Ambrose Bierce in the *Wasp* for February, 1883. Bierce accused James and Howells of building up each other's reputation by publishing laudatory essays about each other in the magazines they controlled. He added that they were trying to rise above the great writers of the past by standing on each other's shoulders.

22. "Modern Fiction," *Atlantic Monthly*, LI (April, 1883), pp. 464-74.

23. "Alphonse Daudet," *Century Magazine*, XXVI (Aug., 1883), p. 506.

24. *Life on the Mississippi* (Boston, 1883), p. 470.

25. "The American Fear of Literature," *Why Sinclair Lewis Got the Nobel Prize*, ed. E. A. Karlfeldt (New York, 1930), p. 20.

1. HOWELLS: MATURITY IN FICTION

1. Cited in *A Bibliography of William Dean Howells*, eds. W. M. Gibson and George Arms (New York Public Library, 1948), pp. 29-30.

2. *Life in Letters of William Dean Howells*, 2 vols., ed. Mildred Howells (New York, 1928), I, p. 282.

3. *Century*, XXV (Nov., 1882), pp. 28-29.

4. *Century*, XXVIII (Aug., 1884), pp. 632-3.

5. *Century*, XXVIII (May, 1884), p. 153. Gibson and Arms cite Tyler Dennett, *John Hay* (New York, 1933), p. 115, as saying the review was "most probably" by Howells. The phrasing and opinions, however, make it virtually certain.

6. *Poets of America* (New York, 1887), p. 239.

7. *Victorian Poets* (New York, 1877), p. 25.

8. *The Letters of Henry Adams, 1858-1891*, ed. W. C. Ford (New York, 1930), I, p. 348.

9. *Nation*, XLI (Oct. 22, 1885), p. 347. This detail illustrates Howells's meticulousness as a historian of manners. He wrote to Mark Twain that he

178

had asked a teacher in a ladies-school how much literature her pupils learned in school. "Some go barely knowing that Shakespeare was an Englishman," was the reply which served as the basis for Howells's observation about Irene Lapham. *Mark Twain-Howells Letters*, eds. H. N. Smith and W. M. Gibson (Cambridge, Mass., 1960), II, p. 499.

10. E. H. Cady, *The Road to Realism, The Early Years of William Dean Howells* (Syracuse University Press, 1956), pp. 232-4.

11. *Andover Review*, IV (Nov., 1885), p. 426. Mabie's article is one of the most completely developed statements of the neo-transcendental critical attitude toward realism. While he praised Howells's technical skill, he proceeded to relegate all the American realists, especially Howells and James, to the perdition of the unregenerate for their denial of the larger sympathies and the imaginative qualities of older novelists and the great tradition of poetic literature. With one side of his mind Mabie says that Howells, in *The Rise of Silas Lapham*, touched upon a stage of social evolution that was "real," "vital," and "not without deep significance." On the other side, Mabie charged him with a lack of faith and some form of "mental or moral disease" in dealing with commonplace people and "trivial themes."

12. *Prejudices, First Series* (New York, 1919), pp. 53, 56.

13. George N. Bennett, *William Dean Howells, The Development of a Novelist* (Norman, Okla., 1959), p. 119.

14. The bits and pieces of which Bartley's character was constructed from Howells's experience suggest that Bret Harte, with his loose borrowings of money, fastidious appearance, and literary cleverness, may have provided the initial source. Mark Twain, half seriously, accused Howells of basing the portrait on him from the evidence of a quotation carved on the mantelpiece of Twain's home (and the Hubbards') saying, "The chief ornament of a house is the guests who frequent it," together with the facts that Twain was a journalist and drank rather steadily, like Bartley. Howells himself many years later told Brander Matthews that he drew Bartley, whom he called a "false scoundrel," from within himself. (See *Mark Twain-Howells Letters*, I, pp. 412-3.)

15. Cady, *The Road to Realism*, p. 213.

16. *Century*, XXV (Jan., 1883), pp. 463-5.

17. *Atlantic Monthly*, L (Nov., 1882), pp. 710-3.

18. A. S. Van Westrum, "Mr. Howells on Life and Love," *Lamp* (Feb., 1904), 26-31. Cited in Cady, *The Realist at War* (Syracuse University Press, 1958), p. 136.

19. According to E. H. Cady, *The Road to Realism*, pp. 48-9, Howells's earliest piece of fiction was in the Horatio Alger pattern, almost fifteen years before Alger himself wrote *Ragged Dick*. Howells's youthful fiction, "A Tale of Love and Politics, Adventures of a Printer Boy," was printed in the Ashtabula *Sentinel*, September 1, 1853. It was a tale of an orphan who saves a judge's daughter from drowning and becomes a successful newspaper man.

20. *Life in Letters of William Dean Howells*, ed. by Mildred Howells, I, p. 361.

21. *Nation*, XLI (Oct. 22, 1885), p. 347.

22. *Catholic World* (Nov., 1885).

23. "William Dean Howells," *Harper's Weekly* (June 19, 1886). Reprinted in Leon Edel, ed., *The American Essays of Henry James* (New York, 1956). See pp. 149-56 *passim*.

24. Cited in Cady, *The Road to Realism*, p. 240. The note states: "Taine quoted by John Durand to Howells, April 10, 1888 (Harvard)."

NOTES

25. "The Progressive Realism of American Fiction," *Literary and Social Silhouettes* (New York, 1894), pp. 71-2, 78.
26. "The American Novelist and his Public," (1886). Reprinted in *Literary and Social Silhouettes*, p. 49.
27. "William Dean Howells," *The Opposing Self* (New York, 1959), pp. 99, 103.

2. JAMES: THE MIDDLE YEARS

1. In the *Letters of Henry James*, ed. Lubbock, Volume I, pp. 82-89, the period in James's career from 1882 to 1888 is called "The Middle Years." For one of his most interesting statements of the ambiguous relationship he felt toward England and America, see his letter to William James, dated October 29, 1888: "I have not the least hesitation in saying that I aspire to write in such a way that it would be impossible to an outsider to say whether I am at a given moment an American writing about England or an Englishman writing about America (dealing as I do with both countries,) and so far from being ashamed of such an ambiguity I should be exceedingly proud of it, for it would be highly civilized."
2. *The Legend of the Master*, compiled by Simon Nowell-Smith (New York, 1948), pp. 1-3, contains "Partial Portraits" of James in the early and middle 1880's from which I have cited the above description of him.
3. See Lubbock, *Letters of Henry James*, I, pp. 88-89.
4. *The Portable Henry James* (New York, 1956), p. 20.
5. *The Great Tradition* (New York, 1954), p. 187.
6. *The James Family*, p. 325.
7. Lubbock, *op. cit.*, I, p. 73.
8. *The James Family*, p. 325.
9. *Washington Square* (New York, 1881), p. 116.
10. *Atlantic Monthly*, XLVII (May, 1881), p. 710.
11. *Scribner's Monthly*, XXI (March, 1881), p. 796.
12. *The Art of the Novel*, ed. R. P. Blackmur (New York, 1934), pp. 49-50.
13. See *The Portrait of a Lady*, chapter VI, where James analyzes his heroine.
14. Ch. LIII.
15. *The Notebooks of Henry James*, eds. F. O. Matthiessen and K. B. Murdock (New York, 1947), p. 18.
16. *Atlantic Monthly*, XLIX (Jan., 1882), p. 127.
17. *Nation*, XXXIV (Feb. 2, 1882), pp. 102-3.
18. *The Art of the Novel*, p. 51. This analysis of the method of *The Portrait* was after the fact. James did not conceive, while writing the novel, of the center-of-consciousness in this sense. In fact, in his Notebooks of the time he worried for fear his novel was "too exclusively psychological" and insufficiently dramatic.
19. *Hawthorne* (New York, 1879), pp. 130-1.
20. "Alphonse Daudet," *Century*, XXVI (August, 1883), p. 503. The whole discussion is of much interest for understanding James's equivocal position on the question of an author "putting people into a book." It is, James says, "what a novelist lives upon," the only restriction being that of "taste." His admiration for Daudet's realism and his close observation of actual history was made palatable for James by a "soft" quality not apparent in Flaubert, Goncourt, or Zola. "Daudet's great characteristic is this mixture of the sense of the real with the sense of the beautiful."

21. Lubbock, *Letters*, I, pp. 115-7.
22. *Henry James's Criticism* (Cambridge, Mass., 1929), p. 32.
23. *Partial Portraits* (London and New York, 1888), p. 3.
24. *Ibid.*, p. 393.
25. *Ibid.*, p. 137.
26. *Ibid.*, p. 287.
27. *Atlantic Monthly*, LXII (Oct., 1888), p. 566.
28. *The Notebooks of Henry James*, p. 51.
29. *The Art of the Novel*, p. 271.
30. *Notebooks*, p. 52.
31. *Atlantic Monthly*, XLIX (Jan., 1882), pp. 126-30. Oscar Cargill, *The Novels of Henry James* (New York, 1961), pp. 124-5, suggests that this review may have provoked James into writing a novel of New England manners in competition with Howells.
32. *Notebooks*, p. 47.
33. *Ibid.*
34. *The James Family*, p. 325.
35. *The Opposing Self* (New York, 1955), p. 104.
36. "James's Portrait of a Southerner," *American Literature*, XXVII (Nov., 1955), p. 315.
37. Lubbock, *Letters*, I, pp. 115-7.
38. *The James Family*, pp. 327-9.
39. *Ibid.*, p. 329.
40. *Ibid.*
41. Lubbock, *Letters*, I, p. 135.
42. *Atlantic Monthly*, LVII (June, 1886), p. 852.
43. *Critic*, V (April 17, 1886), p. 191.
44. See the article, cited above, by Charles Anderson, "James's Portrait of a Southerner." Anderson says James drew upon a "collective myth of the South" which was not the real thing, but which he worked successfully in the texture of his story.
45. Howe in the introduction to *The Bostonians* (New York, 1956) has stressed the connection, in James's interpretation of the feminist phenomenon, between political and sexual life in America. "James was bold enough to see that the two spheres of experience could not be kept apart. . . ." Trilling in *The Opposing Self* discusses the novel as a revelation of a profound social disarrangement, to be traced directly to "the beginnings of sexual disorientation in America." He sees implications behind James's satire of an elaborate ritual of sexual perversion and frustration complete with Lesbian witches, "Bacchae," desexed men, and an erotic mythology.
46. James's comments on *The Bostonians* cited here and in the following discussion are to be found in Lubbock, *Letters*, I, pp. 324-5 and II, pp. 100, 497-9.

IV. POSTSCRIPT: MARK TWAIN AND REALISM

1. A. B. Paine, *Mark Twain: A Biography* (New York, 1912), I, p. 512.
2. *Mark Twain's Letters*, ed. A. B. Paine, I, p. 145.
3. "What Paul Bourget Thinks of Us," *Literary Essays*, pp. 146-7.
4. *Ibid.*, p. 147.
5. Preface, Library Edition (1892) *The Hoosier Schoolmaster* (New York, 1899), pp. 6-7. See for a discussion of the relation of the American novel to

regionalism and nationalism B. T. Spencer, "The New Realism and a National Literature," *Publications of the Modern Language Association,* LVI (Dec., 1941), pp. 1129-31.

6. *New England Magazine,* II, n.s. (1890), p. 243.

7. *Literary News,* IX (1888), pp. 236-7.

8. *Mark Twain's Letters,* I, p. 434.

9. See *Critic,* VI (March 28, 1885), p. 155. For a discussion of the reception of *Huckleberry Finn* cf. A. L. Vogelback, "The Publication and Reception of *Huckleberry Finn* in America," *American Literature,* XI (Nov., 1939), pp. 260-72.

10. *Century Magazine,* XXX (May, 1885), pp. 171-2.

11. *Americanisms and Briticisms* (New York, 1892), pp. 153-61.

12. *Critic,* VII (Nov, 28, 1885), p. 253.

13. *Musical Courier,* XXXVIII (June 28, 1899), p. 23.

INDEX